I0793690

IMAGES
of America

AYER

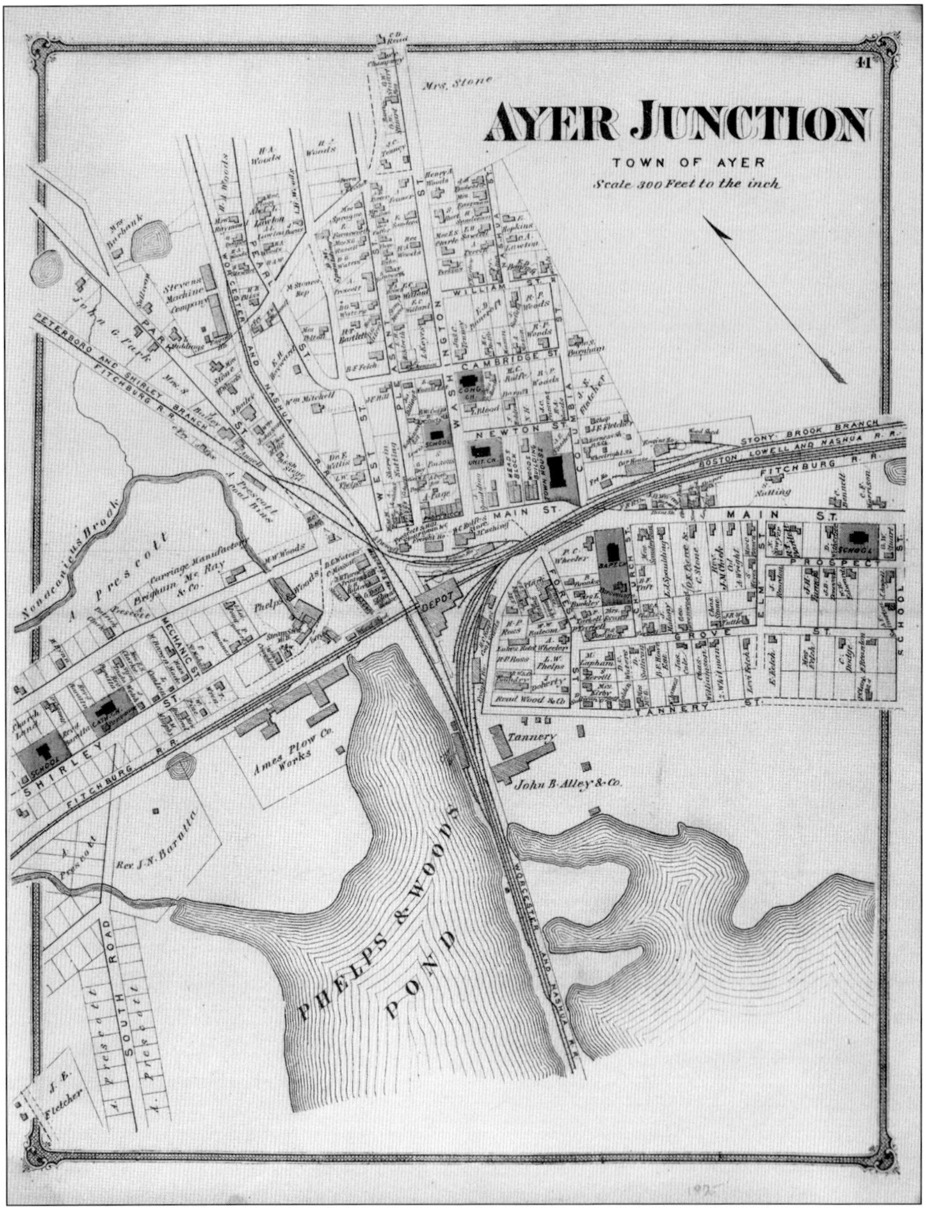

This 1875 map of Ayer shows private residences, businesses, town buildings, schools, and churches. Olive Burbank's property is in the upper left. She was the mother of botanist and horticulturist Luther Burbank. Luther lived in Groton Junction and Ayer with his mother and his sister Emma until he left the area for California in 1875. Olive and Emma left Ayer in 1877 to join Luther in California. (Courtesy of the Ayer Library.)

ON THE COVER: This July 1915 photograph shows a truck decorated for the Fourth of July parade. Charles H. Hardy is standing next to his truck. He was a contractor and builder who also sold and installed plumbing and heating supplies. This photograph was taken in front of his store on Central Avenue, which is now the home of Nashoba Restaurant. (Courtesy of the Ayer Library.)

IMAGES
of America

AYER

Barry E. Schwarzel
with the Ayer Historical Commission

ARCADIA
PUBLISHING

Copyright © 2012 by Barry E. Schwarzel with the Ayer Historical Commission
ISBN 978-0-7385-9152-0

Published by Arcadia Publishing
Charleston, South Carolina

Printed in the United States of America

Library of Congress Control Number: 2011940374

For all general information, please contact Arcadia Publishing:
Telephone 843-853-2070
Fax 843-853-0044
E-mail sales@arcadiapublishing.com
For customer service and orders:
Toll-Free 1-888-313-2665

Visit us on the Internet at www.arcadiapublishing.com

To Ralph H. Richardson and Zelda Moore, who have done much to keep the history of Ayer alive

Contents

ACKNOWLEDGMENTS

This book would not have been possible without the efforts of those who have had the foresight to preserve the local history of Ayer. Some of the articles used in the research for this book came from the writings of local historian Ralph H. Richardson, who wrote a series of articles for the *Public Spirit* on the origins and history of South Groton and Ayer. Thanks to Zelda Moore for sharing articles and photographs from the Page–Moore library. Her work in procuring historical facts, photographs, and her many informative writings were invaluable in the research and content for this book. Thanks to the Ayer Library director Mary-Ann Lucht and to Don Comeau, a volunteer at the Ayer Library and overseer of the Nutting Historical Room. Comeau has compiled an extensive collection of artifacts and images from glass negatives that were used in preparation for this publication.

Thanks to Donald and Josephine Wallace, Ed Kelley, and the Ayer Fire and Police Departments for sharing their collection of photographs, postcards, and memories. Thanks to George Bacon, Tom McLain, Ruth Rhonemus, and Alene Reich—all members of the Ayer Historical Commission, of which I am proud to be a member. They helped me with their ideas, feedback, and personal knowledge of Ayer's history. Unless otherwise noted, all images appear courtesy of the Ayer Library.

Introduction

Ralph H. Richardson, Ayer's town historian, wrote, "Ayer was the Child of the Iron Horse. It owes its origins, perhaps more than any other Massachusetts town, to the use of the railroads." Ayer's beginnings are tied closely with the history of its parent town, Groton, which also included a small corner of what was once Shirley. Formerly called South Groton, Ayer was a small farming village with a few sawmills and two district schools, one being the Sandy Pond schoolhouse. A large part of the downtown area, including the train depot, West Main Street up to Devens, and the middle school and high schools were from the original land grant to Maj. Simon Willard in 1657. This land, which was given the name Nonaicoicus farm, occupied 1,000 acres in the southwest corner of Groton. Before any settlers arrived, this land was called Nonaicoicus by the local Native Americans. It is believed that the translation for the word Nonaicoicus is "earthen pot."

After the death of Simon Willard in 1676, his Nonaicoicus farm was gradually sold and divided up. In 1738, William Farwell and his three sons Henry, William, and Steven purchased the farm. William Park arrived here in 1756, and in 1779, his son John bought a total of 200 acres from Henry Farwell, including the land between St. Mary's Cemetery up to where Page–Hilltop and the regional high school are now. In 1754, David Stone acquired the northwest corner of the Nonaicoicus farm property. By 1813, the remainder of Simon Willard's land, about 250 acres, was sold to Phineas Nutting.

Nutting's property included most of Main Street and East Main Street, the Plow Shop Pond and Grove Pond, north to Highland Avenue, and back to Park Street. John Page's farm extended to the east of Nutting's. Page was the largest landowner next to Maj. Simon Willard, and in 1712, he built the first mill on Sandy Brook Pond. The mill at Sandy Brook Pond was located where the old pumping station was. This was the property on the north side of East Main Street and across from the entrance to Cain's Foods.

In 1717, John Page's son Jonathan sold the mill and the 13-acre farm to Jonas Prescott. Prescott, in turn, gave the mill and the farm to his son-in-law Joseph Stone in 1728. In 1834, the Stone family sold the mill and the farm to Calvin Fletcher. The present-day Fletcher's Pond was so named because Fletcher bought the property from landowners on Sandy Brook Meadow and used the water to power his mill.

In 1844, Fitchburg Railroad constructed a rail line through South Groton, but it was not until 1847 that a passenger train made its way through. The first train station in South Groton was at the intersection of Central Avenue and Groton Harvard Road, on what was known as Flanagan's Crossing. In 1848, the Worcester & Nashua Railroad constructed a rail line to Groton Center through South Groton. This was the crossing that made the junction of the two railroads. There was now rail access east-west and north-south. It is also interesting to note that between the years 1850 and 1860, Henry David Thoreau had been a passenger on the Fitchburg Railroad as well as the other railroads that passed through Groton Junction. He traveled across Massachusetts during these years, giving his lectures on various topics.

By 1870, South Groton, now referred to as Groton Junction, had exceeded Groton Center in population size. People and businesses came to Groton Junction because there was employment and there was easy access for transporting raw materials and finished goods. The increase in population meant there was a need for more homes, schools, churches, and retail stores. In the late 1860s, there was a growing restlessness on the part of the residents in Groton Junction. There was a feeling that the needs of the Junction were not being met, or in some cases, were ignored. Many wanted to break free from Groton Center. In 1863, Groton Junction residents petitioned the school department for a high school, until finally, in 1868, the new East Main Street School was built where the courthouse is today.

On November 10, 1870, a petition to the General Court for the incorporation of the town of Groton Junction was signed by 270 people. On January 24, 1871, it was voted at a town meeting 191 to 123 that the towns of Groton not oppose the petition. The town of Shirley voted to release its territory east of the Nashua River to the new town for a fee of $500 as its share of the debt. The name Ayer was chosen for the town, which was incorporated on February 14, 1871. The first Ayer town meeting was held on March 6, 1871, and was followed by an elaborate celebration.

Ayer's history is short in comparison to the other towns that surround it, but it is no less important. The following photographs tell the history of Ayer and its people and how a small village was transformed from a farming to a railroad economy. The arrival of a military installation was yet another time for Ayer's townspeople to readjust and adapt its economy. This is not meant to be a complete history of Ayer, but rather a glimpse of some of the events and people that helped shape this community. There are people, places, and events that are not represented in the following photographs. Although they are not depicted or mentioned in this book, they are still an important part of the history and character of this community.

One

Groton Junction and the Iron Horse

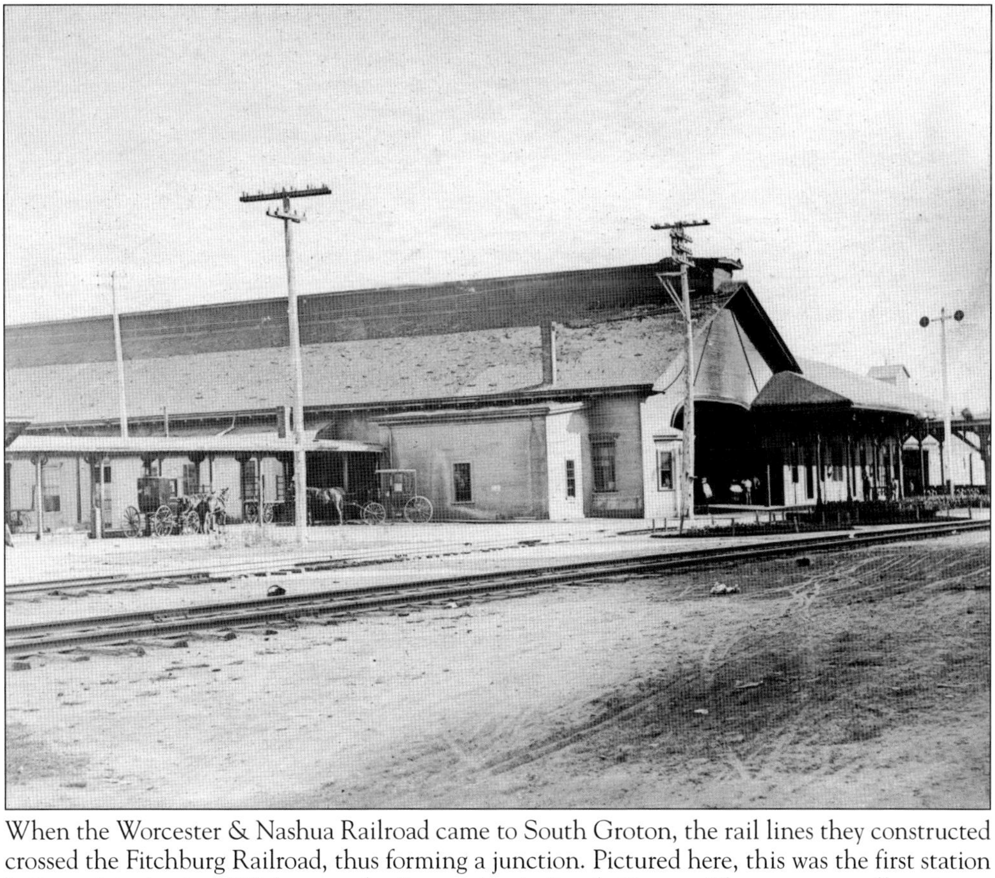

When the Worcester & Nashua Railroad came to South Groton, the rail lines they constructed crossed the Fitchburg Railroad, thus forming a junction. Pictured here, this was the first station built on this site, in 1848, but not the first station in South Groton. There was a small station at the intersection of Central Avenue and Groton Harvard Road.

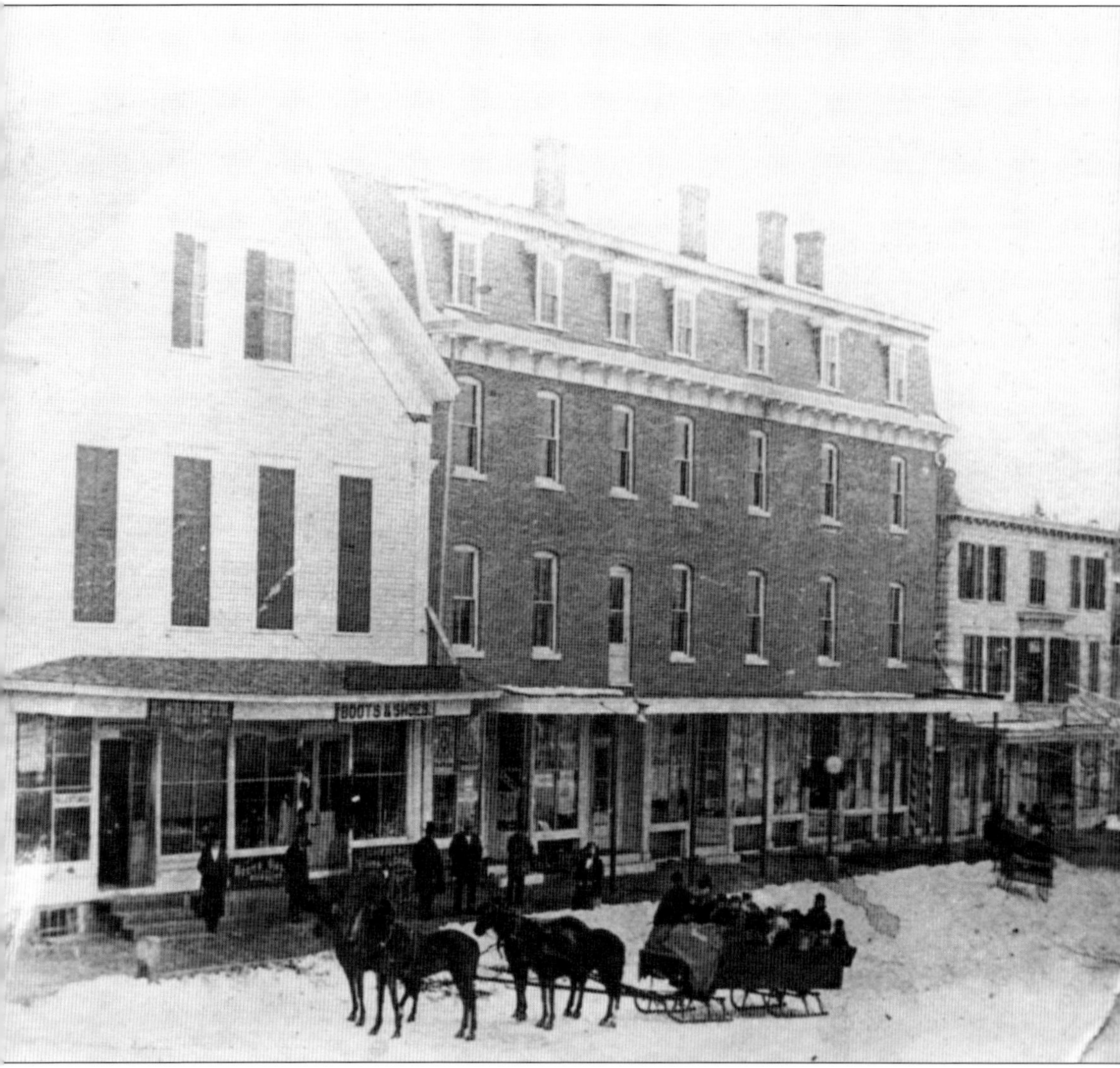

This easterly view of Main Street shows the block between Pleasant and Washington Streets. This is the old Page Block, pictured before the fire of April 1872 in which 40 buildings were destroyed. After the fire, Alfred and Thomas Page were one of the first to rebuild their property on Main Street, which today is the centerpiece of the downtown area. It is now known as the Page-Moore Building.

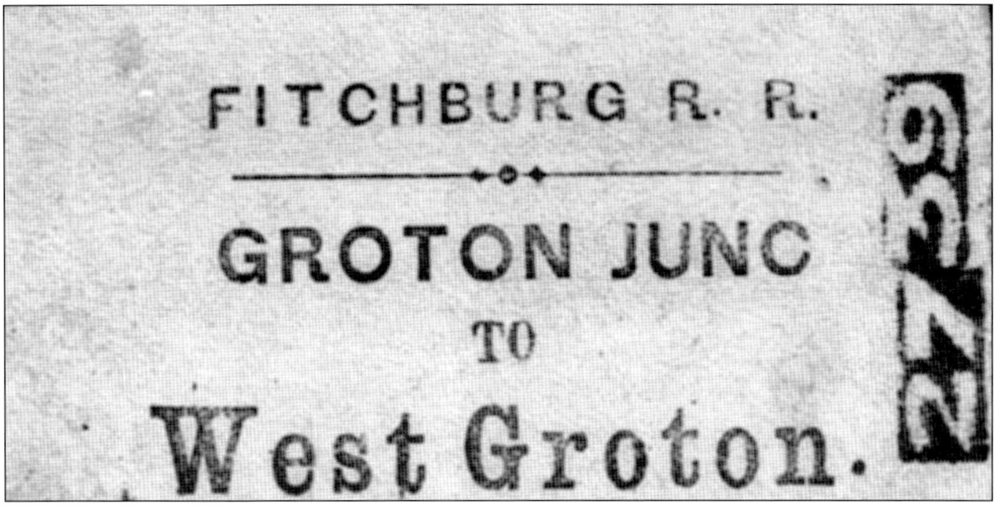

This train ticket was purchased in March 1863 at the Groton Junction station. Issued by the Fitchburg Railroad, the ticket displays the destination on the front; not shown here, the month and year of purchase is stamped on the reverse side of this ticket. The ticket is one of the many artifacts housed at the library.

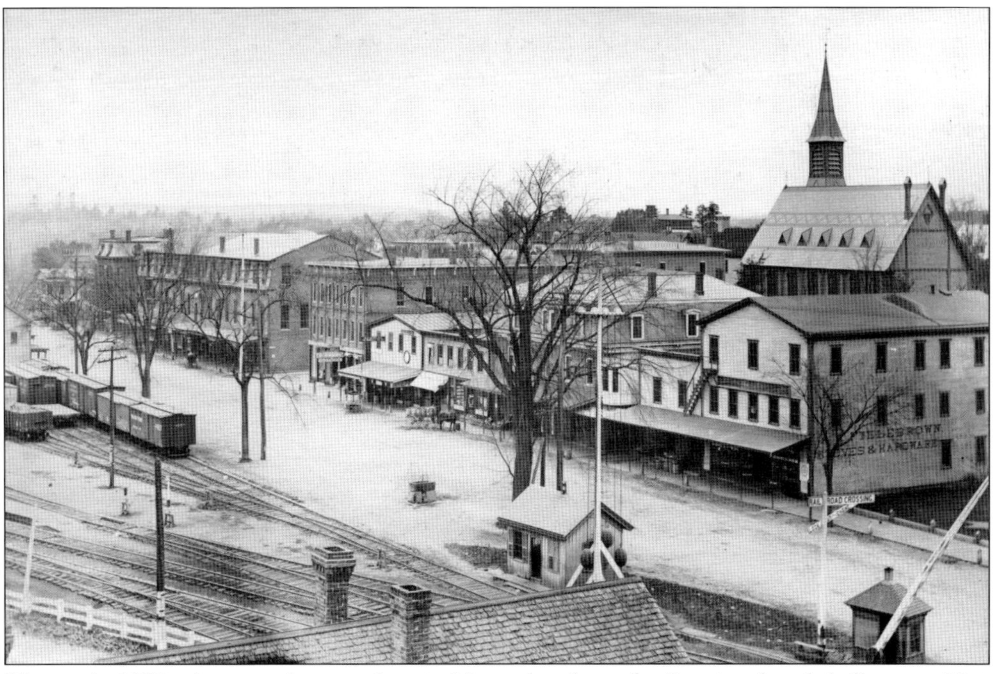

This early 1890s photograph was taken in November from the Baptist church bell tower. This church was on the corner of Church Street and East Main Street.

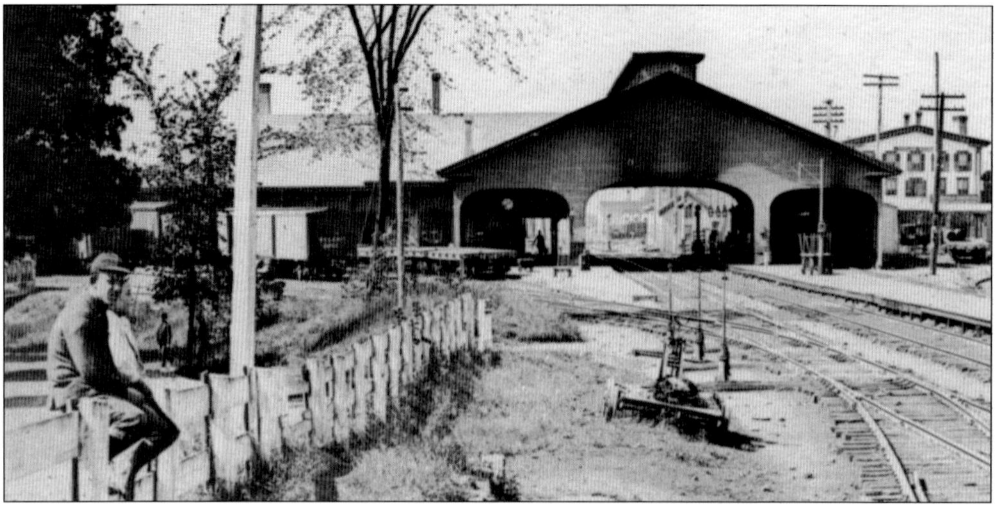

Shown here in September 1895, this young man had no idea that his photograph would be viewed more than a century later. This was probably one of the last photographs of the old train shed, torn down that same year to make way for the construction of a train depot.

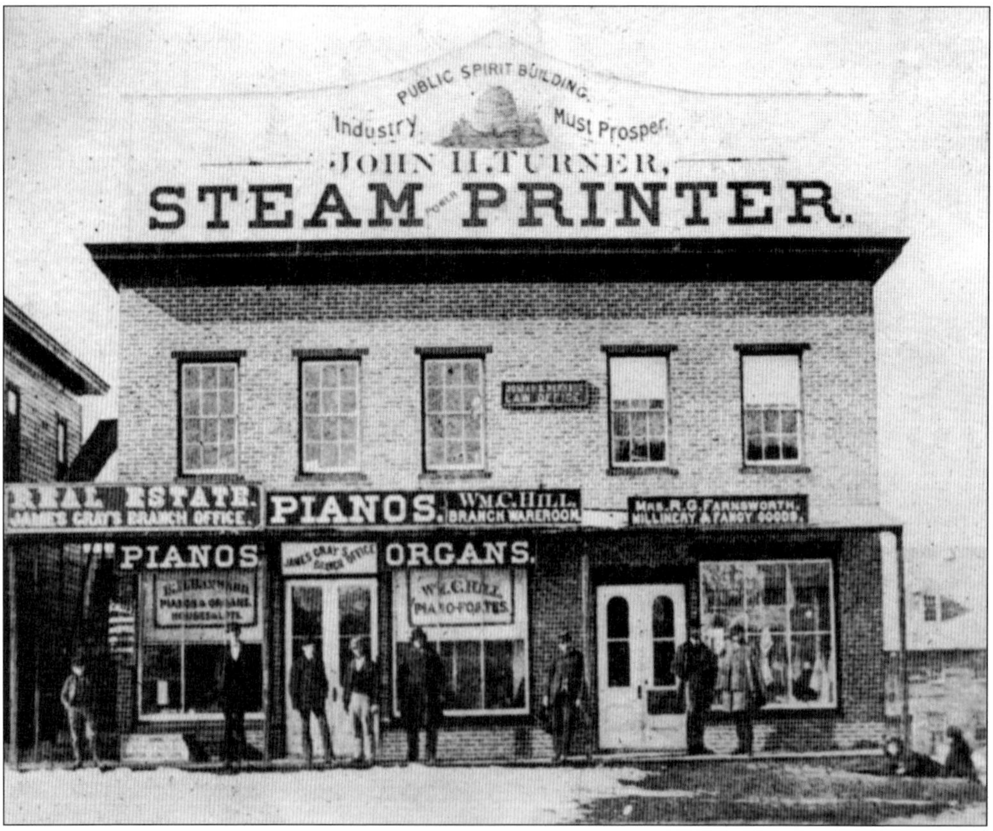

Here, John Turner's Public Spirit Building appears in Merchant's Row. The *Public Spirit* was first published in 1869, and in 1870, Turner had William Baker construct this building. In 1878, Turner had this building moved to the corner of West and Main Streets. In 1854, the *Railroad Mercury* was the first publication in this area.

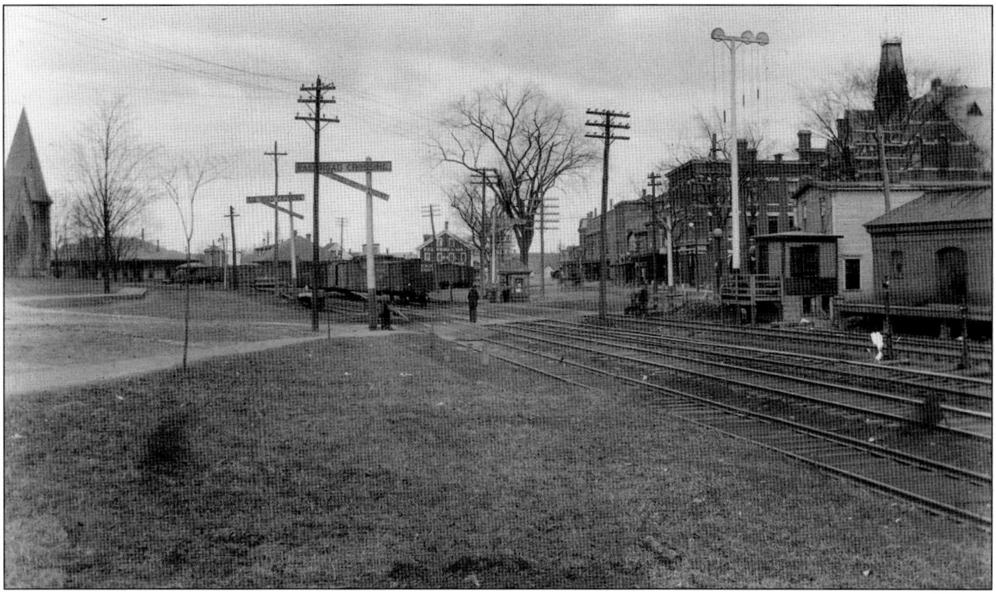

This is an easterly view of the Main Street crossing, which connects Main Street to East Main Street. This crossing is the road that those travelling west and north of Ayer must pass through when coming from the Littleton area. In this particular photograph, the crossing gates appear to have just come down and one can see the gatekeeper in the center.

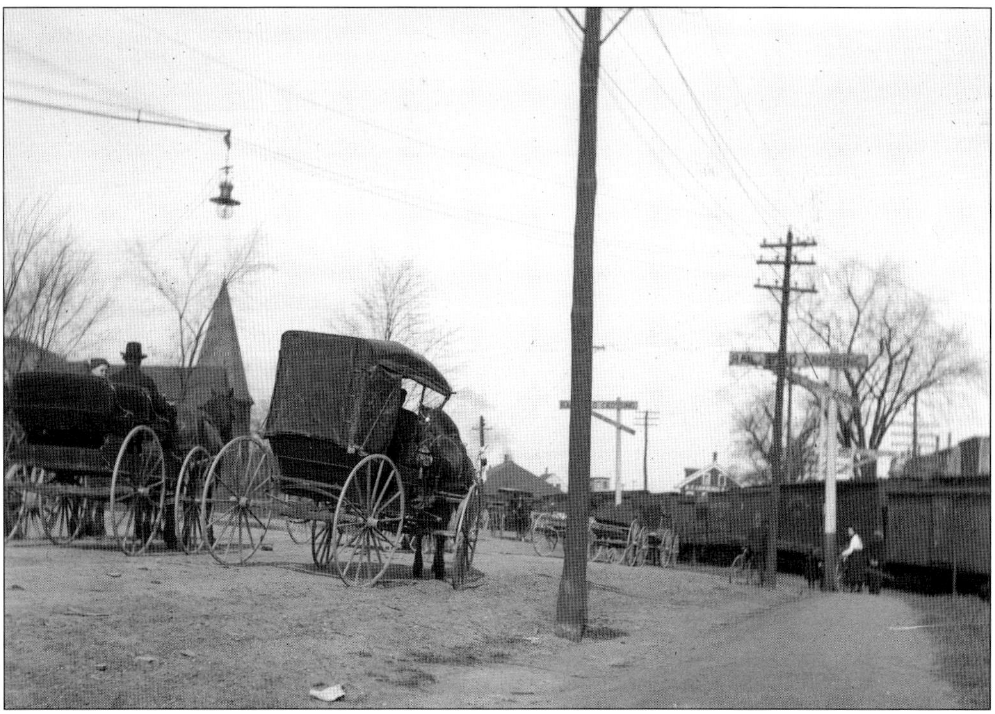

This photograph of the Main Street crossing shows traffic waiting for the passing freight train. In 1904, there was no other access from East Main Street to Main Street. Not only is there the horse-and-buggy traffic, but also there are a few people waiting with bicycles. Note carriages in both directions are waiting to pass.

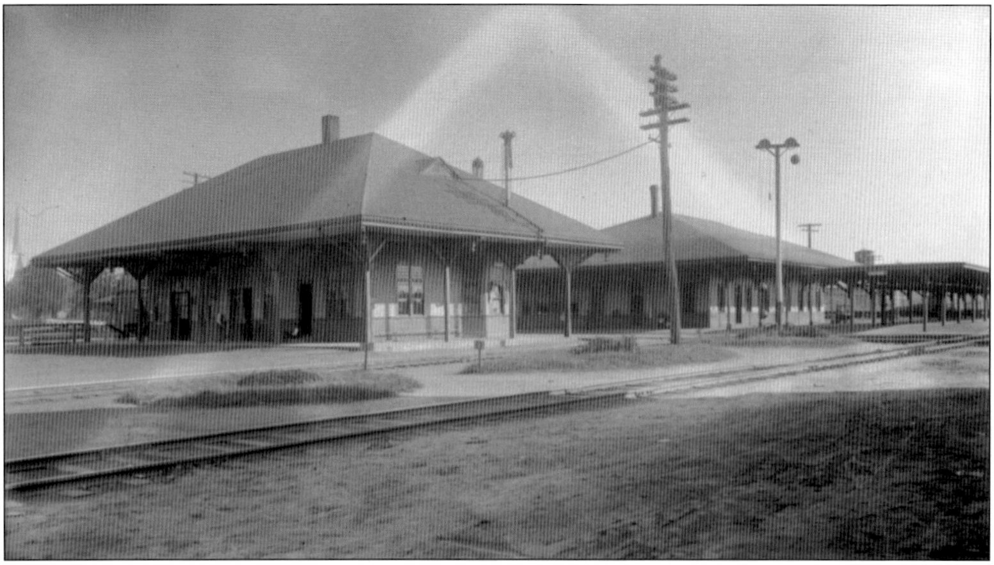

Construction started on the train depot in 1895, after the demolition of the old train shed, which had been in use since 1848. This September 1905 photograph was taken from Merchant's Row facing southeast. Merchant's Row occupied the present-day westerly side of the Mobil Station parking lot.

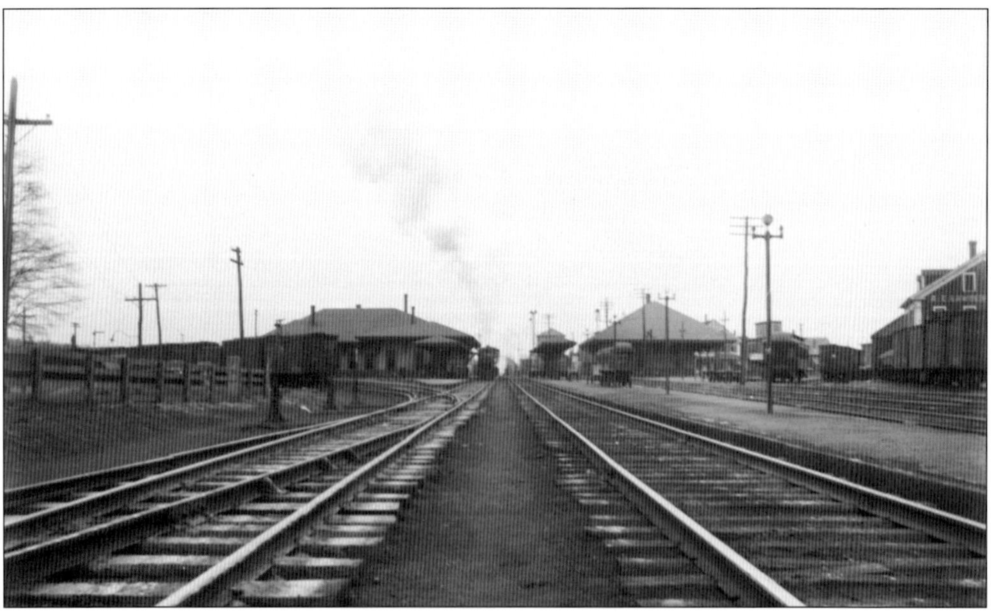

This November 1905 photograph by Charles Kennison shows a west-facing panorama of the station. Kennison lived next to the train tracks on East Main Street. There have been many photographs reproduced for this publication from his glass negatives. This photograph also shows the two buildings at the station. One was a passenger terminal; the other was a freight terminal.

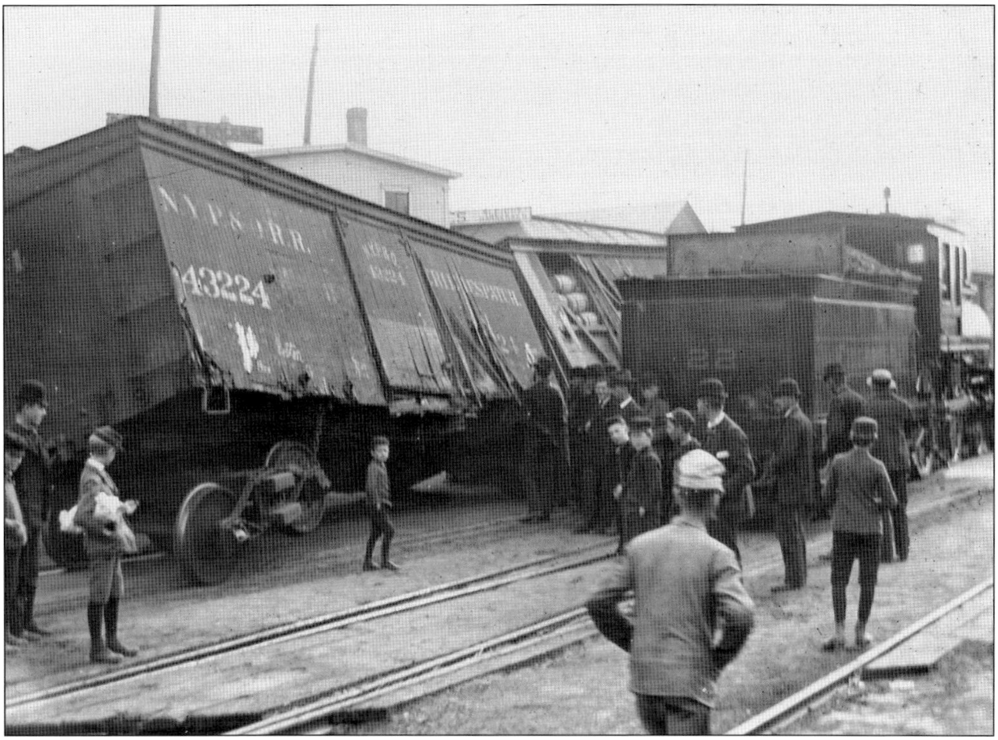

This derailment occurred at the Main Street crossing by the town hall. At the top of the photograph and to the left of center can be seen the roof of the harness shop. To the right of the harness shop, the roof of the freight house can just barely be seen. The freight house was taken down in 1906 when the overpass was erected.

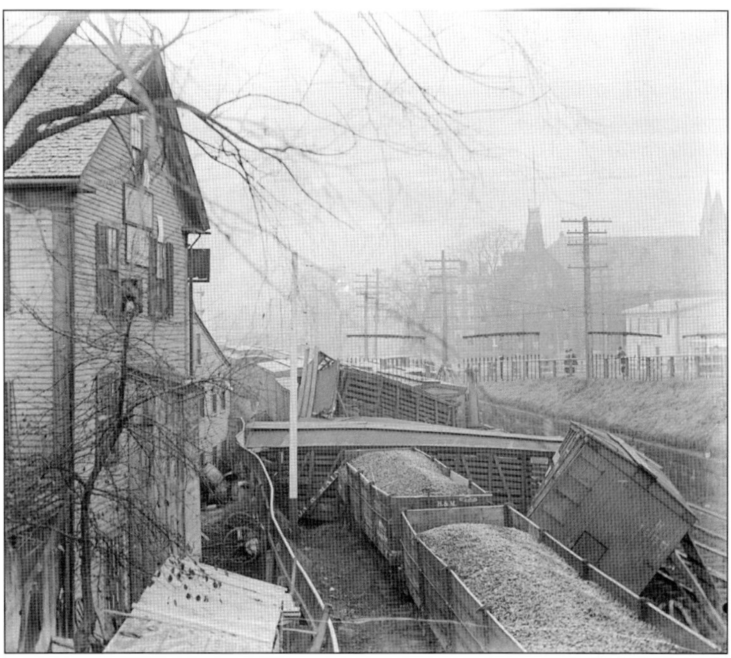

This derailment happened after 1906, which is evident at the right of the photograph where the road rising up to the bridge overpass can be seen. Fillebrown's Store is on the left. Just beyond Fillebrown's is Charles Kennison's home, where a window faced train traffic coming in and out of the rail junction in Ayer.

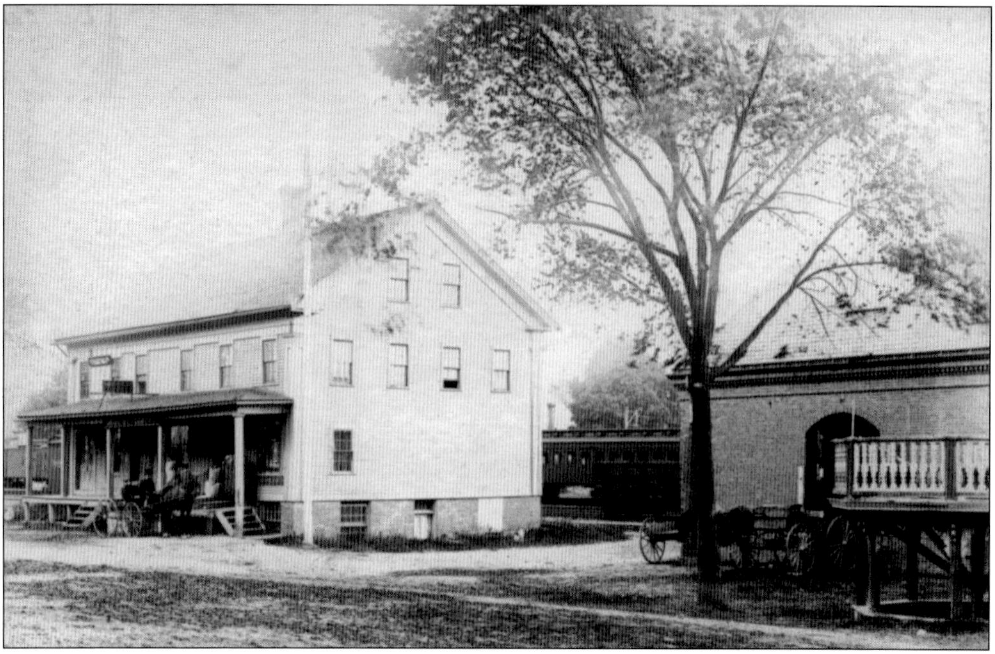

The Harvey A. Woods building on the left was erected in 1853 on the south side of Main Street and just east of where is now the Ayer Package Store. Woods later sold this store in 1867. He was the first to build on the north side of Main Street after the fire of 1872. Ironically, this new wooden structure was the first to be destroyed by fire in 1879.

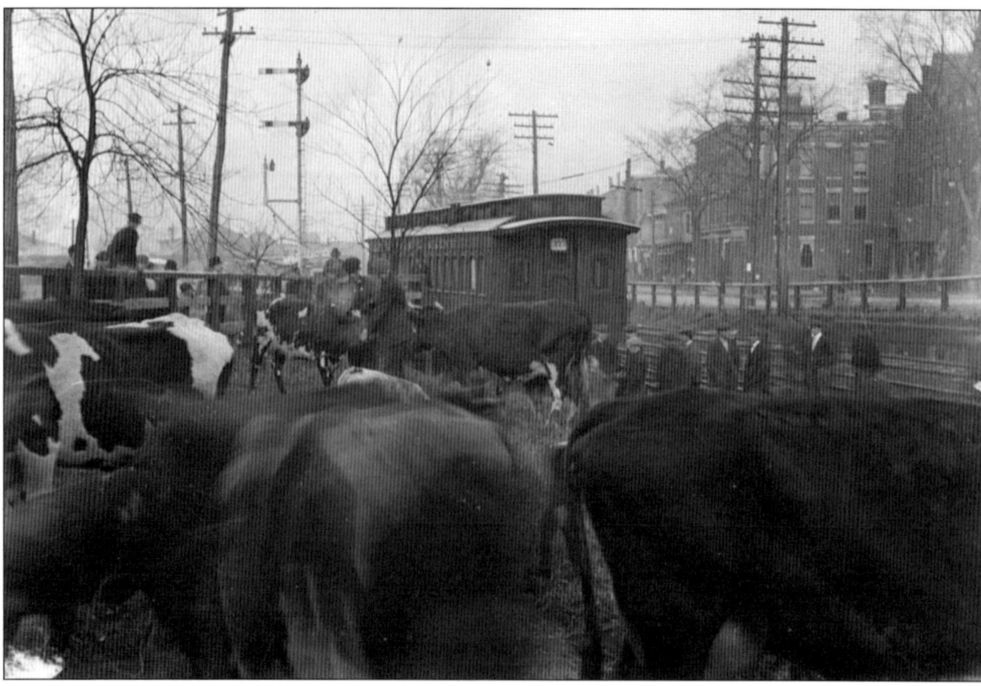

In this c. 1907 photograph, two men in the center left try to persuade one cow to move along. A few young boys on the fence seem to be enjoying the entertainment. Cows too close to the railroad tracks were probably not a common sight.

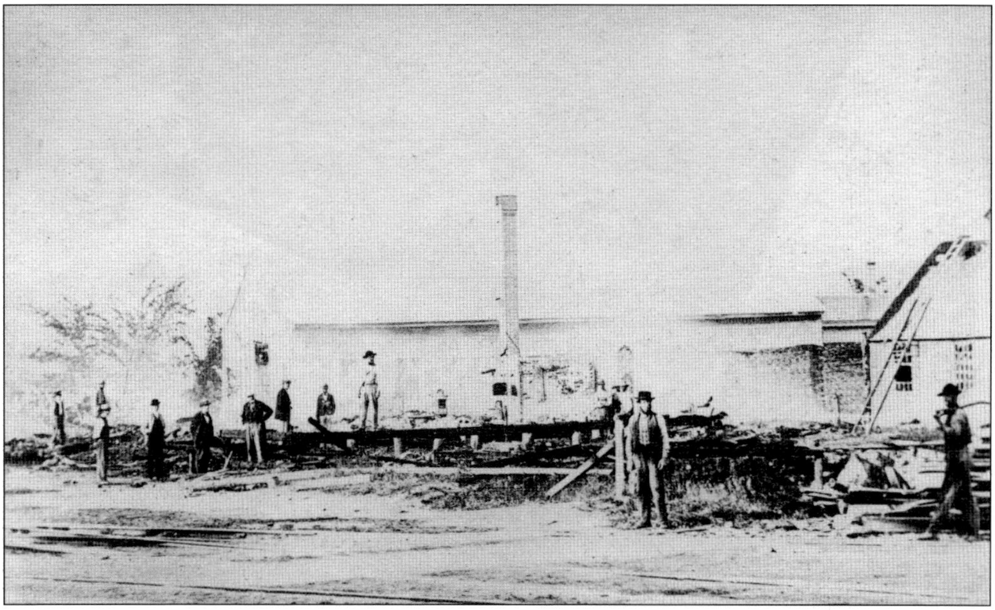

The July 1870 fire destroyed all of the buildings on Merchant's Row, with the exception of one structure. Although the hose companies had received a new hand engine in April 1870, it was not enough to fight back this sweeping fire. After this fire, many business owners relocated to Main Street. Merchant's Row never regained the substantial business it once had before the fire.

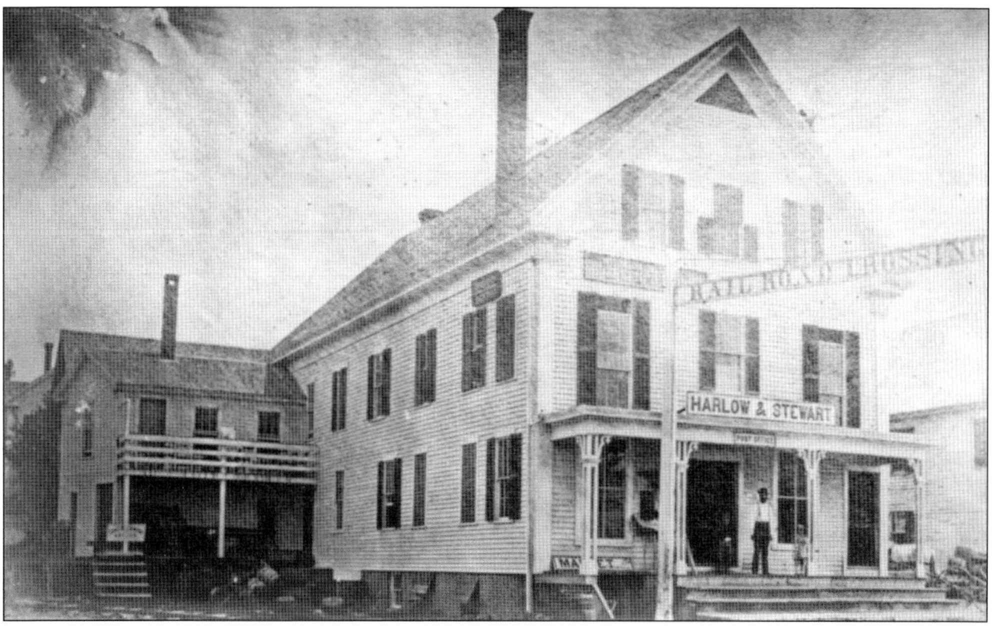

The Harlow and Stewart Building was one of the first to house the post office. It was located at the corner of West Street and Main Street where the Subway restaurant currently sits. It was built in 1858; the first postmaster was Andrew Boynton Gardner.

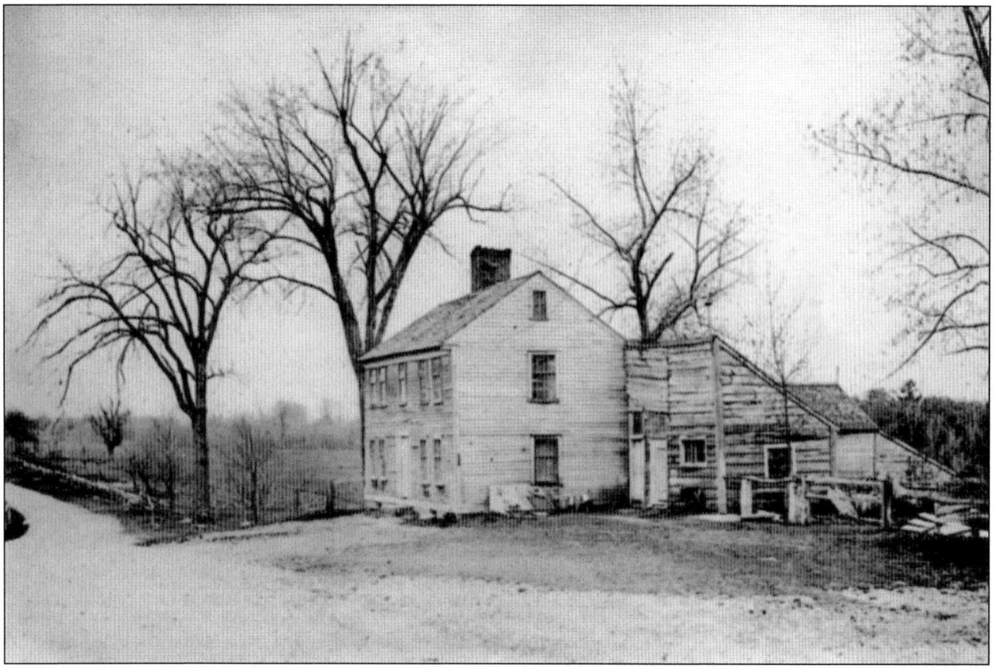

The Abel Stone house, pictured here in May 1895, was one of the oldest homes in Ayer. Located on Harvard Road on the Harvard and Ayer line, the house was built before 1729. Over the years, it fell into such disrepair that it was necessary to demolish the home in the fall of 2011.

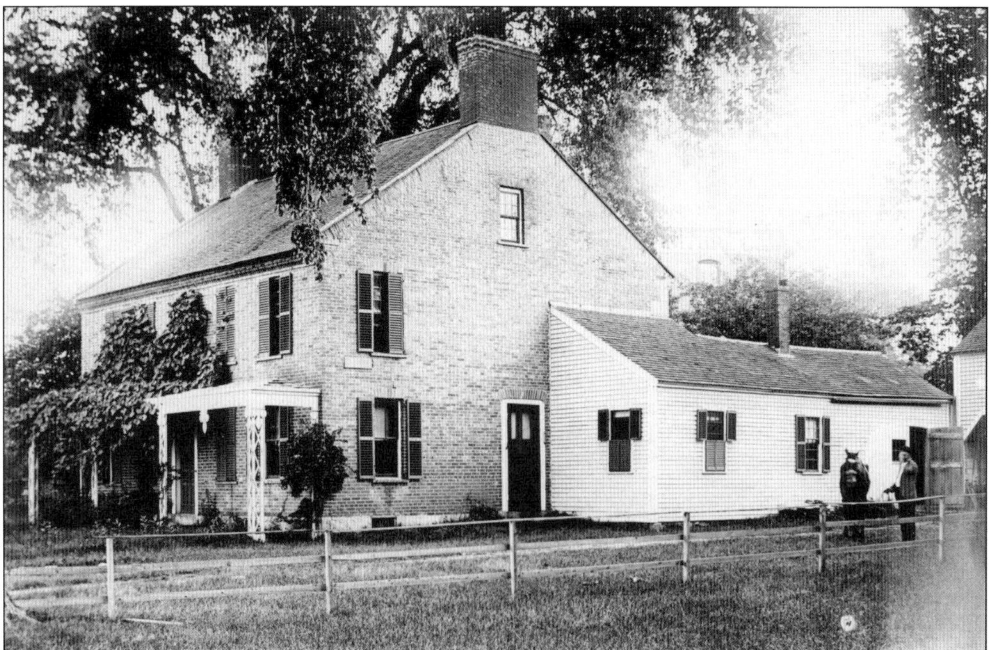

Pictured here in July 1894 on the corner of Park Street and Groton Street, the John Park home was built in 1791. Presently, it is partially hidden, as it is part of the auto parts store. The front of the store wraps around the home with its entrance located on Park Street.

Two

A New Town Emerges

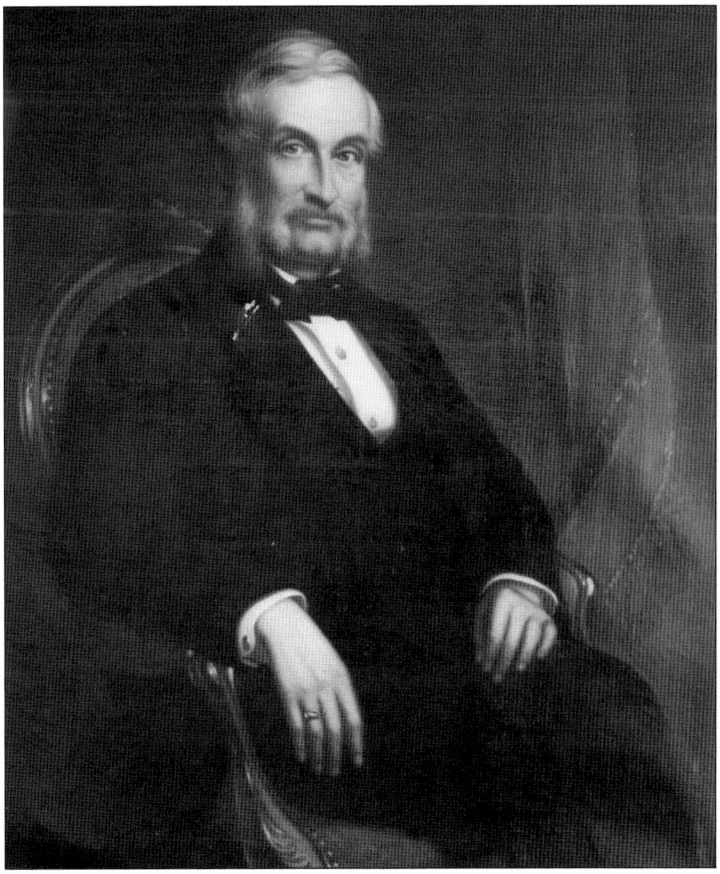

This portrait of Dr. James Cook Ayer is hanging in the town hall. Dr. Ayer was a prominent resident of Lowell, Massachusetts, and a producer of hair tonics and elixirs. Aside from owning his factory in Lowell, he also invested in sawmills in Florida and iron mines in Michigan. (Courtesy of Jason Holmes.)

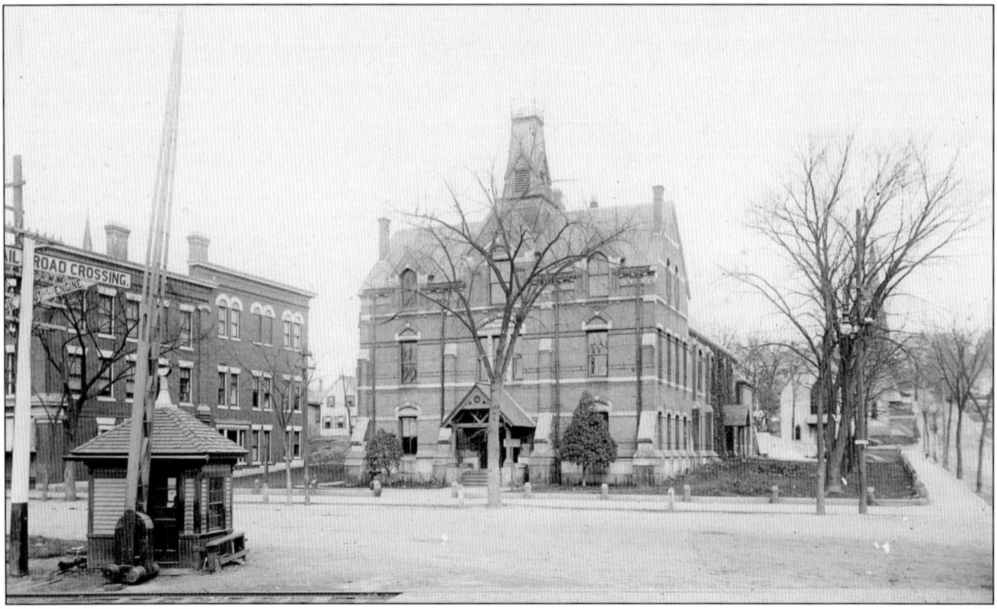

The construction of the town hall was partially funded by a generous gift of $10,000 from Dr. Ayer. The architects were Weston and Rand. Prior to construction, the town had to purchase enough land on which to erect the new building. In June 1872, five lots were approved for purchase at a cost of $8,148.73. Construction began in 1873 and was completed in 1876.

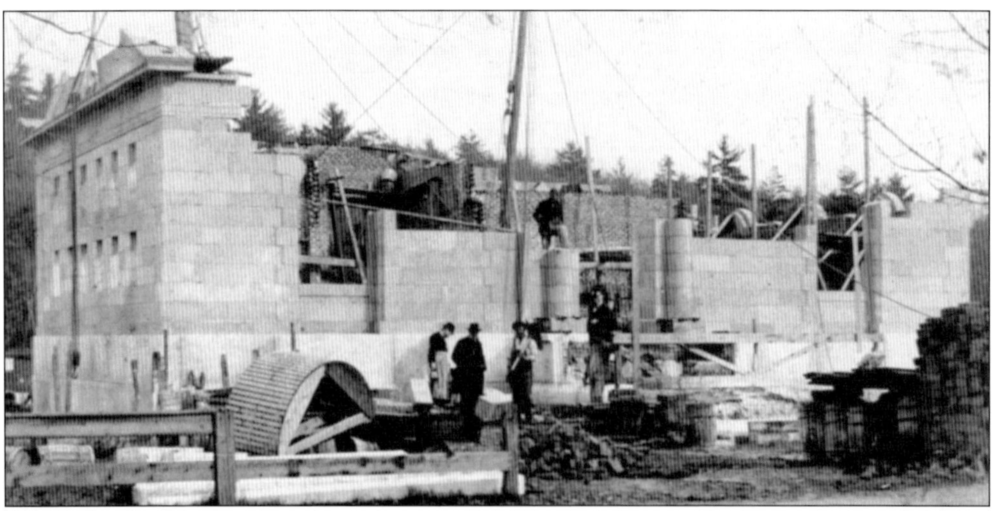

Built on East Main Street in 1893, Ayer Library was presented to the town on January 13, 1894, by Frederick Fanning Ayer, who continued his father's generosity. To design the library, Frederick Ayer hired Alexander S. Jenny, a member of a Boston firm of architects who designed the Boston Public Library.

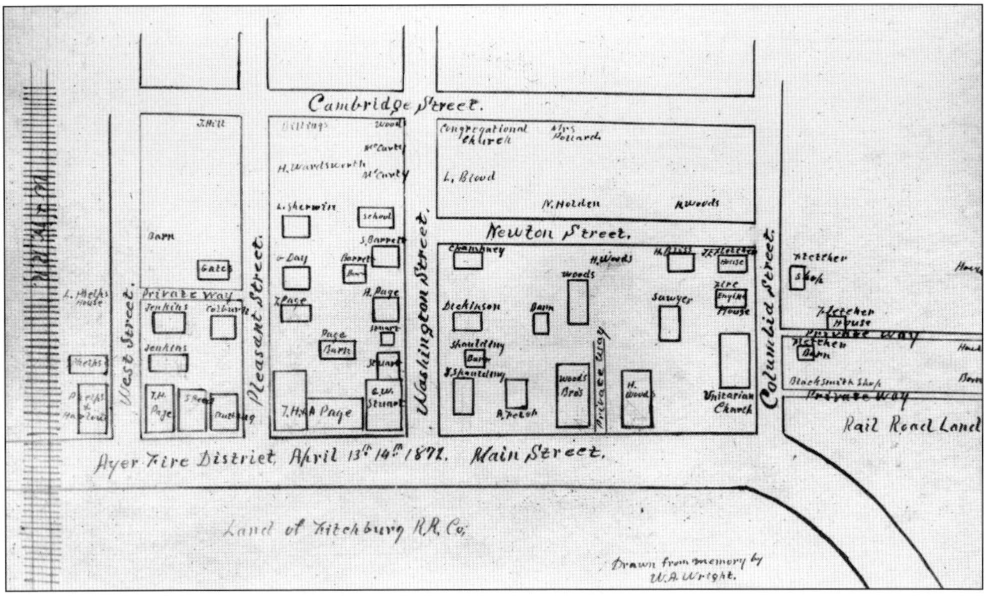

This drawing by William A. Wright shows the Main Street area prior to the fire of April 14, 1872. At that time, the town was looking for land to build the proposed town hall. After the fire, the required land was purchased for the new town hall.

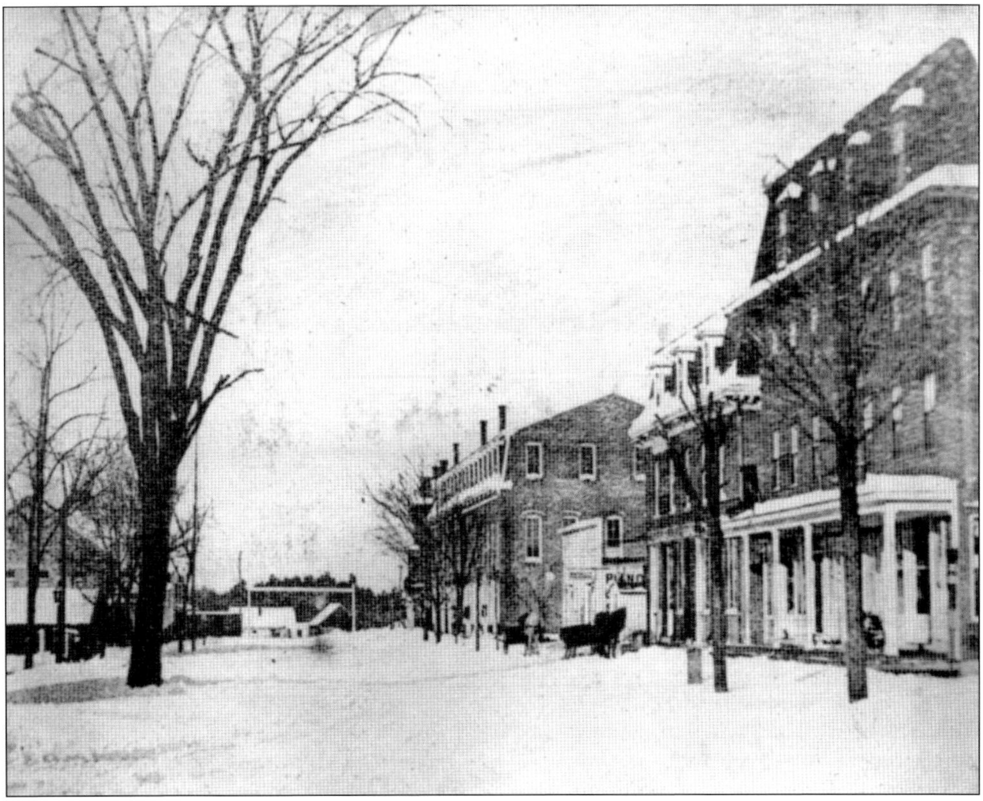

This 1875 photograph shows reconstruction of the business district to the west. Only three years earlier, the entire north side of Main Street was destroyed by fire.

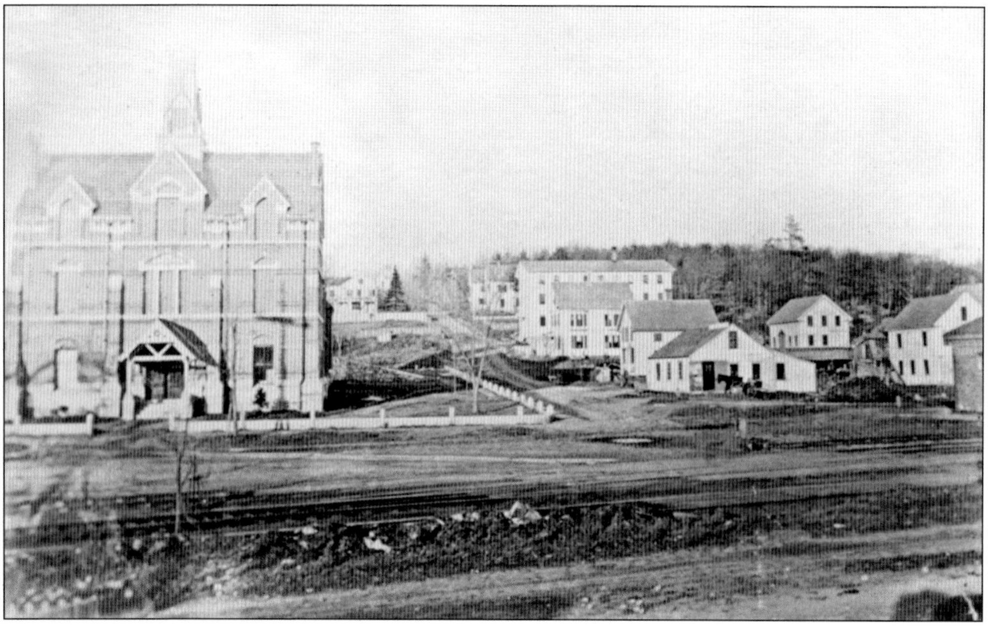

This early 1879 photograph shows the town hall nearly three years after the initial dedication. At this time, there is no gate at the crossing at the end of Columbia Street. Whitcomb's blacksmith and wheelwright shop is located across from the town hall. This photograph shows the growth occurring in Ayer at the time.

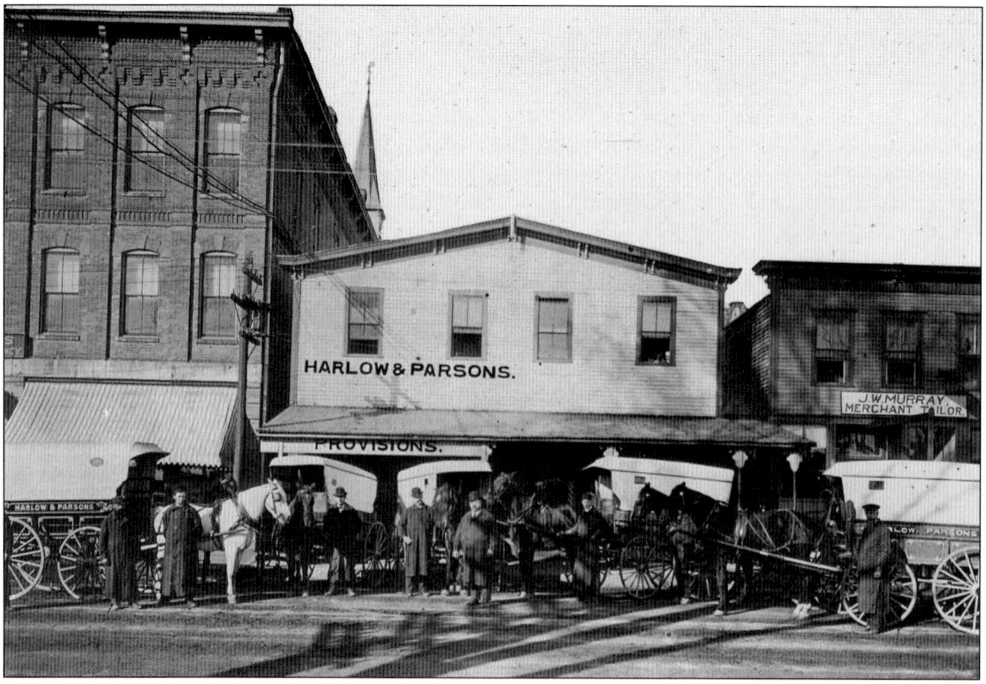

This late 1890s photograph is of the Harlow & Parsons store located on Main Street and next to the Spaulding building on the left. Harlow & Parsons sold provisions and was successful, as can be seen by the amount of wagons ready to deliver its goods to local patrons.

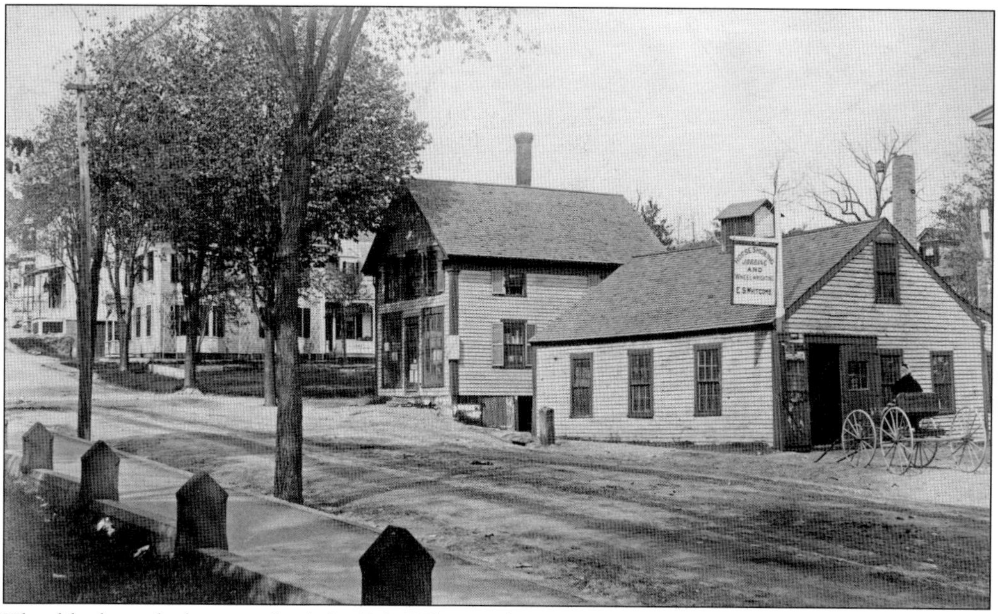

This blacksmith shop was built by E.S. Whitcomb in 1850. This shop was located approximately between where Central Avenue and the post office are now. On the right-hand side of the photograph, a woman sits in the seat of her carriage. The horse is absent; it may be getting shod while she waits.

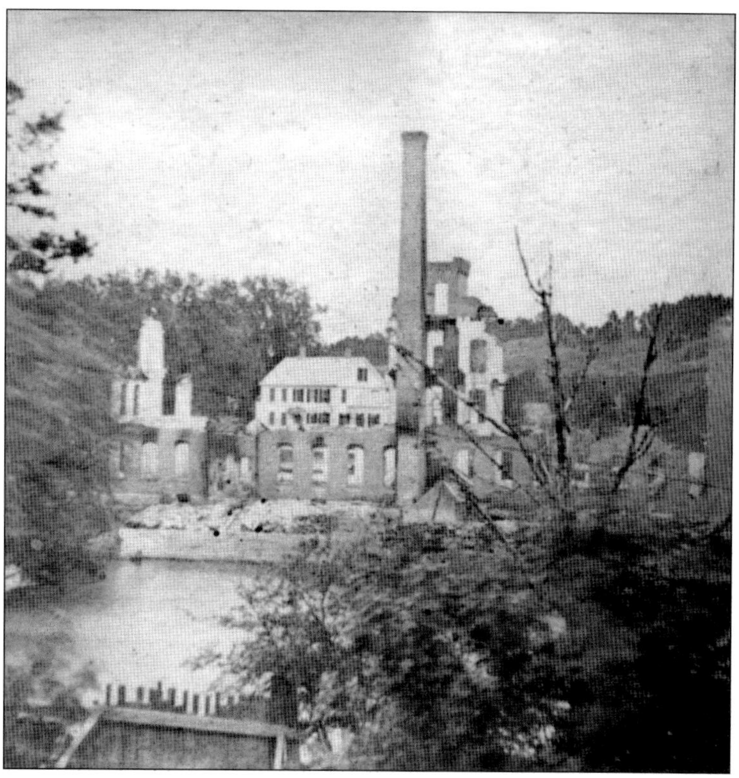

The ruins at Mitchellville are shown here after the fire of 1873. William Mitchell purchased this three-story woolen mill in June 1871 for $20,000. At the time of the fire, there were 75 people employed at the mill, and the business was clearing $1,000 a week.

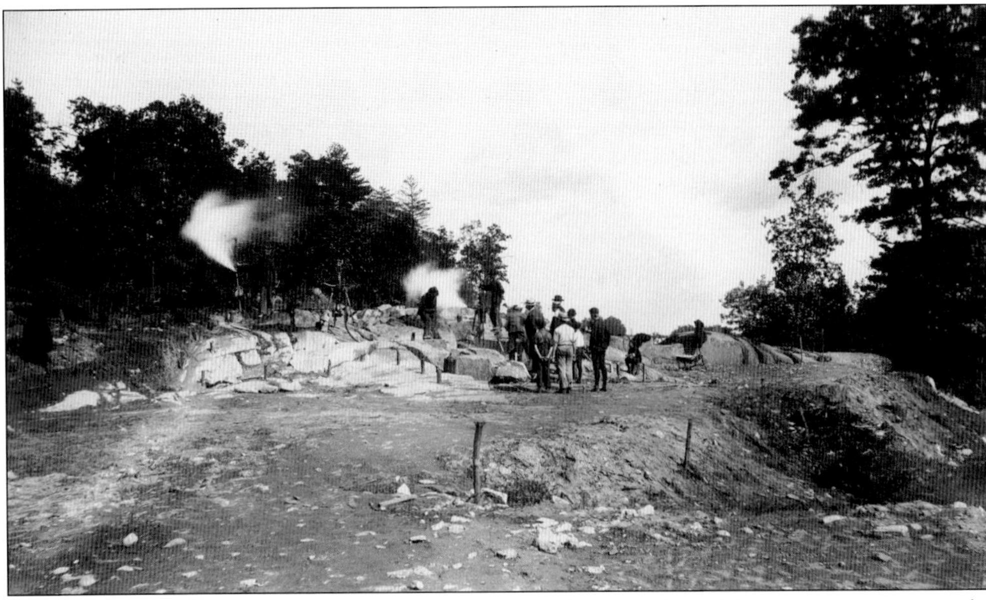

This August 1905 photograph shows the clearing and excavation of Central Avenue. On the left side, steam drills make holes for explosives. The explosives are the tubes sticking up from the ledge that can be seen in front of the steam drills.

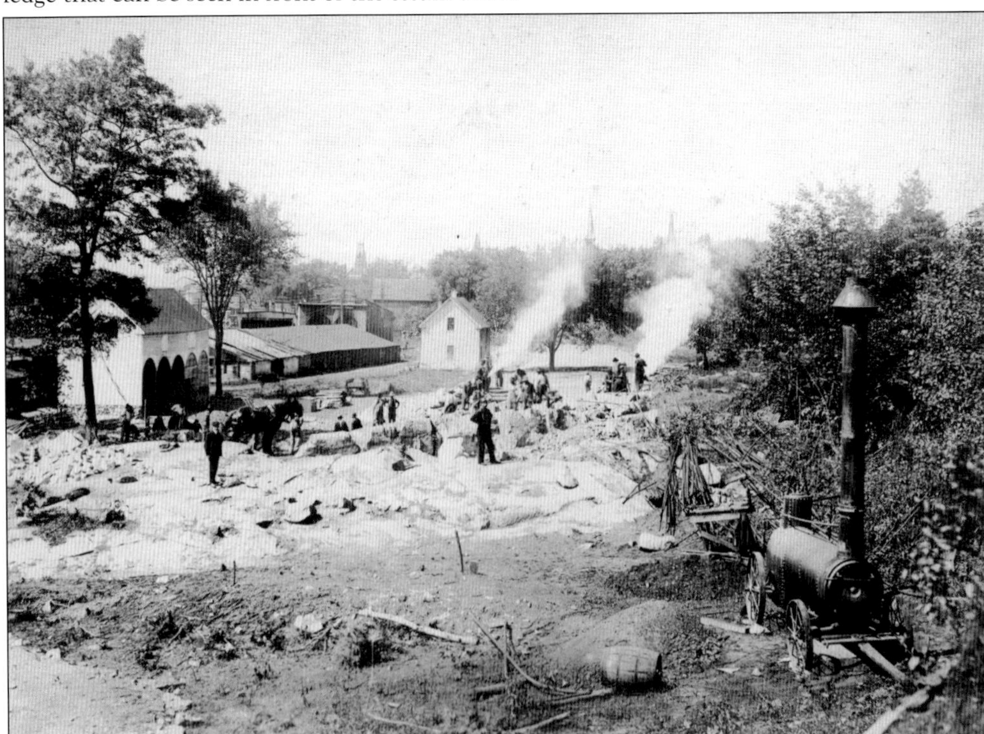

This is an opposite view of the blasting for the new Central Avenue in September 1905. This will be the location of the new trolley line for the Lowell & Fitchburg Street Railway to Lowell and the suburbs, including North Chelmsford. In the upper left, the distant outline of the town hall is visible. In the foreground to the right is a boiler for one of the steam drills.

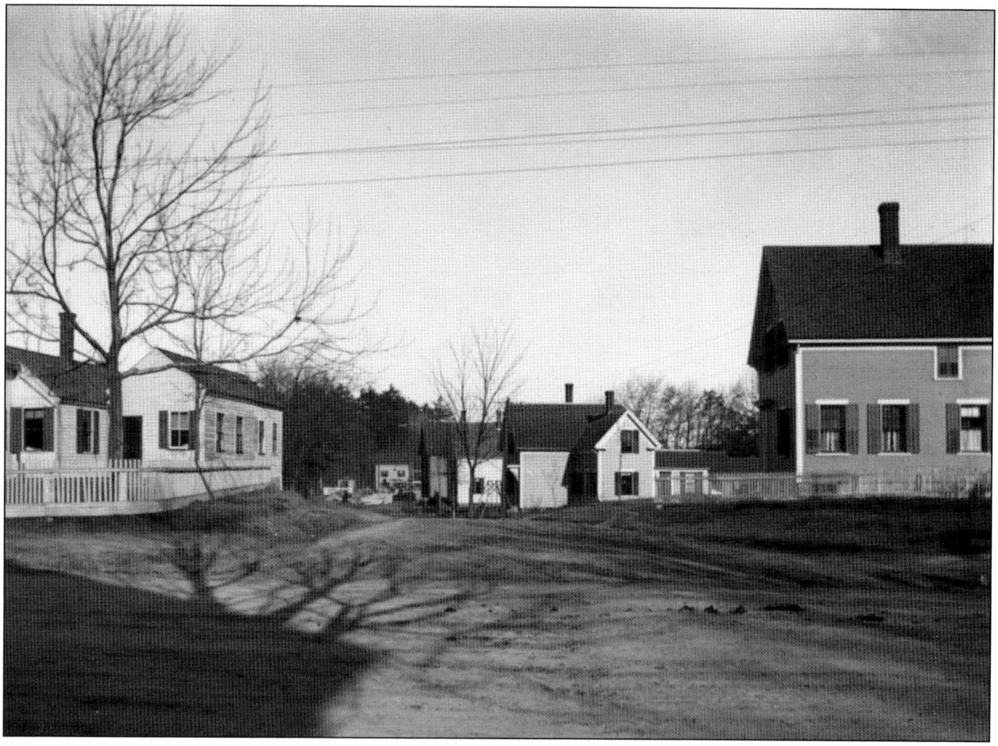

This December 1906 photograph shows the Groton Harvard Road from East Main Street. This road was often referred to as Flanagan's Road, as John Flanagan lived at the intersection of Groton Harvard Road and the new Central Avenue. He was also the gatekeeper at the rail crossing at that intersection referred to as Flanagan's Crossing, and it was the site of the first train depot in Ayer.

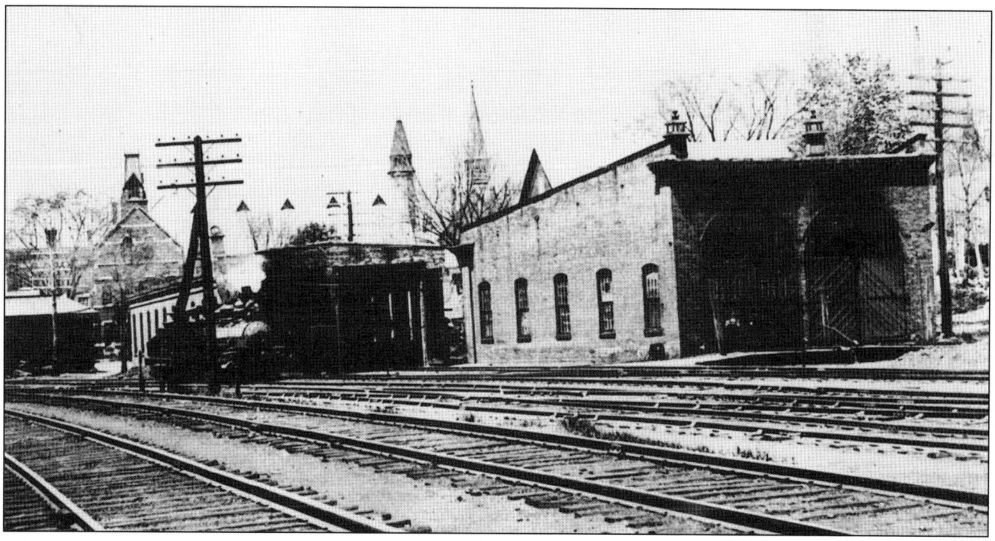

This c. 1903 photograph shows town hall to the west and to the left of the telephone pole. The Stonybrook Railroad engine house is on the right. There is a switcher engine behind the engine house and next to the freight house. The freight house is in about the same place as the present-day post office but was demolished in 1906 when the bridge overpass was erected.

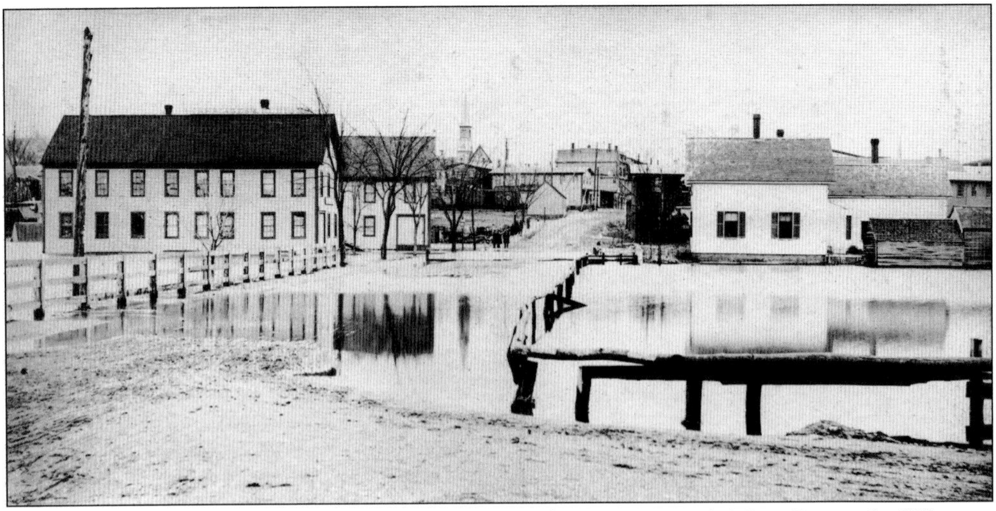

West Main Street appears flooded in March 1896. Looking east towards Main Street, the Whitney Carriage Company is on the left. Farther up, the Page Building can be seen on Main Street. The steeple of the Unitarian church can also be seen toward the left of the Page Building.

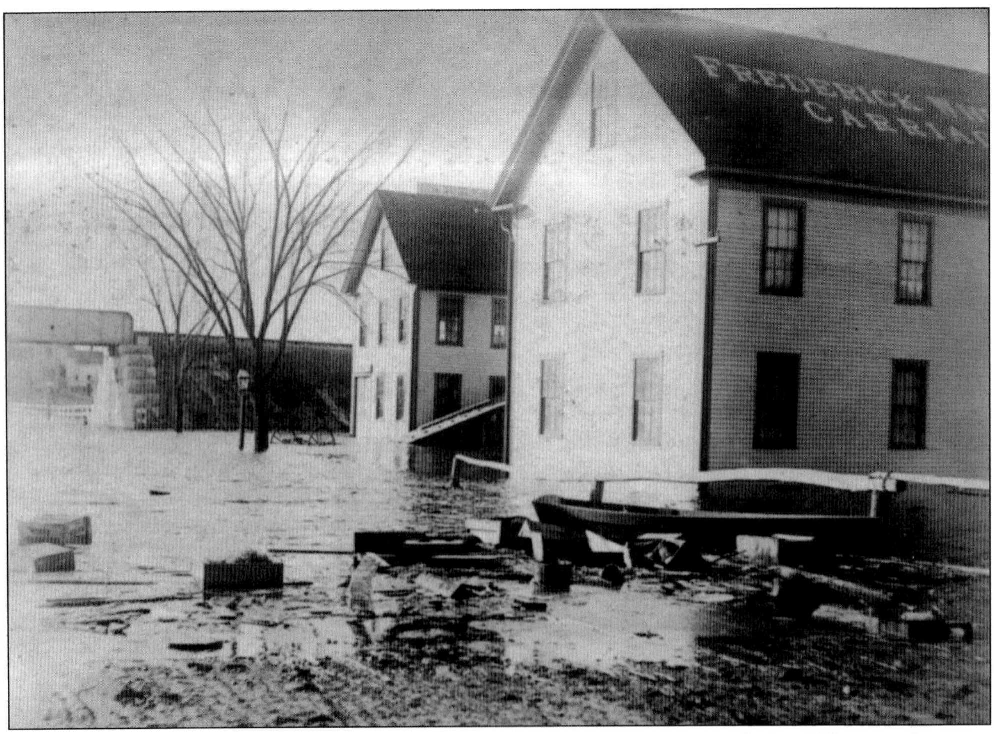

Another flood is shown here in February 1900 on West Main Street with the Whitney Carriage Company to the west. The railroad bridge in this photograph was erected just three years earlier in 1897. Next to the carriage company, there is a rowboat tied to the fence that someone may have used to get to work.

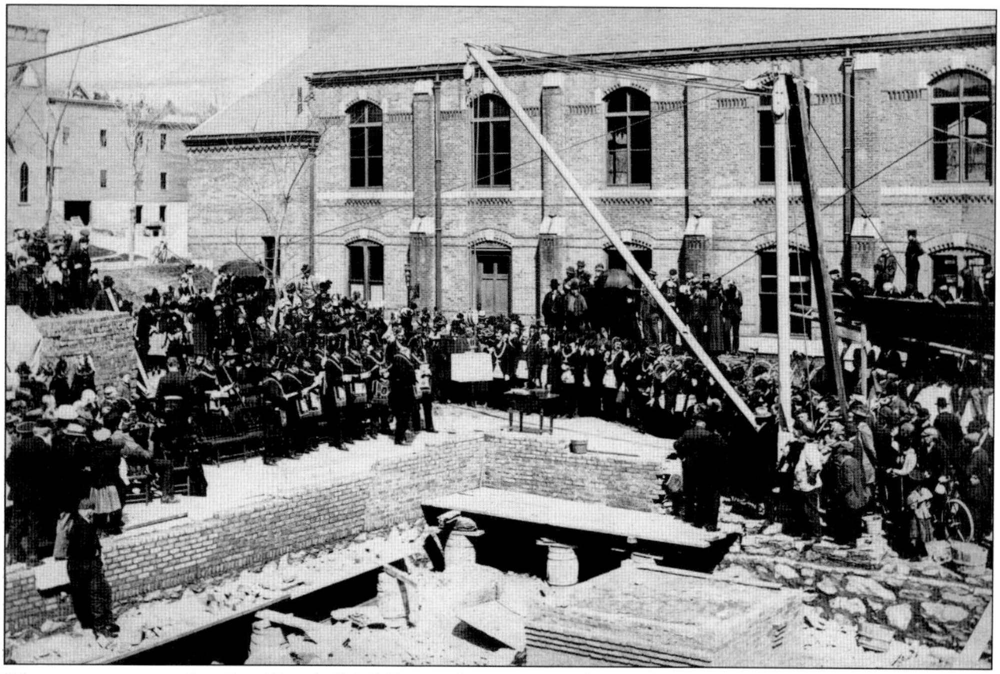

The cornerstone for the North Middlesex Savings Bank was laid in May 1898. This bank has been an integral part of Ayer for over 110 years. It was incorporated in 1885 as a mutual savings bank and operated for the benefit of its depositors.

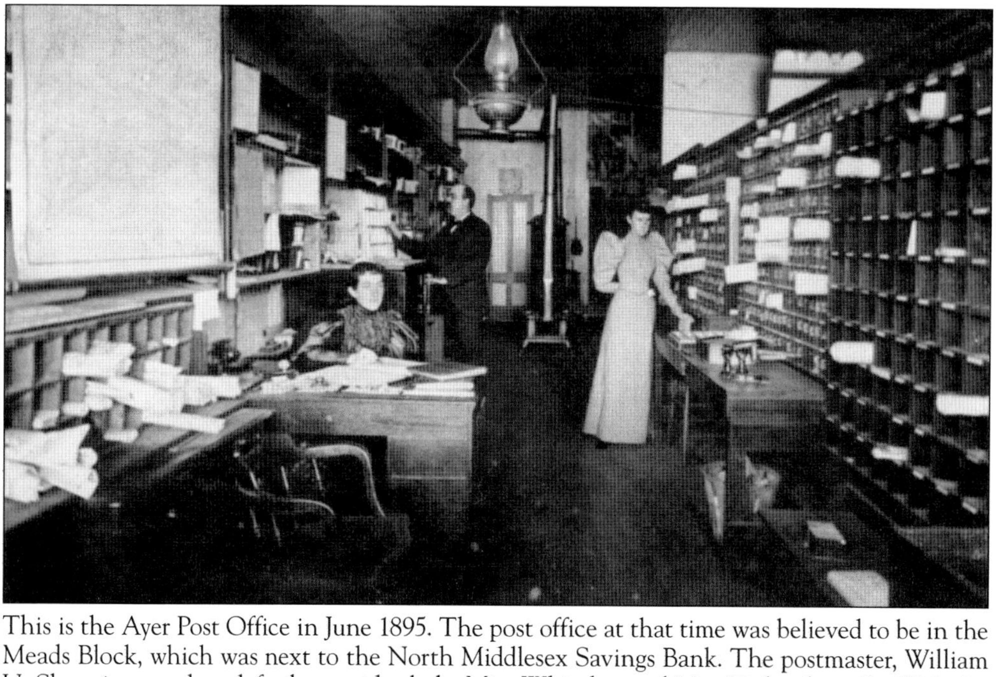

This is the Ayer Post Office in June 1895. The post office at that time was believed to be in the Meads Block, which was next to the North Middlesex Savings Bank. The postmaster, William U. Sherwin, stands at left along with clerks Miss Whitaker and Mrs. Richardson. In 1896, the post office moved to the town hall.

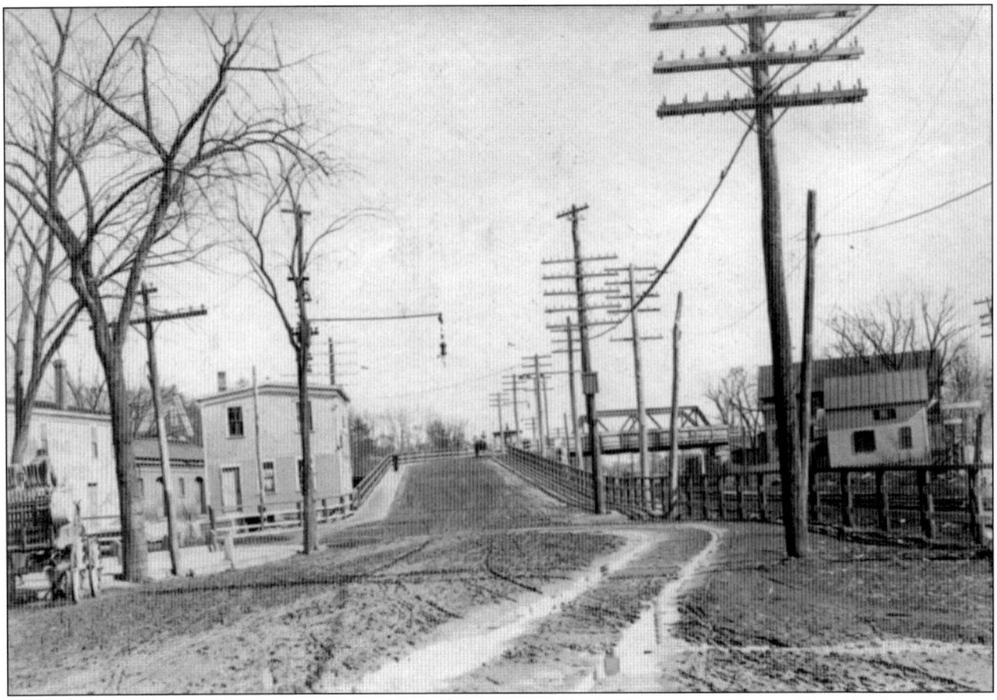

The bridge over the railroad tracks opened in 1906. This allowed traffic to flow freely, without stopping for passenger or freight trains. On the left of the photograph, there is a large tub on the side of the wagon and a row of brooms lined up in the back. The owner may have been a street cleaner. This bridge was replaced in 1950.

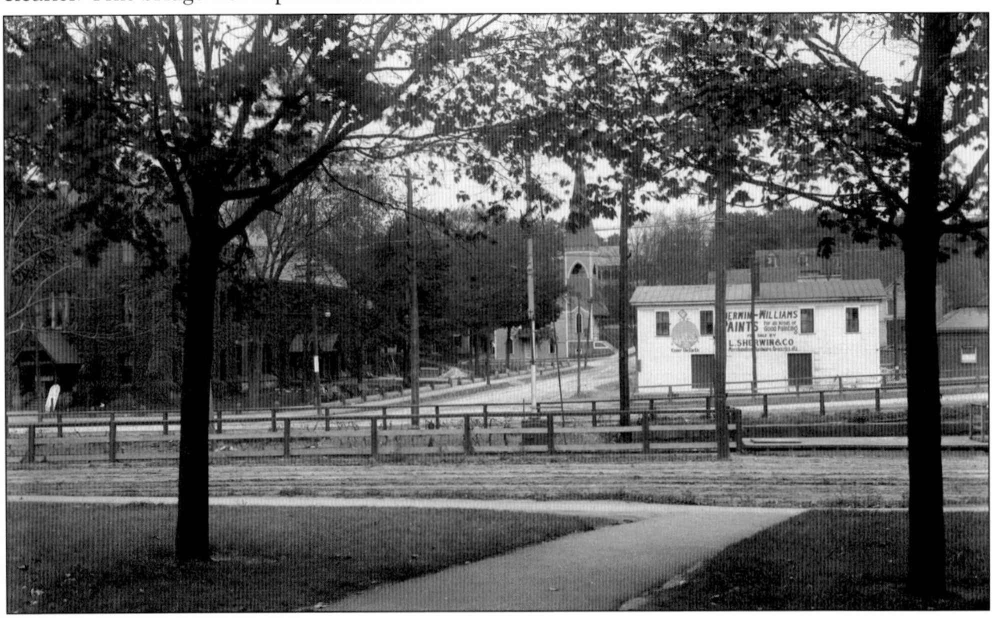

This October 1911 photograph was taken at East Main Street facing Columbia Street, five years after the Main Street crossing closed. Note that the church on Columbia Street has a steeple, but the church today does not. William U. Sherwin's store, started by his father, Levi, in 1871, is directly across the tracks.

Three

Economic and Commercial Growth

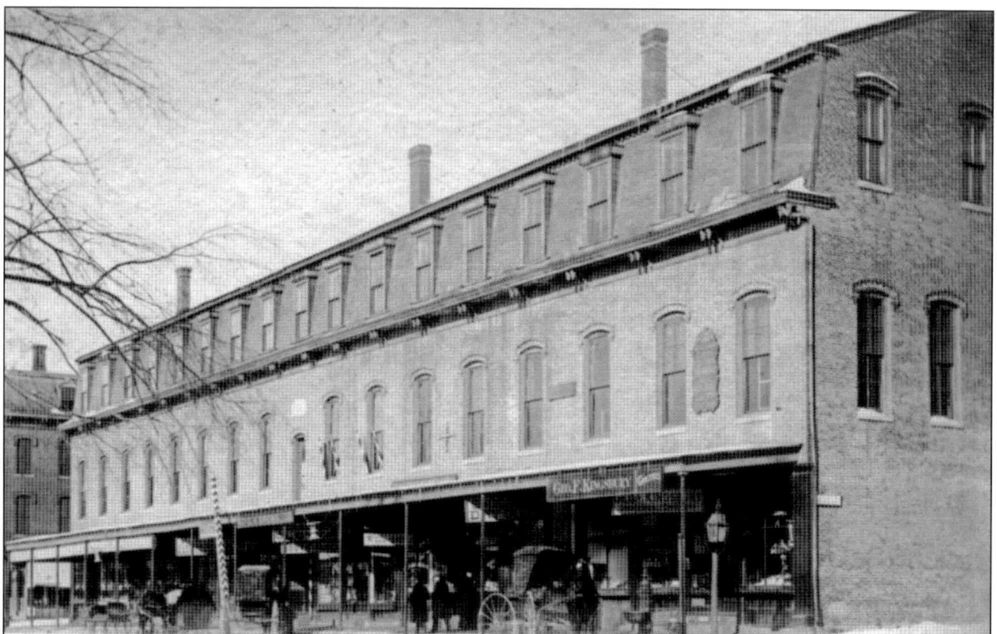

After the fire of 1872, Thomas and Alfred Page constructed a new building on the site of the one lost in the fire. This building has been home to many stores and offices. Upstairs, Page Hall was not only a place for dancing and music, but also a showplace to display new cars in the 1930s. The Page-Moore Building, as it is known today, is the centerpiece of the downtown area.

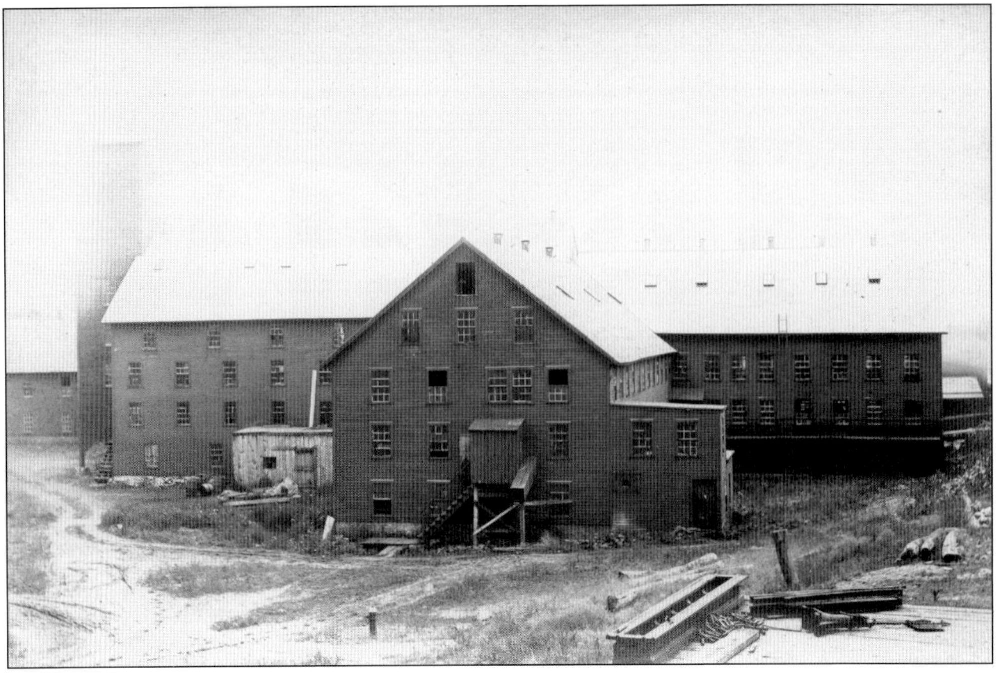

Since 1854, the Tannery employed many South Groton, Ayer, and surrounding town residents until it burned down in 1961. It had seen its good times and bad, but through it all, it did manage to survive. The Tannery fire burned for almost a week, taking other businesses and private residences with it.

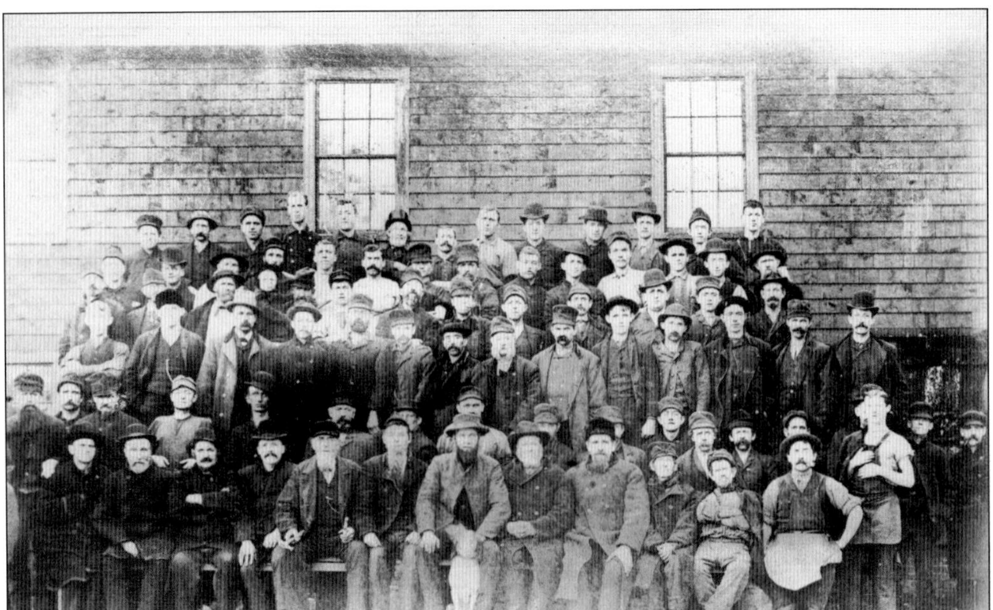

This photograph shows a group of Tannery workers in 1887. A closer look at these workers reveals they appear to be of all ages, young and old. Although he is difficult to see, note the fourth man from left in the fourth row holding a young child.

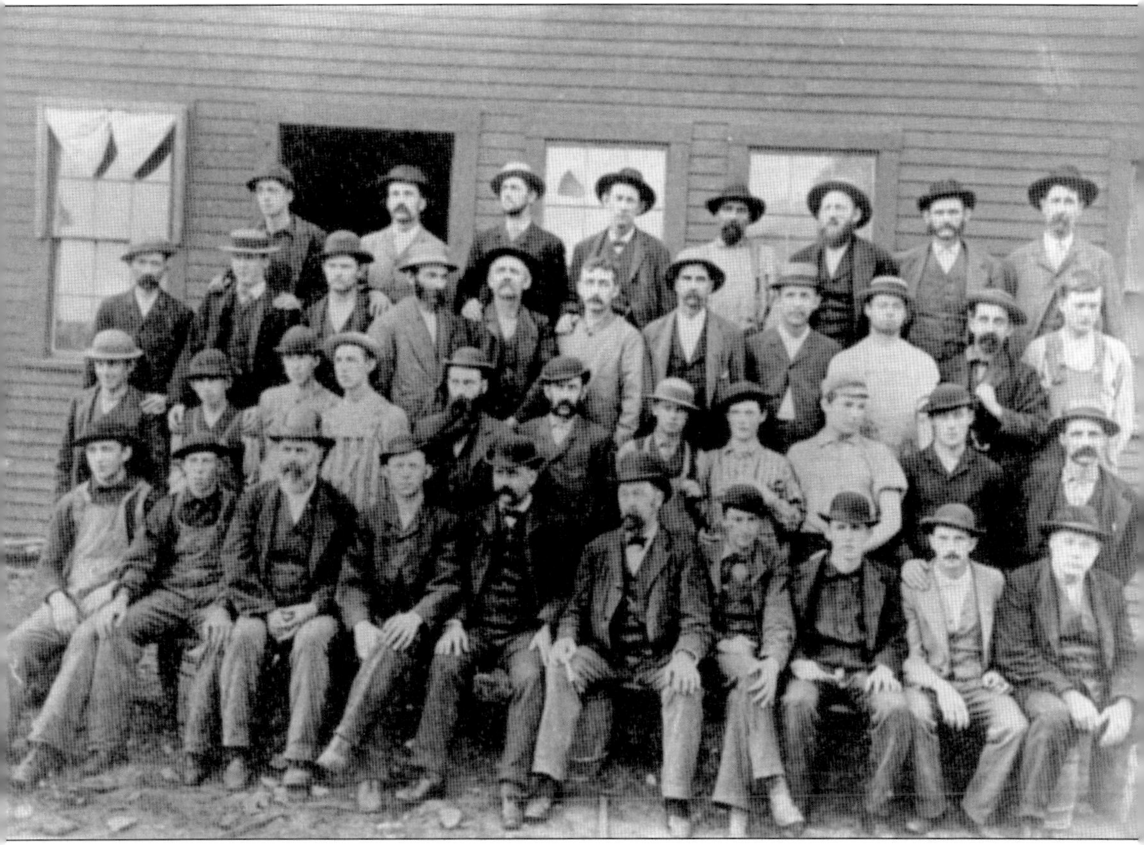

This c. 1886 photograph shows a group of workers from the Ayer Furniture Company. The workers of this time mostly came from Ayer and its surrounding towns and usually worked very long hours and sometimes under grueling conditions. The Ayer Furniture Company workers are, from left to right, (first row) Timothy O'Connell, George Barrett, Charles Lawton, Mark Page, Lewis Dion, William B. Fenner, Henry Firmin, William Barrett, Charles Chase, and James Sands; (second row) Adelbert Burns, Edward Carman, Edward Rivers, George Wadsworth, George Newton, Charles Bruce, Gillman Carman, Charles Dwinell, Parker Sprague, Walter Stuart, and Lewis Clark; (third row) Carl Page, Burleigh Richardson, a Mr. Tupper, Frank Smith, Luther Osborn, Frank McNulty, Jonathan Turner, Charles Ware, Robert Lawton, Nelson Russell, and Byrus Warren; (fourth row) John Gilday, Charles Wood, Frank Thayer, Henry Glasby, Allen McCurdy, Richard Pierce, Elbridge Whitaker, and William C. Wood.

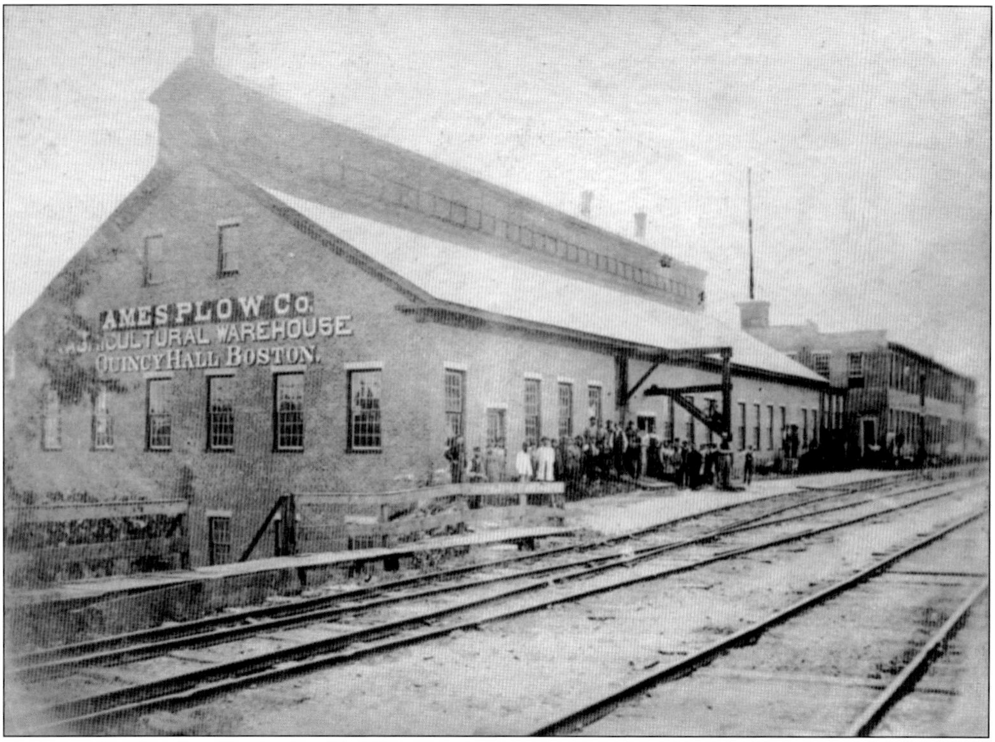

The Ames Plow Company sold agricultural supplies, such as plows and other agricultural equipment. This building was constructed in 1850 and originally housed the H.Q. Bean Company. In 1862, the Ames Plow Company constructed 23 buildings at Camp Stevens, a Civil War camp on the South Groton and Shirley line off the Great Road.

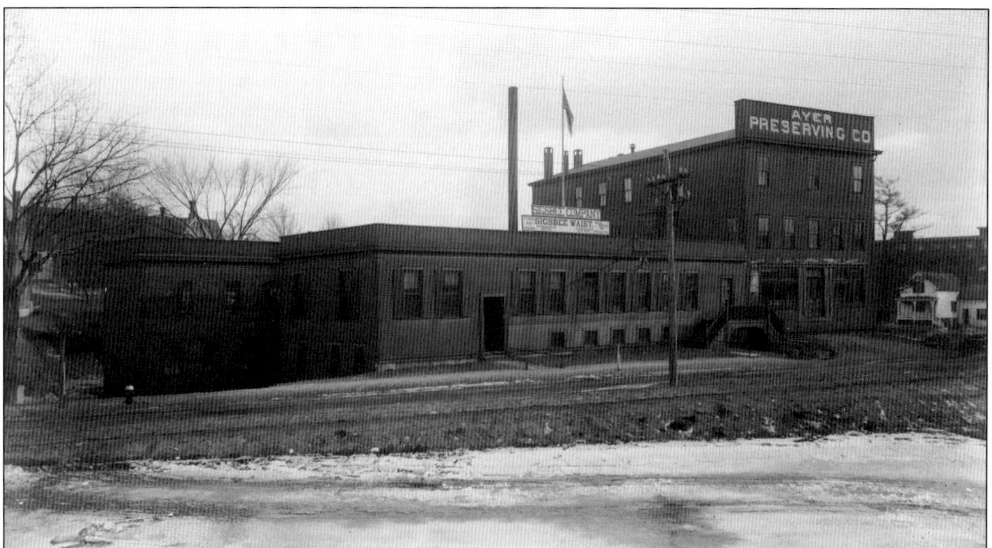

This photograph shows the Ayer Preserving Company and the Sigsbee Company. The Ayer Preserving Company produced syrups, jellies, preserves, and extracts. The Sigsbee Company manufactured flags and ensigns. The buildings were located on Tannery Street. The photograph was taken in March 1904, and in March 1915, both buildings fell victim to a fire and burned.

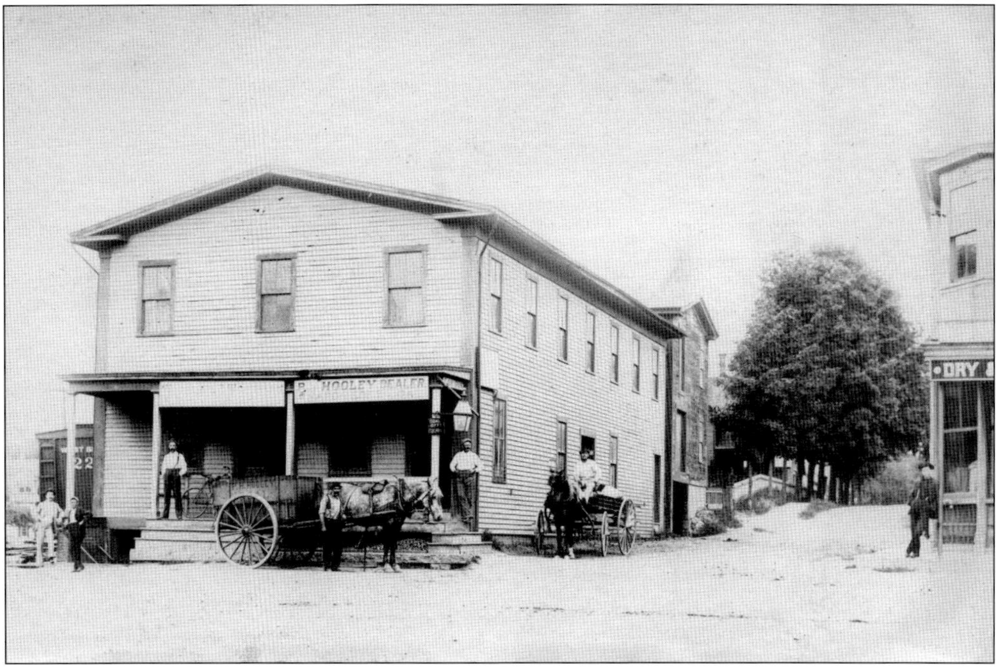

The original building constructed in 1858 was owned and operated by Stewart and Harlow and had burned in the fire of 1872. It was rebuilt on the same foundation. In 1894, P.H. Hooley occupied this building where flour, grain, and coal were sold. At that time, businesses that sold coal would often provide delivery. Note the delivery wagons in front and beside the store.

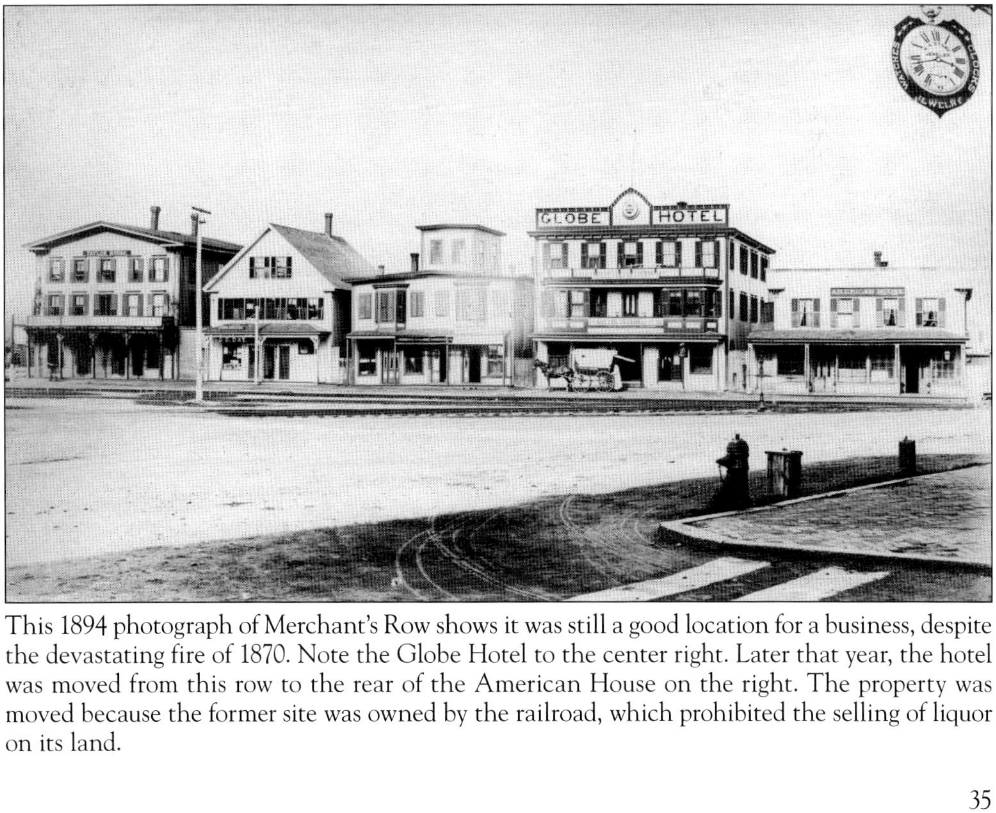

This 1894 photograph of Merchant's Row shows it was still a good location for a business, despite the devastating fire of 1870. Note the Globe Hotel to the center right. Later that year, the hotel was moved from this row to the rear of the American House on the right. The property was moved because the former site was owned by the railroad, which prohibited the selling of liquor on its land.

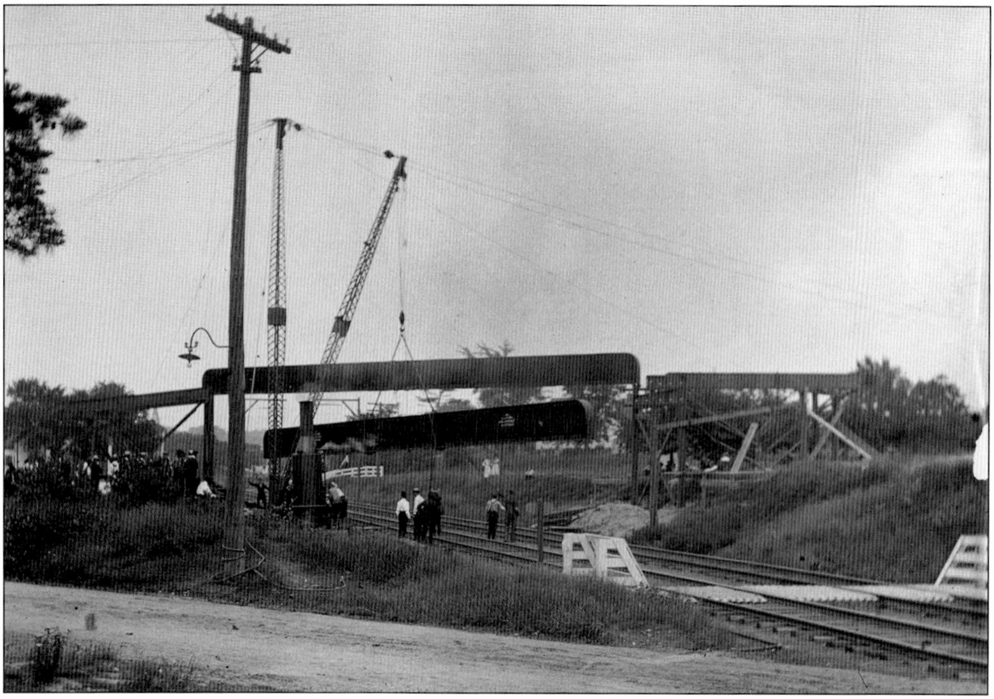

In this 1904 photograph, the Fitchburg and Leominster Street Railway Company installs a trolley line over the railroad tracks crossing West Main Street. The trolley line connected Ayer to parts of Shirley, Leominster, and Fitchburg. Under the bridge, the steam power for the crane is visible.

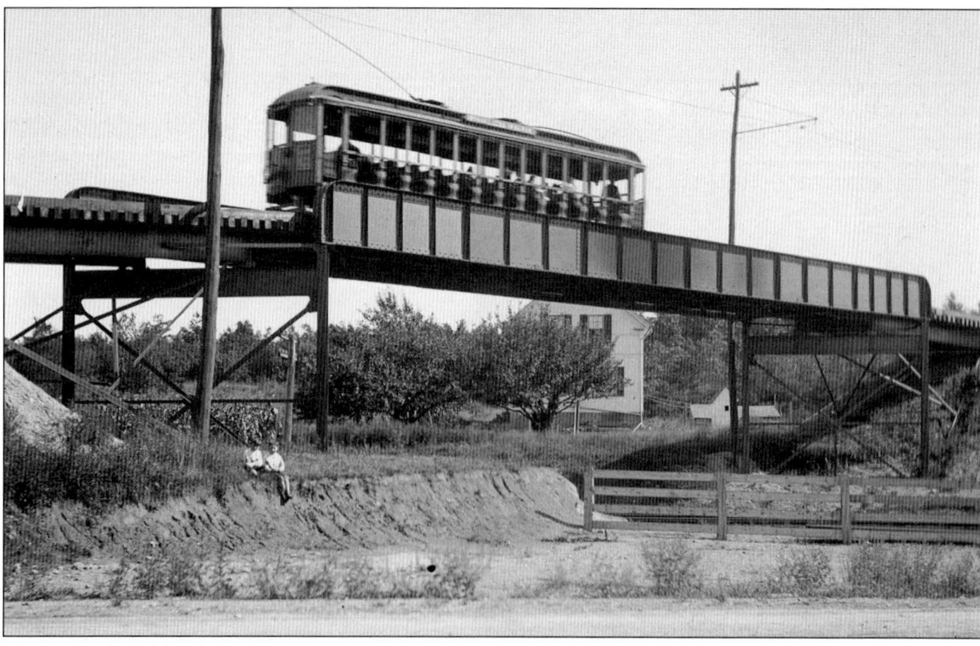

The completed bridge appears here in August 1905. With the completion of this bridge, people could ride this trolley to Shirley, Leominster, Fitchburg, and Lunenburg. Not all people or families could afford an automobile, so public transportation was used to access areas in Ayer and surrounding towns.

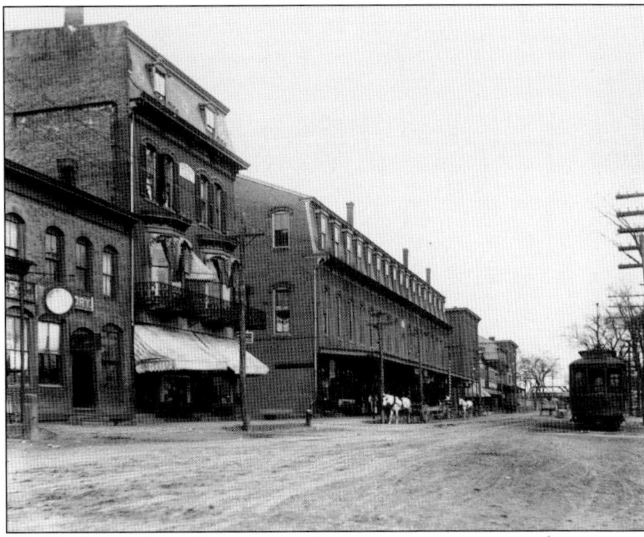

Construction began on two electric trolley lines in 1902. The Lowell and Fitchburg line connected Ayer with Lowell and suburban areas up to North Chelmsford. The Leominster, Shirley, and Ayer line, which crossed with the Leominster, Fitchburg, and Worcester lines at North Leominster, connected Ayer to many towns in the surrounding area. Pictured here around 1910, the recently erected bridge overpass is barely visible in the background.

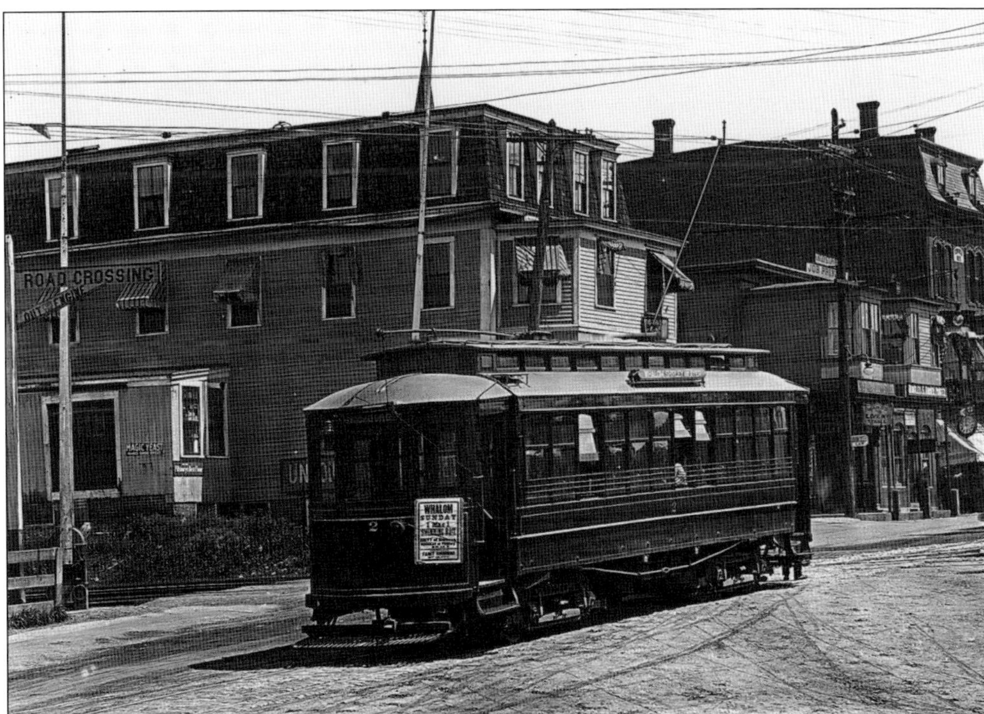

This photograph shows a trolley stopped on Main Street. From here, one could take the trolley to Whalom Park in Lunenburg. In the early 1900s, the park was a favorite destination for swimming, picnicking, and entertainment. (Courtesy of Ed Kelley.)

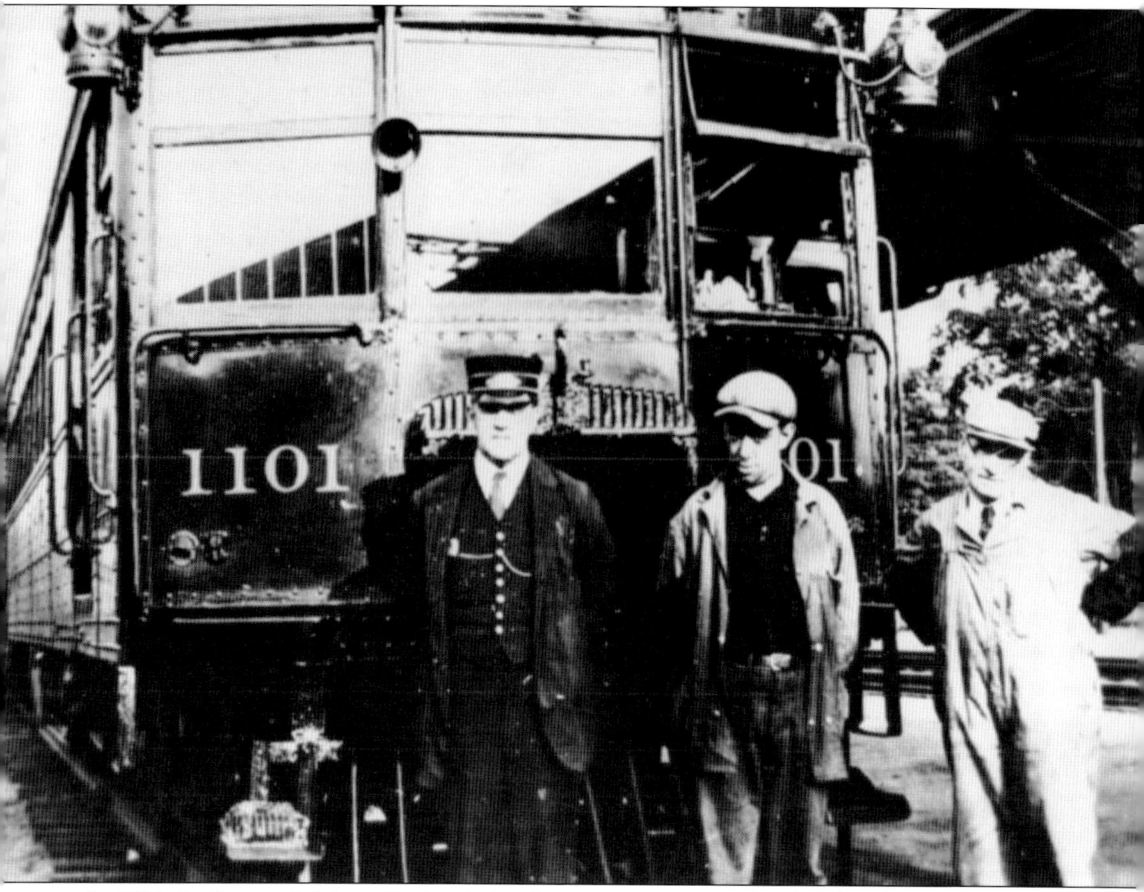

In 1927, the Boston & Maine Railroad closed its maintenance and railroad yards. This was a large blow to the area, as it had been the biggest employer in Ayer since 1849. Ayer's early growth as a town was due in large part to the railroad. The railroad attracted manufacturing companies who relied on the railroad to move merchandise and finished goods more easily. These companies attracted a new workforce who, in turn, required more homes to be built and rooms to be rented. If the railroad had not come to the area, Ayer might have remained a small farming community in South Groton. This 1930 photograph shows a Boston & Maine train of the Milford, New Hampshire, branch at the Ayer train depot. The engineer of engine No. 1101 is Red Hall on the far right, and its conductor is Eddie Hills on the far left. The man in the center is unidentified.

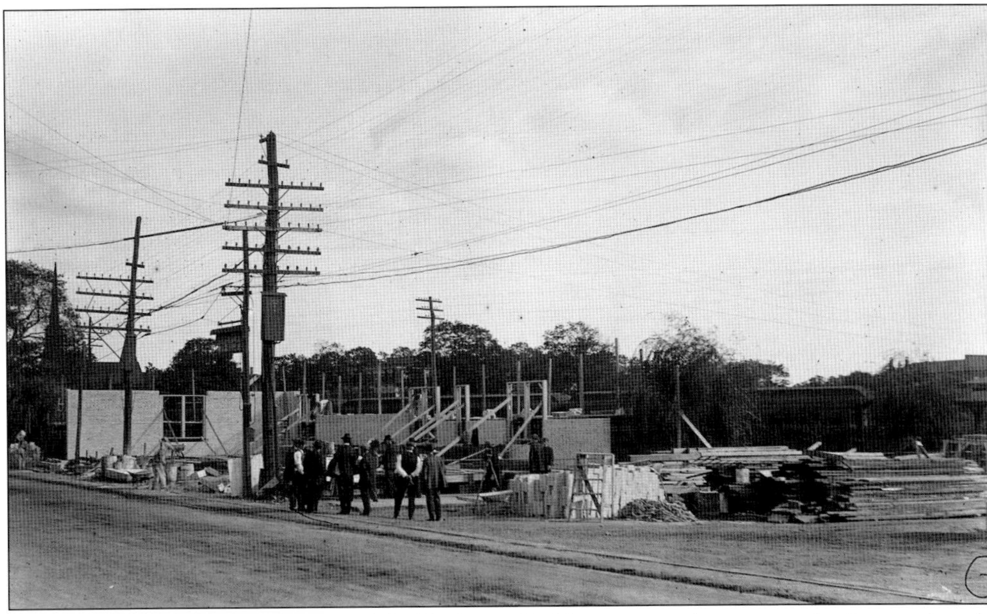

In October 1, 1914, construction of the J.J. Barry Building was under way on the former site of a railroad freight house. Almost a century later, this is still a family-owned business and is an active part of the downtown business community. This building is believed to be the only commercial structure on the south side of Main Street at this time.

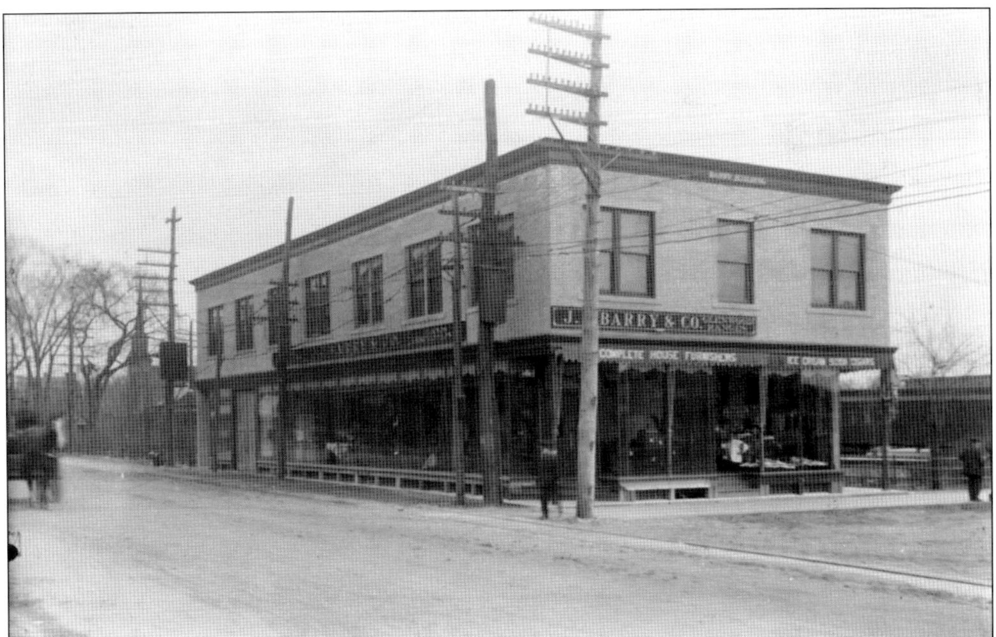

Here, construction of the J.J. Barry Building is complete. The business offered home furnishings, gas ranges, gramophones, and pianos. There is also an ice cream soda and cigar shop at the store. Today, it is the home of the Ayer Package Store, and it is still an important part of the local economy.

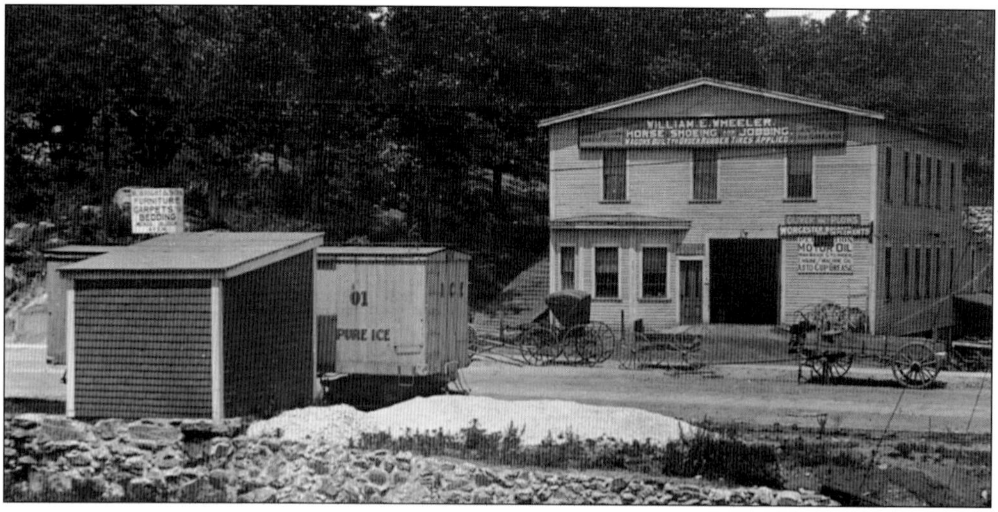

Pictured here in June 11, 1913, this shop was owned by William E. Wheeler, a blacksmith and wagon builder. Wagons wait to be repaired in the front. In the foreground, next to the train car, is an icehouse that was owned by a Mr. Pere. Ayer had two or three icehouses that shipped ice to places like Boston and Brookline, New Hampshire.

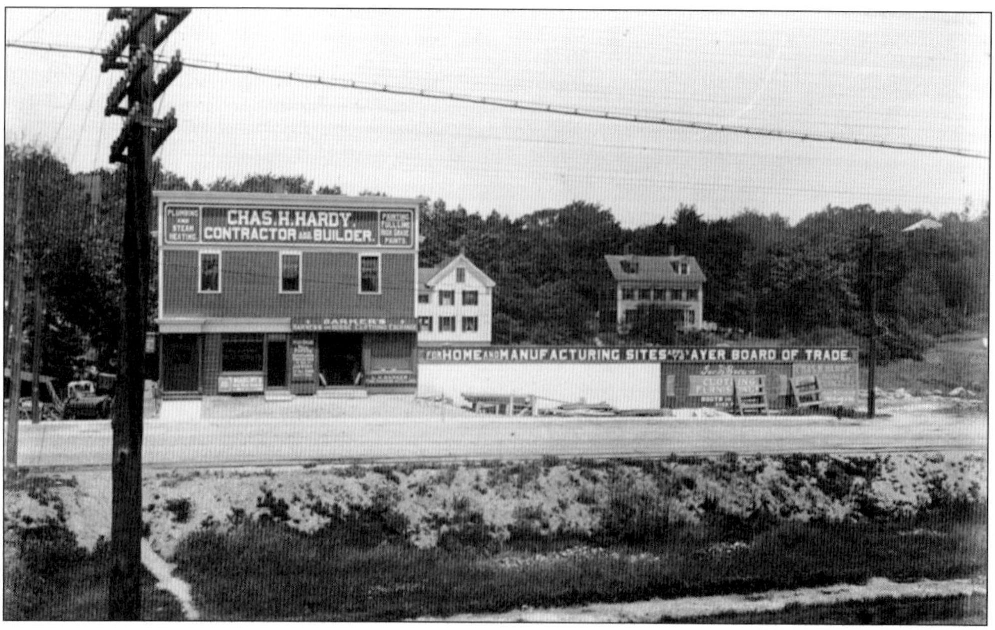

The Charles H. Hardy Building was constructed in December 1911. Hardy was a plumbing and heating contractor as well as a real estate agent. Charles Kennison took this photograph in June 1913.

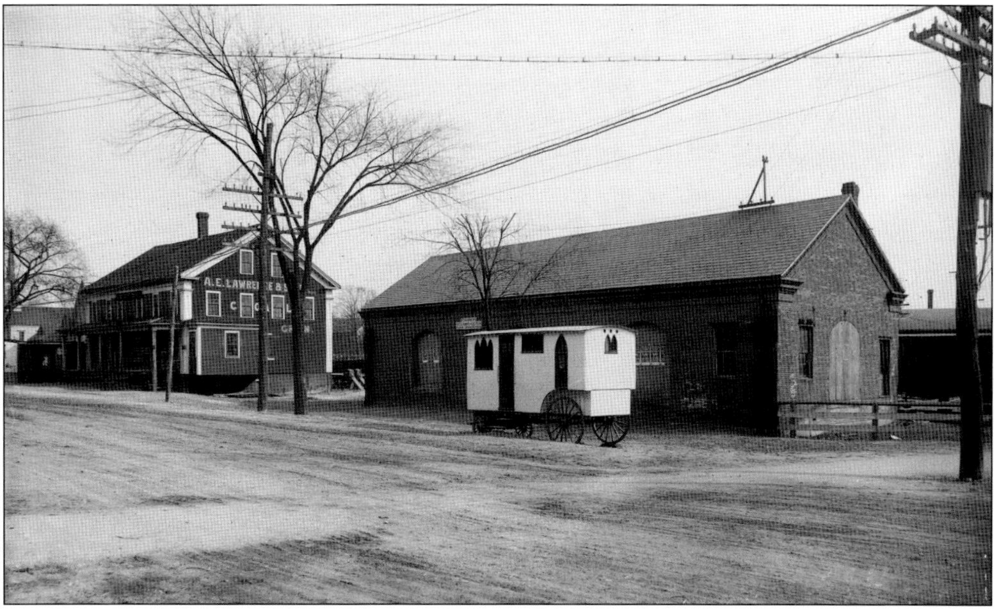

A.E. Lawrence & Sons appears here in 1906, selling feed, flour, grain, and coal. At the time, it was the only store on the south side of Main Street. The rail line right behind the store made off-loading goods convenient. The lunch wagon business must have been profitable, as there is one in front of the freight house and another beyond Lawrence's store near the Main Street crossing.

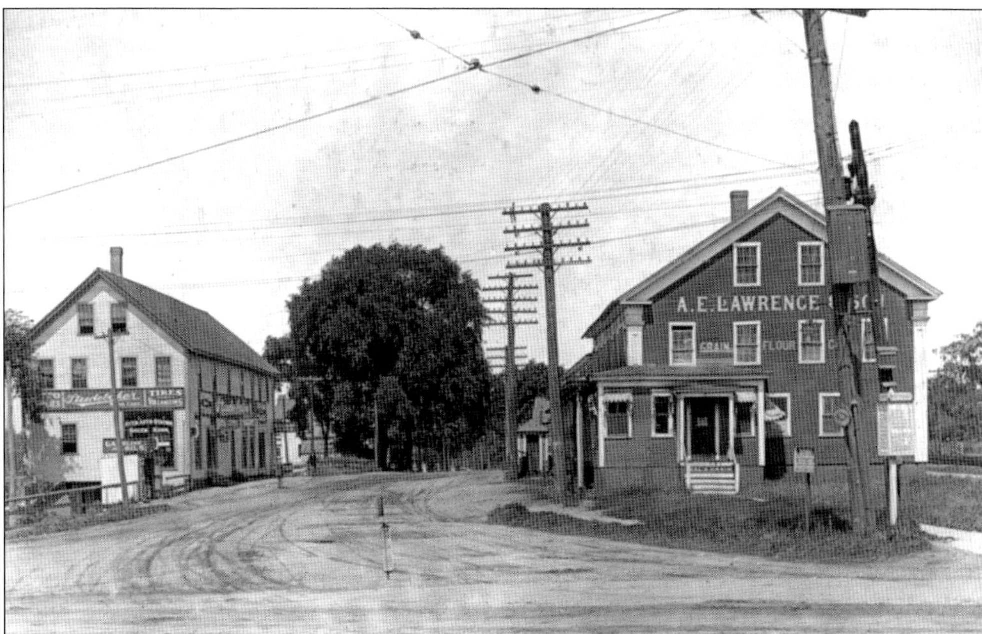

Lawrence's feed and flour store is pictured here in August 1916 on the corner of Main Street and Park Street. The store was moved from the south side of Main Street to this convenient location adjacent to the railroad.

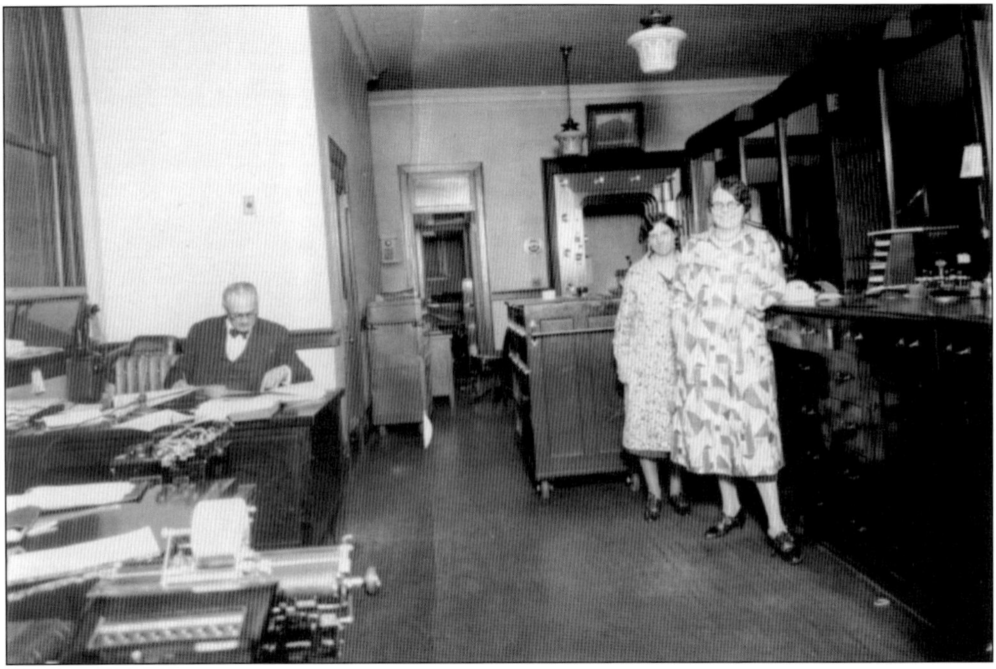

This photograph of the employees of the North Middlesex Savings Bank may have been taken in the 1920s. Note the absence of any electric office equipment.

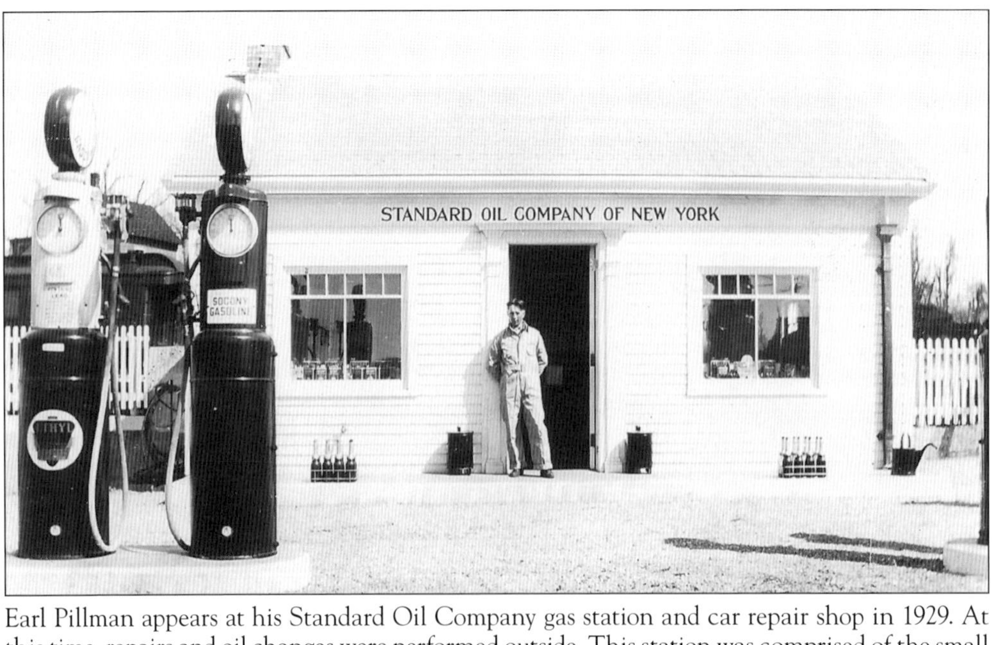

Earl Pillman appears at his Standard Oil Company gas station and car repair shop in 1929. At this time, repairs and oil changes were performed outside. This station was comprised of the small building seen here. Repair work had to be done outside on a lift that is not visible here. Today, Don Chapman's Nu-Kar automobile dealership occupies this Park Street location.

Four

THE FACES OF AYER'S HISTORY

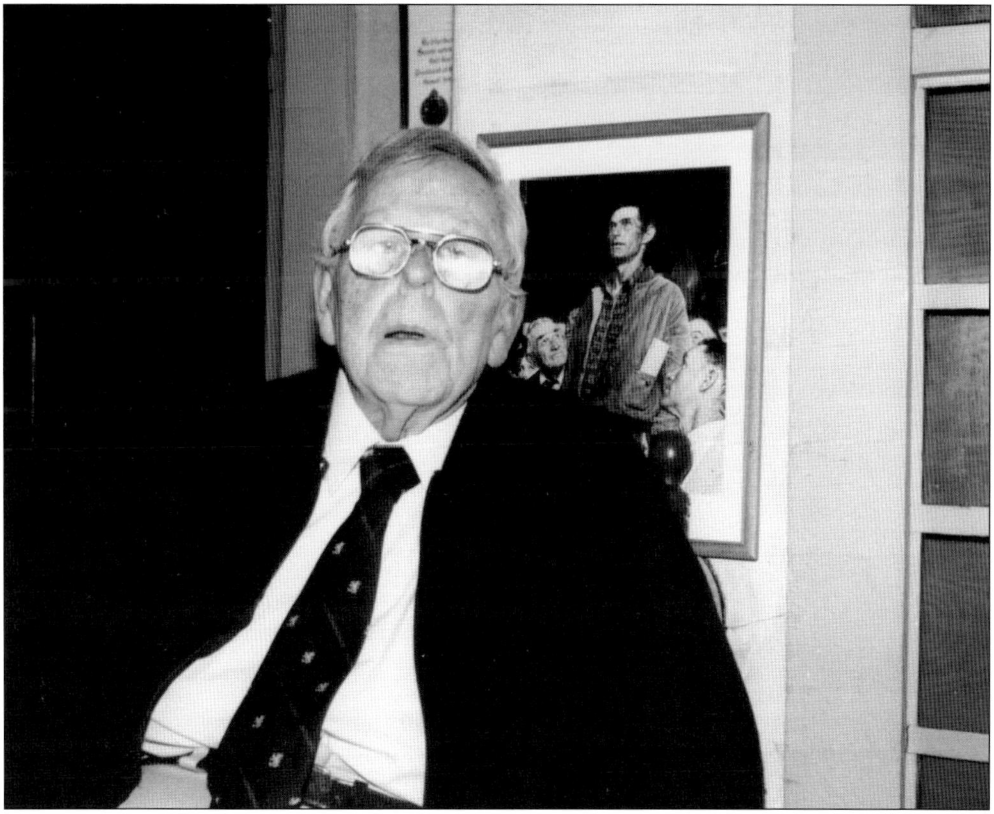

Ralph H. Richardson was a longtime resident and a respected historian of Ayer. He wrote many articles for the *Public Spirit*. These articles are still available in the Ayer Library and are as much a tribute to the history makers of Ayer as they are to Richardson for writing them. In 1927, he became the town moderator at the age of 25 and held that post for 53 years. (Courtesy of Janet Lewis.)

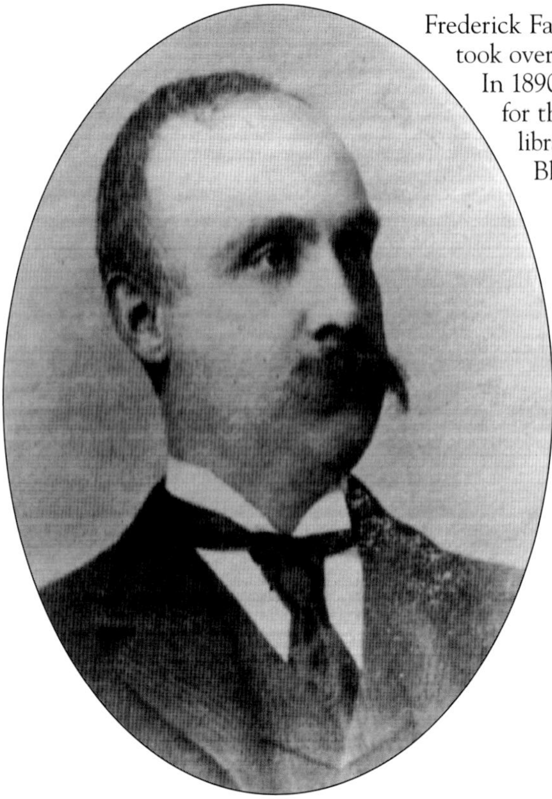

Frederick Fanning Ayer, son of Dr. James Cook Ayer, took over his father's estate upon his death in 1878. In 1890, he presented $5,000 to the town of Ayer for the purchase of library books. By 1882, the library had moved from the post office in Mead's Block to the town hall.

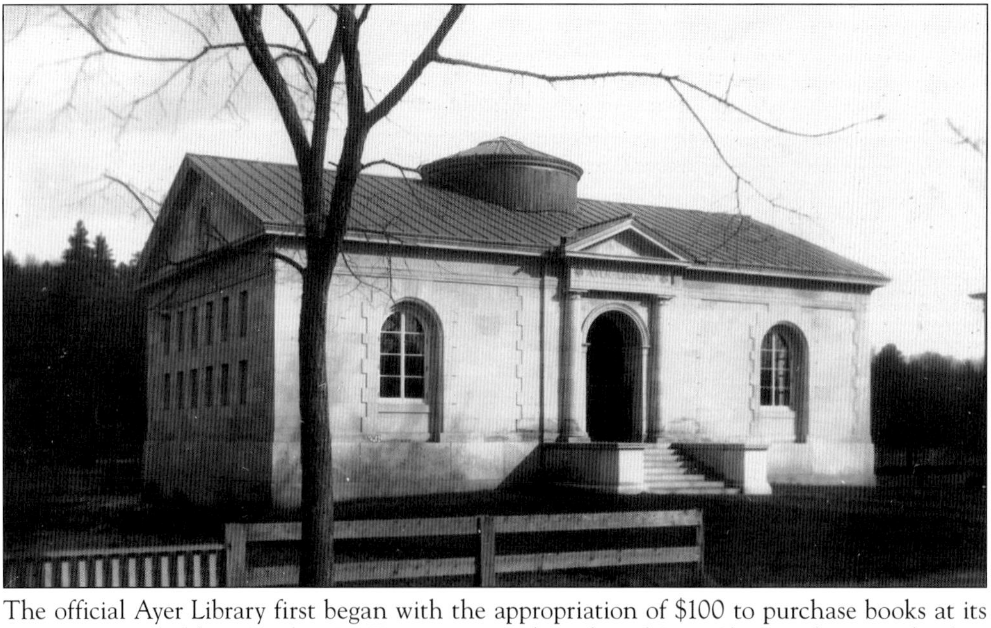

The official Ayer Library first began with the appropriation of $100 to purchase books at its town meeting held in April 1871. Trustees were elected, and Levi Sherwin became the first librarian. He then housed the library at his store on Main Street. The Literal and Musical Club and Benjamin H. Hartwell donated money, and the club presented their newly formed library to the town of Ayer.

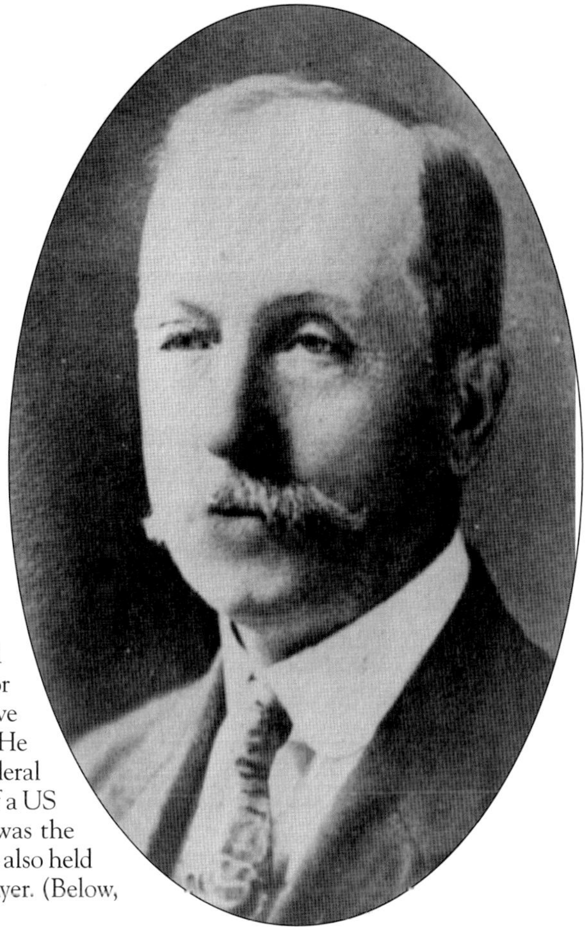

Edward A. Richardson was a landowner and a well-respected public official in the town of Ayer and in the state legislature. He was at the 1917 Constitutional Convention and, at the same time, ran for a seat in the 12th Middlesex Representative District, a position that he later held. He was instrumental in working with the federal government regarding the placement of a US Army cantonment camp in Ayer. He was the father of Ralph H. Richardson, who was also held in high regard by the townspeople of Ayer. (Below, courtesy of Zelda Moore.)

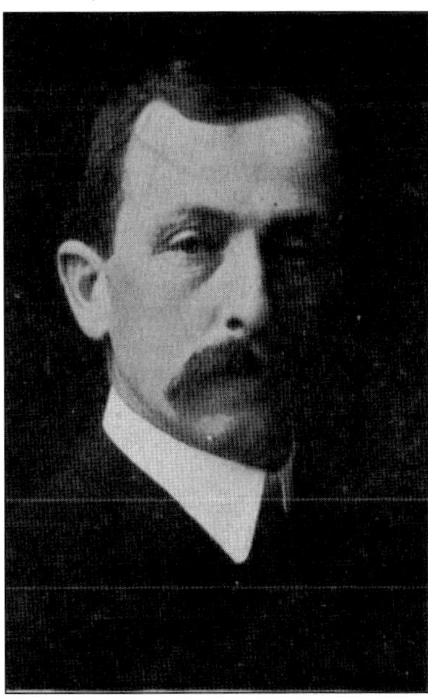

AT THE

State Primaries Tuesday, Sept. 25, 1917

Republican Voters and all others who wish to declare themselves as such will select a candidate for Representative in the Twelfth Middlesex Representative District to be voted for in November.

As a candidate I wish to announce to my friends in Ashby, Ayer, Dunstable, Groton, Pepperell, Shirley and Townsend that I am unable to make a personal canvass in the towns comprising the district.

My duties as a member of the Constitutional Convention now in session and affairs connected directly with the establishment of the U. S. Army Cantonment at Ayer demand my attention prior to the primaries.

I wish to express my appreciation for whatever efforts may be made in my behalf.

Very sincerely,

EDWARD A. RICHARDSON,

6 Washington St., Ayer, Mass.

Please Remember: A Primary Nomination THIS YEAR is probably equivalent to an election

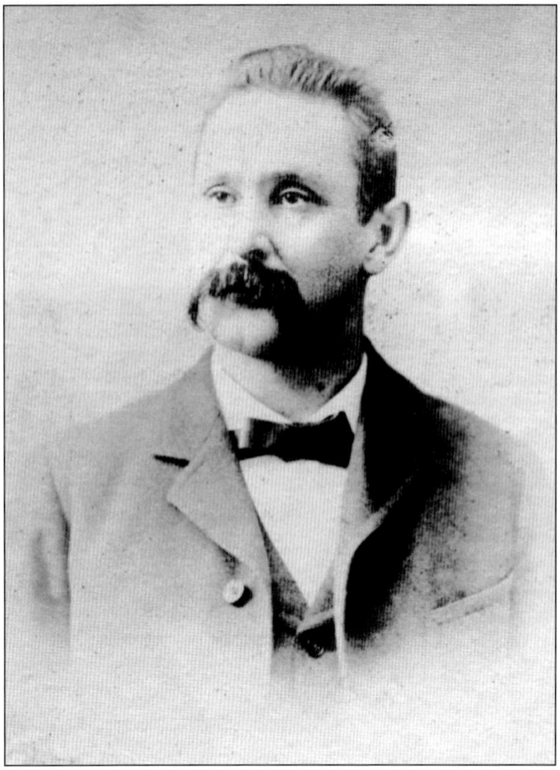

William U. Sherwin was born in Townsend, Massachusetts, in 1851. He was the son of Levi and Mary Jane Sherwin. His father opened up a store in Groton Junction that sold periodicals, wallpaper, and toys. After Levi died in 1889, William and his brother Charles took over the store. They enlarged it, offering hardware, dry goods, and groceries. William became selectman in 1887, serving six terms.

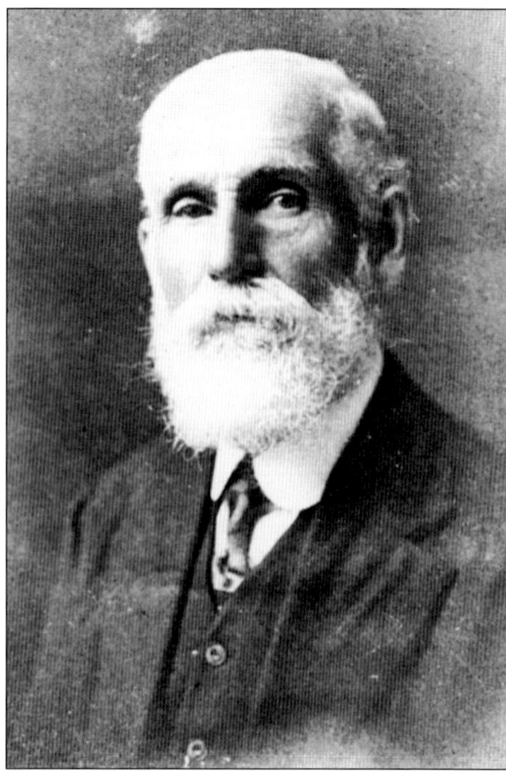

John H. Turner established his printing business in Groton Junction in 1865. In 1868, he established the *Groton Public Spirit*. Over the years, the newspaper grew in popularity and increased in circulation. It was later called *Turner's Public Spirit*. Now the *Public Spirit* weekly, it continues to report local news and events.

Benjamin Franklin Taft was born in 1823 in Northbridge, Massachusetts. He came to Groton Junction in 1853 and worked at the H.Q. Bean Company, a manufacturer of agricultural implements. The company was succeeded by the Ames Plow Company, where Taft was manager of operations. In 1862, he oversaw the construction of 23 buildings at Camp Stevens, which were completed in 12 days.

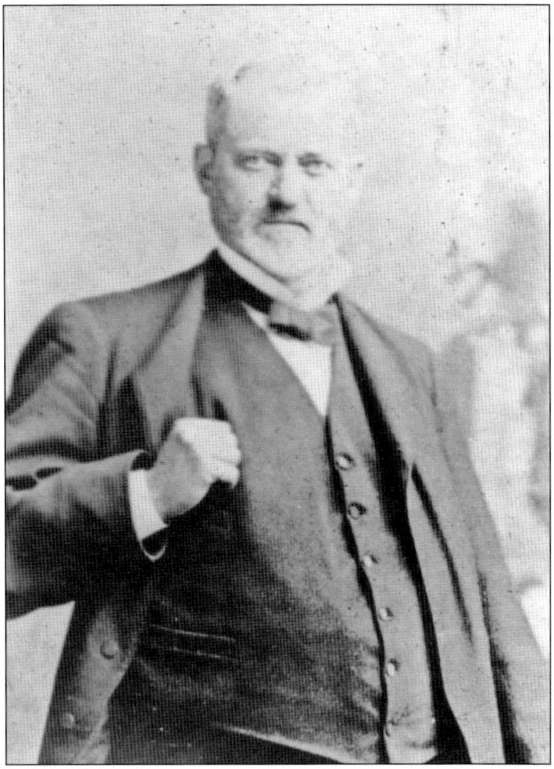

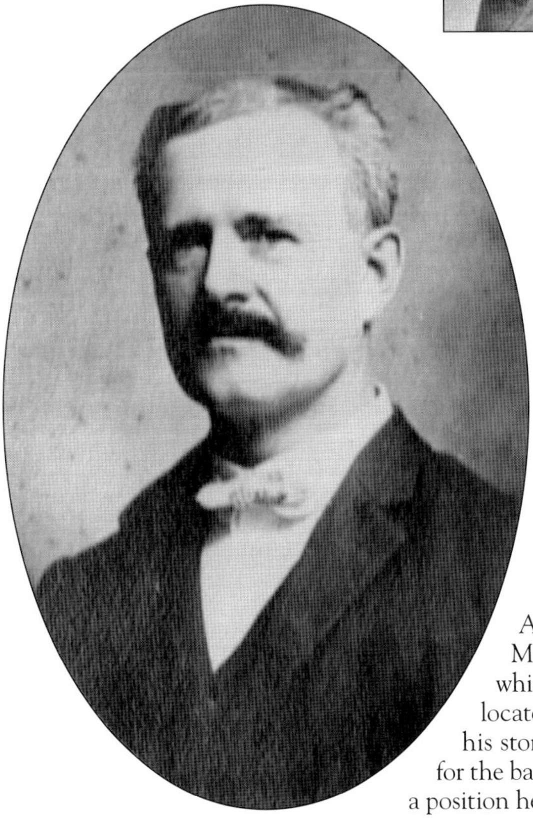

Albert A. Fillebrown came to Ayer in 1884 from Maine. He opened up a store on Main Street, which sold tin, hardware, and stoves. His store was located where the Bank Block is today. He moved his store to East Main Street in 1898 to make way for the bank. In 1908, he was appointed deputy sheriff, a position he held until his death 12 years later.

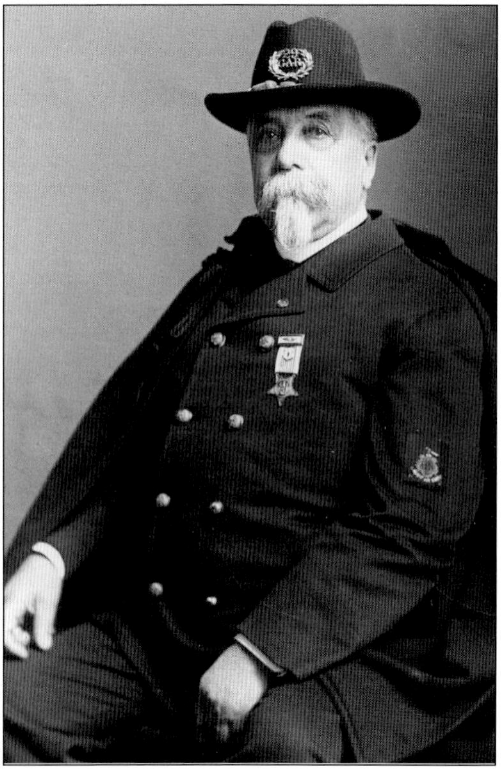

Dr. John Quincy Adams McCollester came from Deerfield, Massachusetts. He settled in Groton Junction in 1857, where he had a large medical practice. He served in the Civil War from 1860 to 1865 and was a regimental surgeon for the 53rd Regiment Massachusetts Volunteer Infantry at Camp Stevens. He was appointed examining surgeon for pensioners in 1864 and held that position until 1876. He was then appointed to the US Examining for Pensioners in 1898, with an office in Waltham.

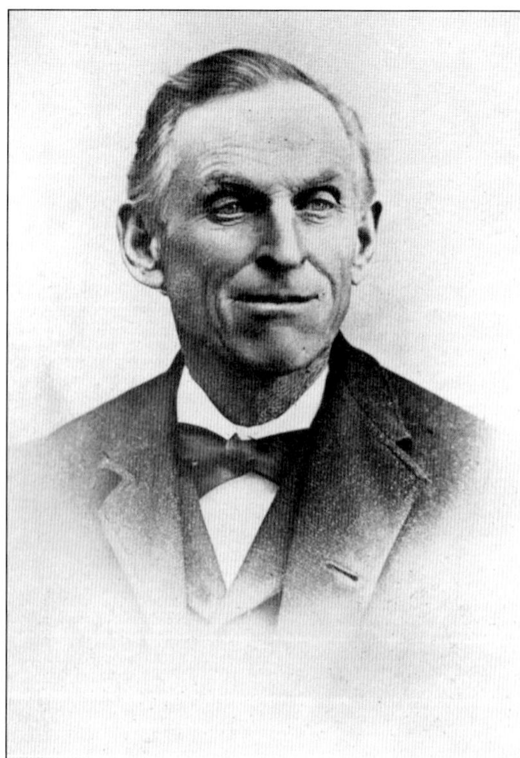

Levi W. Phelps was born in 1821 in Lancaster, Massachusetts. At the age of 14, he began his apprenticeship in the lumbering business in Leominster with a salary of $35 a year. He came to the area in 1854 as a contractor, manufacturer, and supplier of lumber products. At 94, he supervised a building project in Mitchellville. His descendants own the Moore Lumber Company in Ayer. (Courtesy of Zelda Moore.)

William M. Sargent came to Ayer in 1875, where he started a booking and publishing company. He published a book about Ayer called *Town of Ayer, some of the leading industries, principal buildings and prominent citizens*. It was published in 1902.

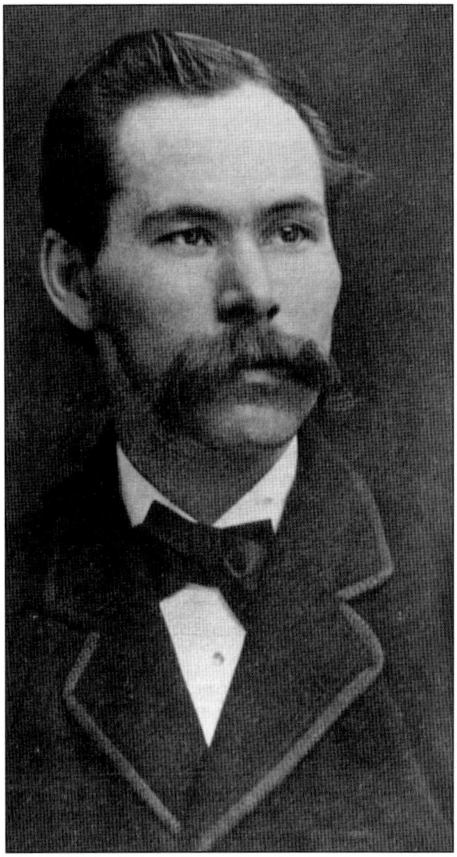

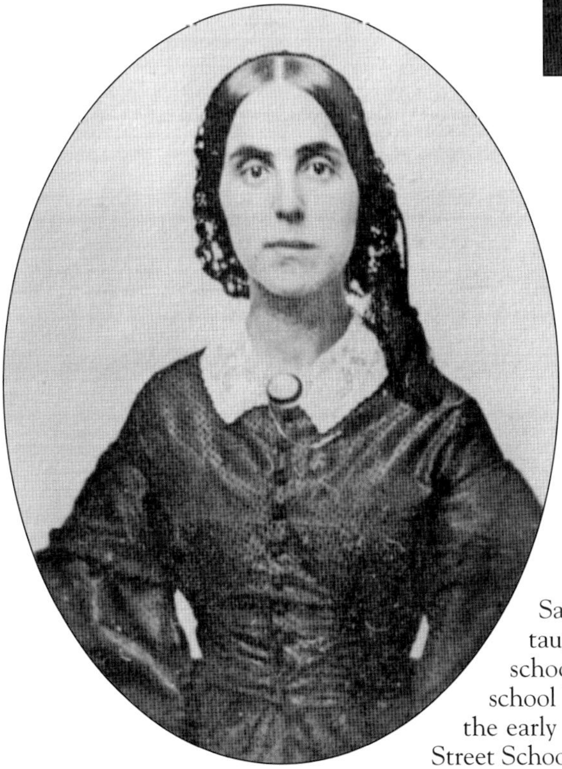

Sarah Rice Brooks was a schoolteacher who taught school at the Sandy Pond one-room schoolhouse in 1851. At about that time, the school burned and was not rebuilt until 1868. In the early 1860s, Brooks taught at the Washington Street School.

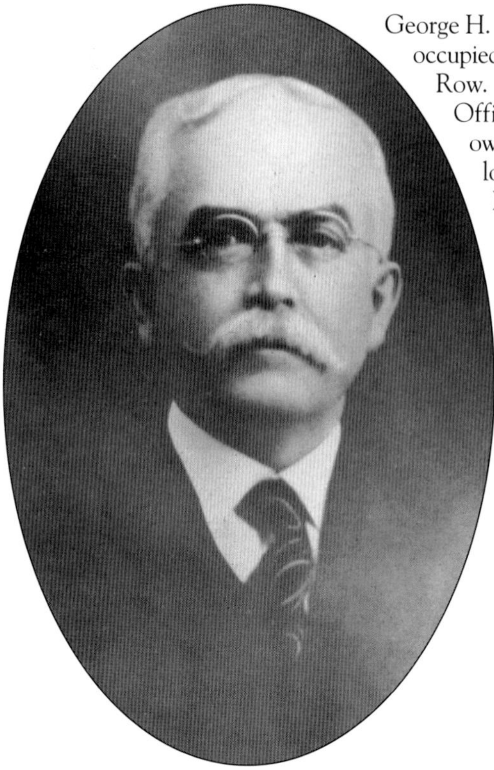

George H. Brown was born in Groton in 1858. His business occupied the first floor of the north building on Merchant's Row. The store also held the Groton Junction Post Office, where Brown was postmaster. He was also owner of a large clothing store and a pharmacy. The longest continuous ownership and operation of a Massachusetts pharmacy by several generations of the same family, Brown's Pharmacy was located on Main Street.

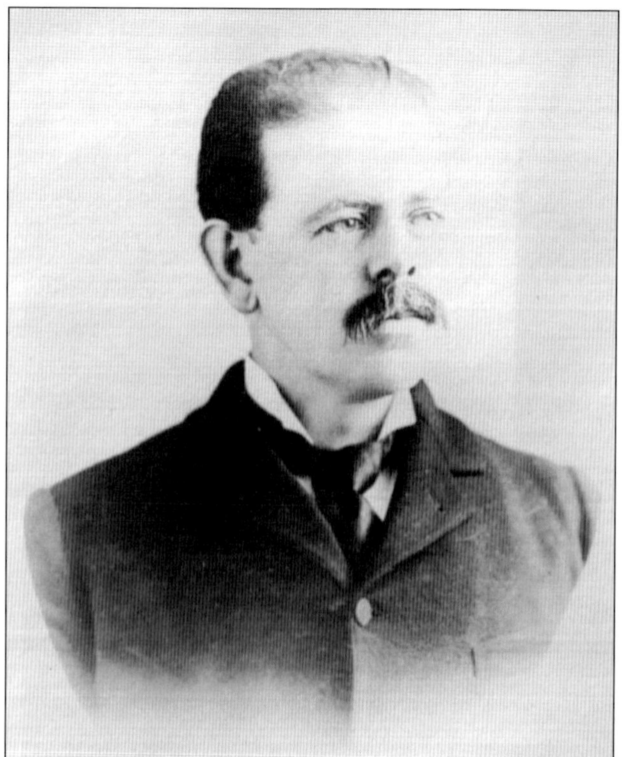

Born in Westford, Massachusetts, on July 14, 1855, George J. Burns was educated in Ayer and was in the first graduating class of Ayer High School in 1875. He attended law school at Boston University, received his degree in 1878, and was admitted to the bar that same year. He authored the chapter about Ayer in Volume Two of the *History of Middlesex County*, published in 1890.

Susanna Whitney Reed came to South Groton in 1856. She approved books submitted to the library. Showing her public spirit, she personally solicited money to have the town install water at the Woodlawn Cemetery.

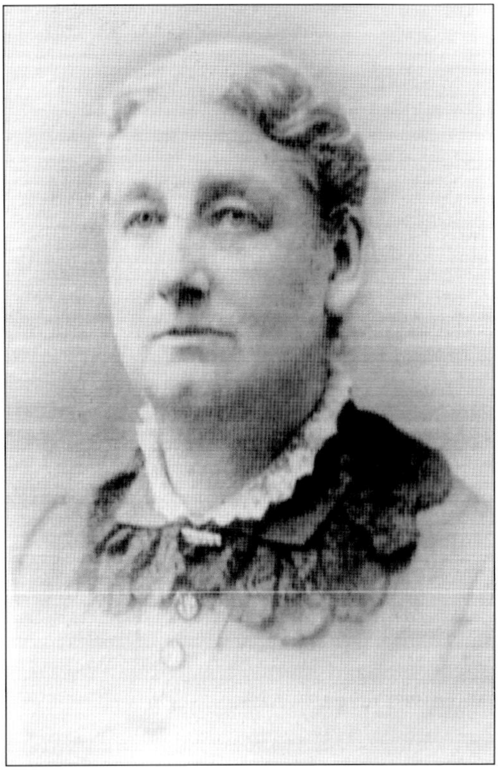

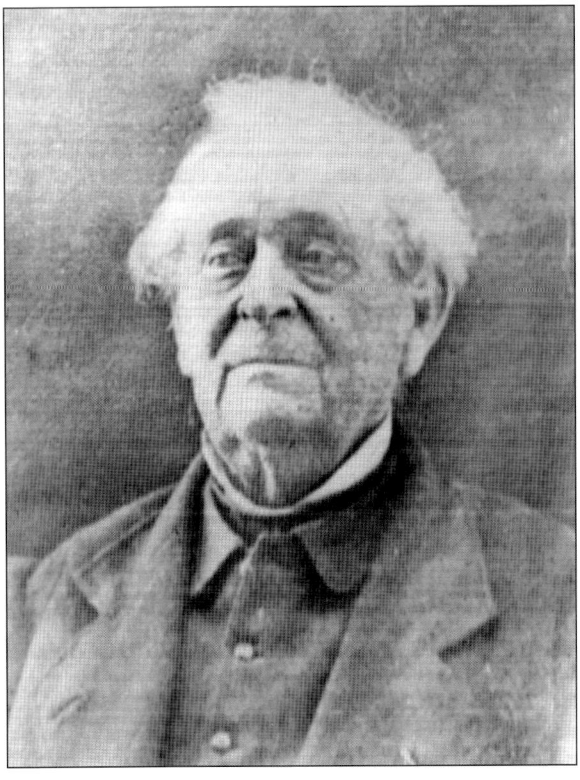

Harvey A. Woods was born in 1807 in Townsend, Massachusetts. After moving to South Groton, he purchased a dry goods business on the north side of Main Street in 1852. In 1867, he moved the business to a new building across Main Street. Woods also sold real estate. He purchased land and constructed a building where the North Middlesex Savings Bank now stands. This wooden building was destroyed by fire in 1879.

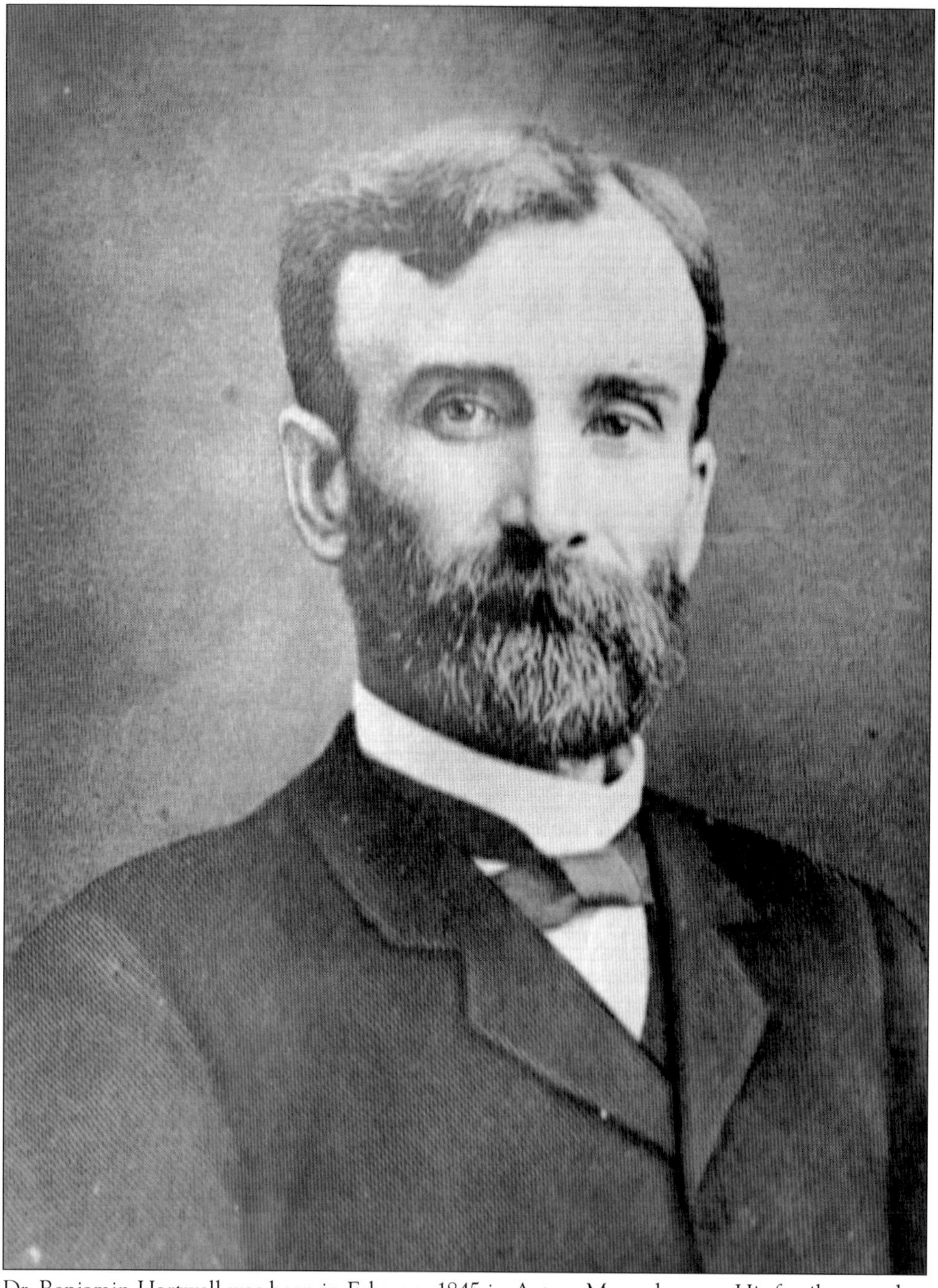

Dr. Benjamin Hartwell was born in February 1845 in Acton, Massachusetts. His family moved to South Groton when he was two years old. He attended schools in Ayer and graduated from Lawrence Academy in Groton. He taught school at the Sandy Pond schoolhouse and at the high school from 1866 to 1867. He went back to school to earn a degree in medicine. In 1869, he returned to South Groton, where he set up his medical practice. He was a member of many professional medical groups and was on the school board in Ayer for many years. He organized a private circulating library in 1869 and presented it to the town of Ayer in 1871 as its first official library.

Silas Nutting was born in South Groton in 1818 and lived his entire life in the same home. His estate encompassed most of what is East Main Street today. In 1910, his daughter Sarah J.S. Nutting Bennett conveyed to the town her Nutting's Grove to be used as a public park. Today, it is known as Pirone Park.

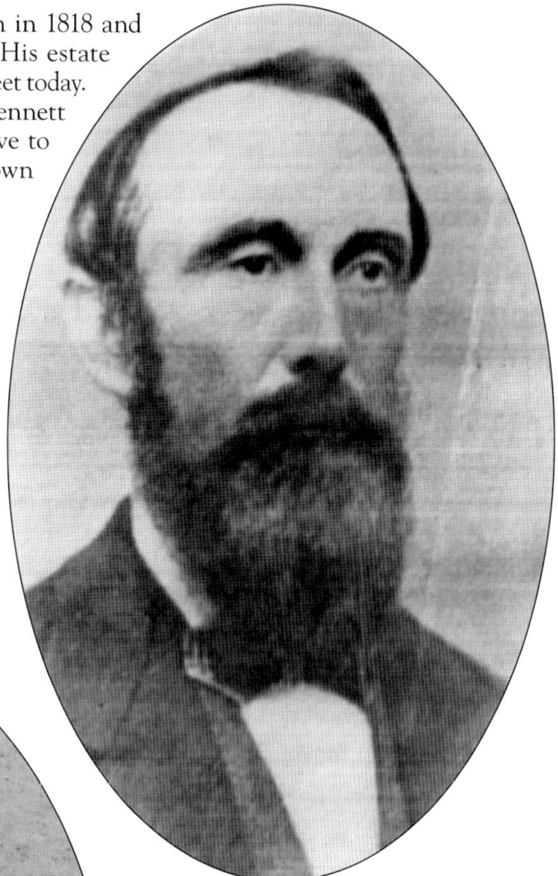

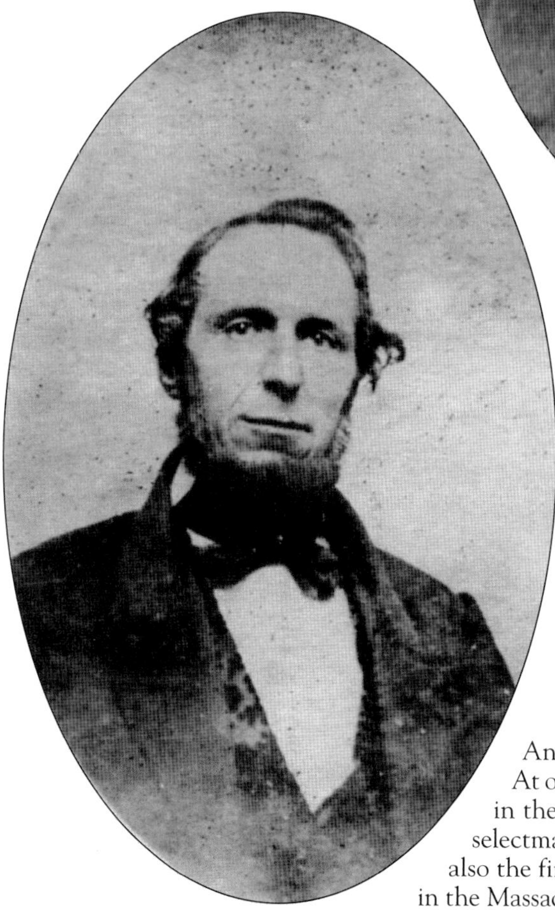

Andrew Felch first came to the village in 1843. At one time, he taught school and also engaged in the meat business. He was one of Ayer's first selectman, holding that position in 1873. He was also the first town clerk and represented the district in the Massachusetts Legislature.

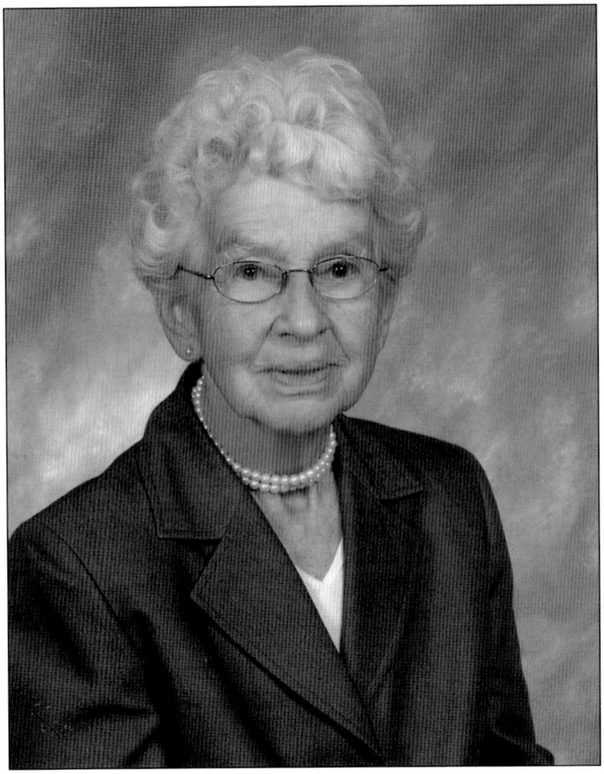

Zelda Moore has always found time for the community. Involved in Scouting, high school programs, Freedoms Way, and church organizations, she was also a Red Cross Volunteer at the Fort Devens Hospital for Vietnam War Veterans. She also spent many years interviewing Ralph H. Richardson in an effort to chronicle the history of Ayer. Her personal Page-Moore Library is a tribute to her love for the town and provides a valuable resource for history. (Courtesy of Calvin Moore.)

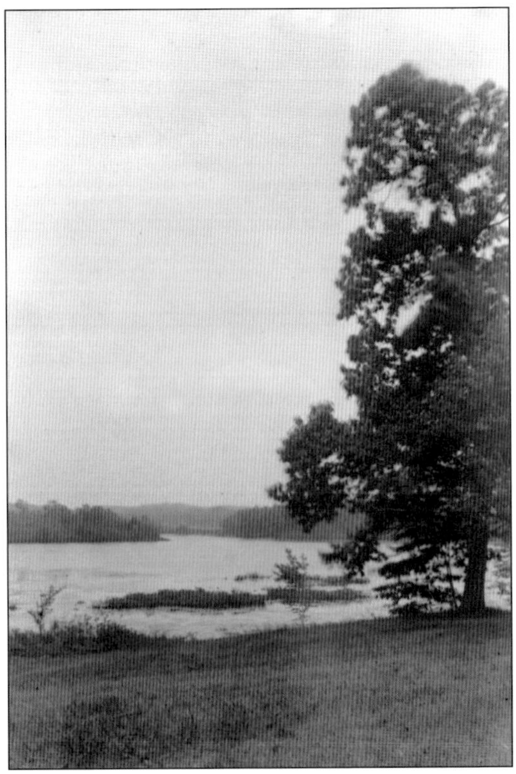

This chestnut tree was located on the north side of Central Avenue at Flanagan's Pond. Some say that it was really Fletcher's Pond, but because John Flanagan had a boat for hire folks would say, "Let's go down to Flanagan's," meaning to rent a boat there. Eventually, the name Flanagan was used in reference to the pond.

Five

In Service to the Public

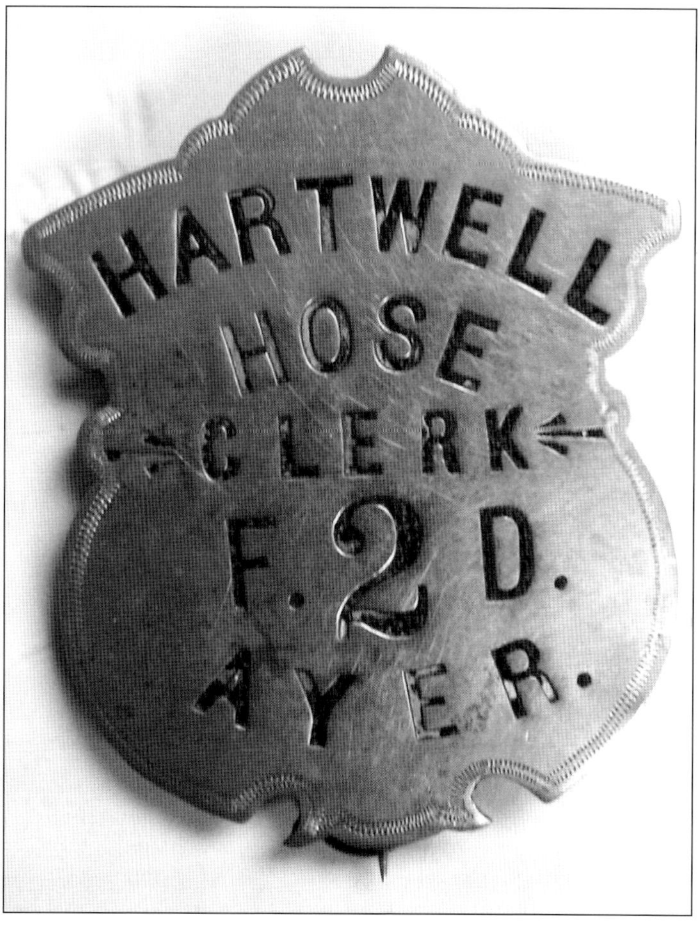

This is a photograph of the original badge worn by the members of the Hartwell Hose Company. At that time, there were two hose companies—the Page and Hartwell and the George J. Burns Hook and Ladder Company. This well-preserved badge is part of the Ayer Fire Department's collection. Once the fire department received their first gas-powered engine, all hose, hook, and ladder companies were disbanded. (Courtesy Ayer Fire Department.)

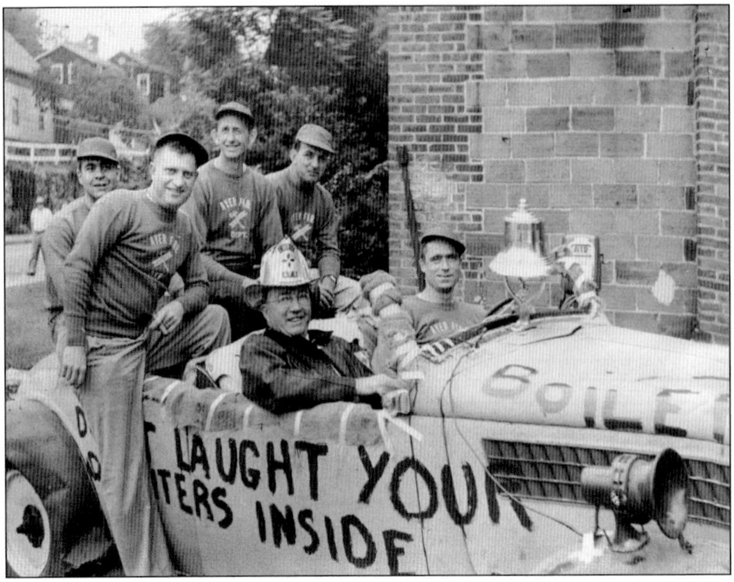

Pictured here in 1954, the Ayer Fire Department participates in a parade in Saugus as part of a Firemen's Muster. Chief Oikle is in the passenger seat. (Courtesy of the Ayer Fire Department.)

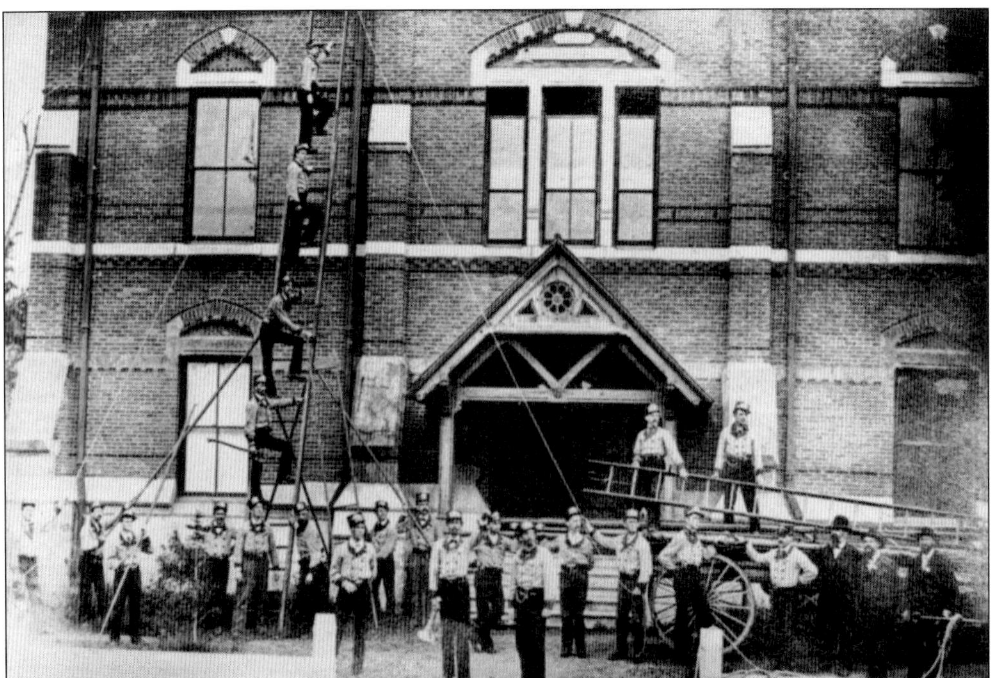

Members of the Alert Hook and Ladder Company demonstrate their ability to set up ladders against the town hall around 1880. In the lower right of the photograph, the wagon carries ladders and hooks. This photograph was taken before the fire company changed its name to the George J. Burns Hook and Ladder Company.

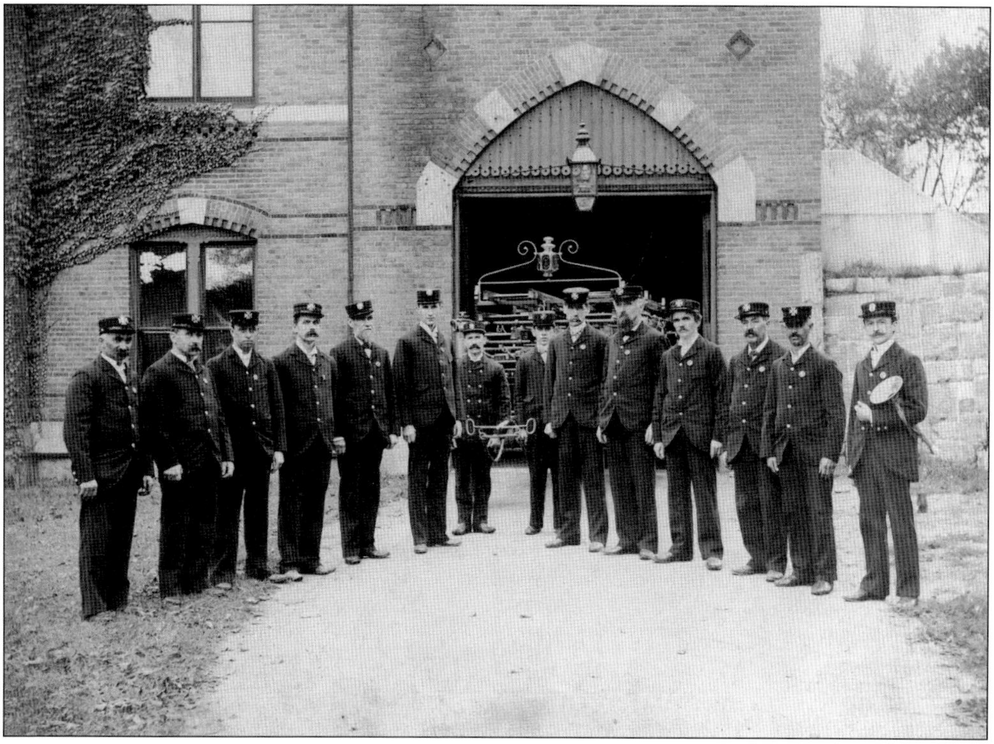

This is the Alert Hook and Ladder Company in front of the firehouse at the rear of the town hall in 1899. In this same year, the fire company changed its name to the George J. Burns Hook and Ladder Company. Behind them is the Colonel Needham hand-pump engine. This hose company was located at a firehouse on the corner of West Main and Park Streets.

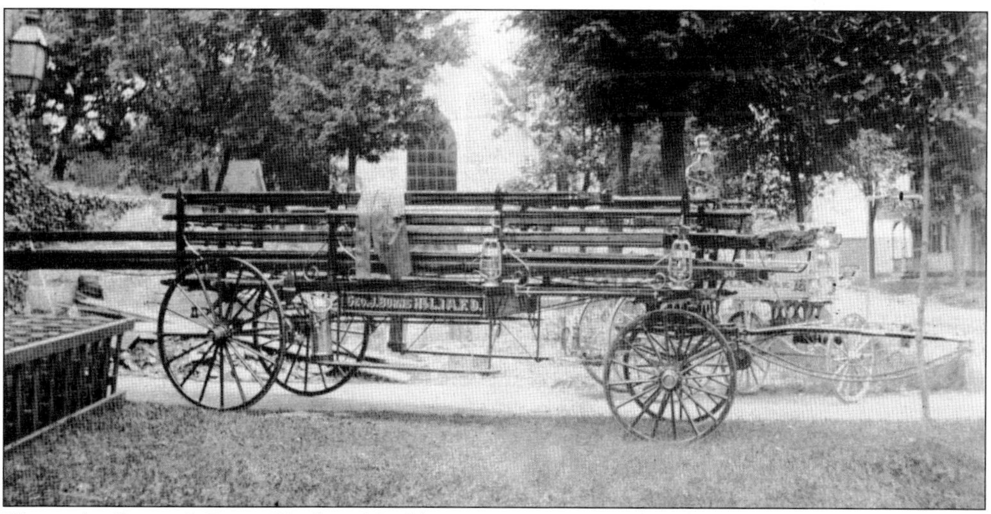

This is the George J. Burns Hook and Ladder wagon. As seen in this photograph, the wagon is longer than most to accommodate the ladders. This is in the driveway of the town hall with the Baptist church in the background on Columbia Street. (Courtesy of the Ayer Fire Department.)

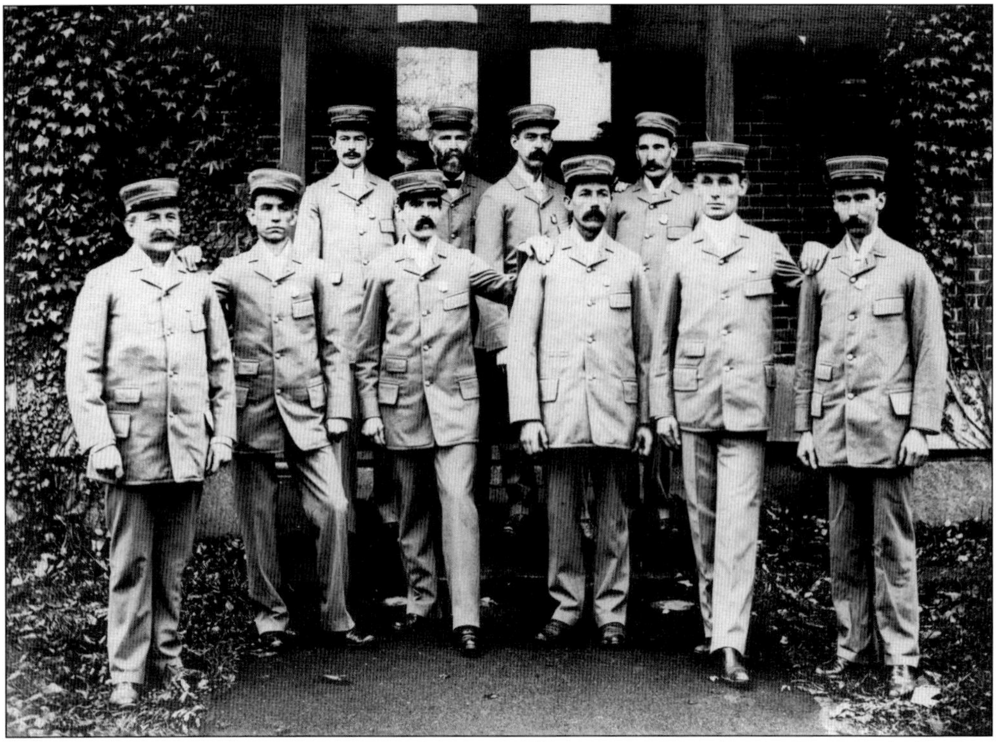

This December 1898 photograph shows the Hartwell Hose Company beside the town hall. They were representative of the privately funded hose companies in Ayer at the time. Members of the fire companies were required to show up to fight working fires. Failure to do so resulted in a fine. (Courtesy of the Ayer Fire Department.)

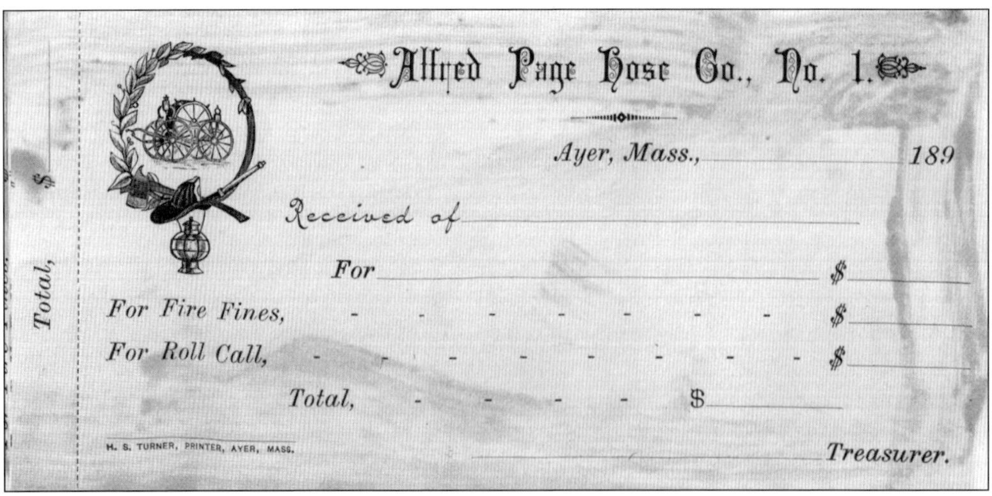

Alfred Page Hose Co., No. 1.

Ayer, Mass., ______ 189

Received of ______

For ______ $ ______

For Fire Fines, - - - - - - - - - $ ______

For Roll Call, - - - - - - - - - $ ______

Total, - - - - $ ______

______ Treasurer.

H. S. TURNER, PRINTER, AYER, MASS.

Total, $

Alfred Page Hose Company issued receipts such as these to collect fines from those who did not show up at a fire or who missed roll call. Huntley S. Turner printed this receipt in the 1890s at his local printing and publishing shop on the present-day location of Kelley's Hallmark Store. (Courtesy of the Ayer Fire Department.)

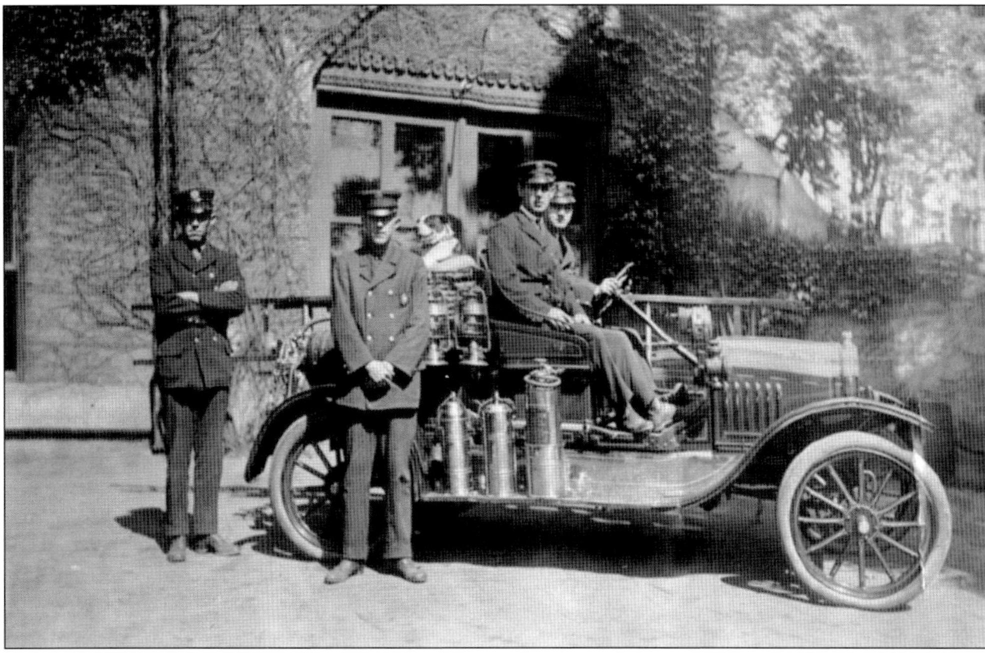

This is the first gasoline-powered hook and ladder truck purchased in 1919 for the Ayer Fire Department. This 1916 White Motor Company fire engine replaced the Colonel Needham hand-pump. The hose companies of the Hartwell, Page, and Burns were then disbanded. (Courtesy of the Ayer Fire Department.)

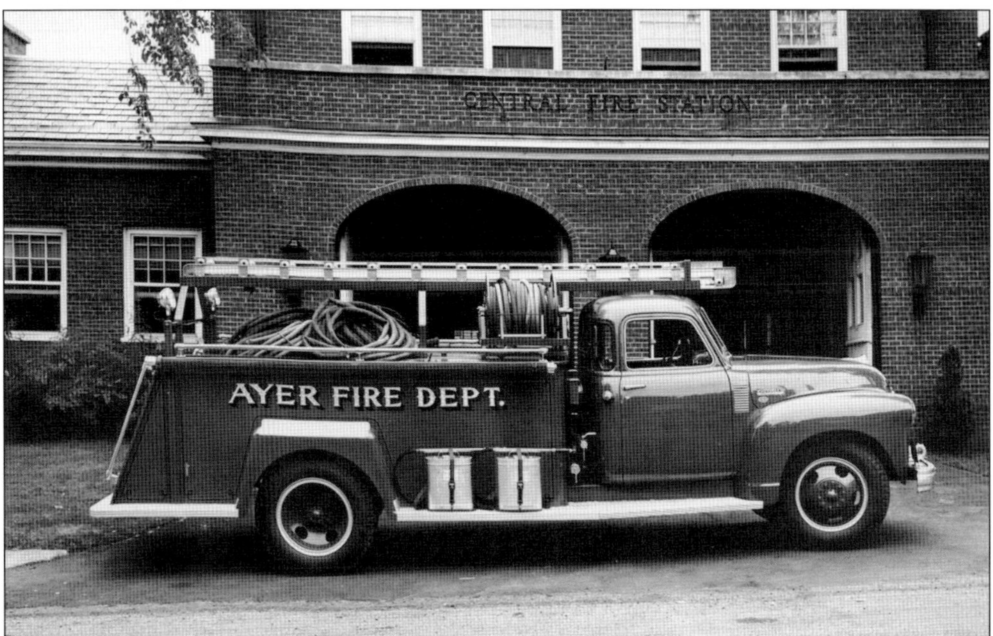

This new 1949 Chevrolet fire engine has just been delivered. The Ayer Fire Department not only protected the community, but also the military families who were housed at Devenscrest. This vehicle became a brush truck after it was replaced with newer equipment. (Courtesy of the Ayer Fire Department.)

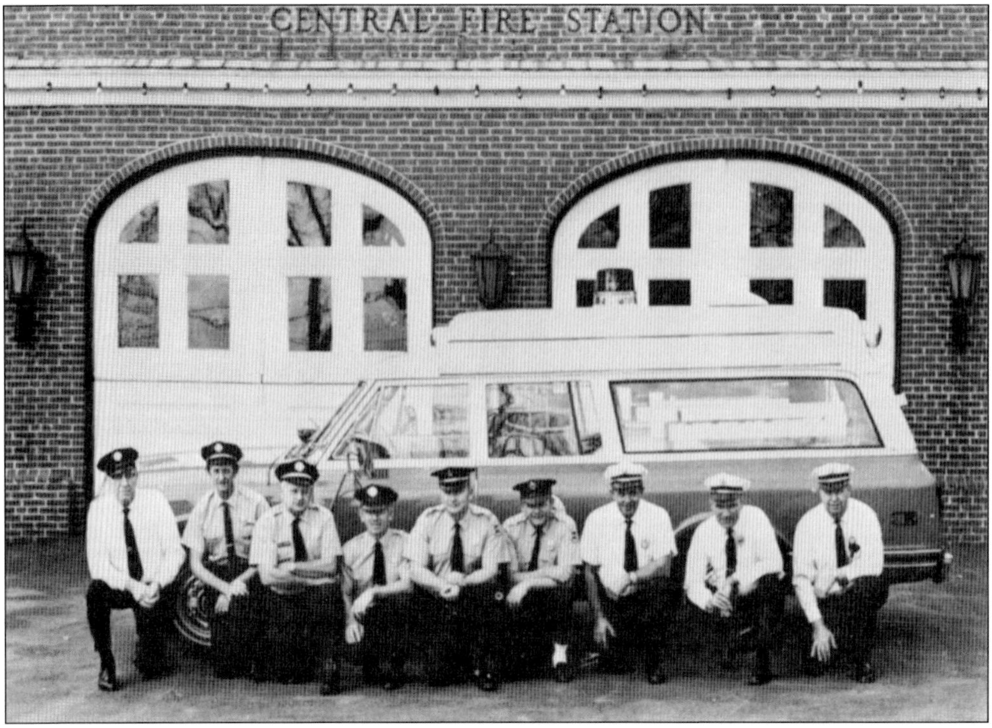

The Ayer Fire Department appears with its new ambulance in this 1969 postcard. In front of the former Central Fire Station on Washington Street are, from left to right, Clarence Craft, Bob McDowell, James Devers, Dave Schute, Arthur Pedrazzi, Albert Tooker, Rodney Kidder, George Donahue Jr., and John Guthrie. (Courtesy of the Ayer Fire Department.)

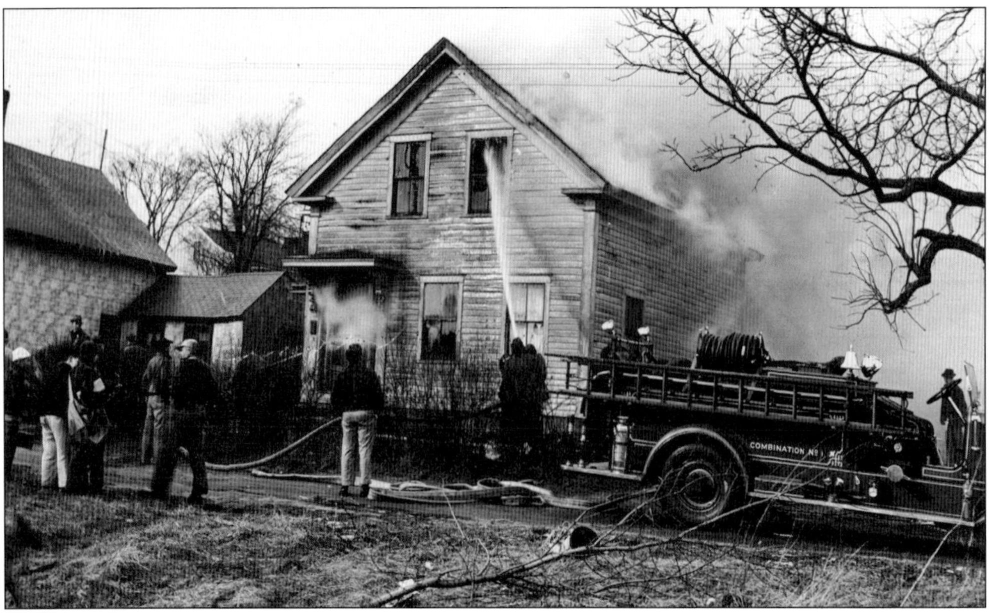

This 1949 house fire took place on Bligh Street off School Street. The fire truck was a combination of a ladder truck and hose. The firemen would be directed to the site by a series of whistles blown a certain number of times. (Courtesy of the Ayer Fire Department.)

This fire alarm call card was used to help firemen find the location of the fire. The card shows street intersections in each box that correspond with the number of whistles being blown. The whistle was also used to alert residents when school was cancelled. (Courtesy of the Ayer Fire Department.)

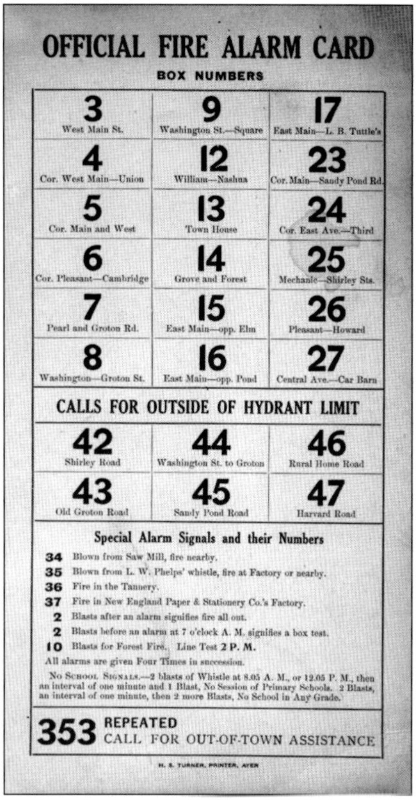

OFFICIAL FIRE ALARM CARD

BOX NUMBERS

3 West Main St.	9 Washington St.—Square	17 East Main—L. B. Tuttle's
4 Cor. West Main—Union	12 William—Nashua	23 Cor. Main—Sandy Pond Rd.
5 Cor. Main and West	13 Town House	24 Cor. East Ave.—Third
6 Cor. Pleasant—Cambridge	14 Grove and Forest	25 Mechanic—Shirley Sts.
7 Pearl and Groton Rd.	15 East Main—opp. Elm	26 Pleasant—Howard
8 Washington—Groton St.	16 East Main—opp. Pond	27 Central Ave.—Car Barn

CALLS FOR OUTSIDE OF HYDRANT LIMIT

42 Shirley Road	44 Washington St. to Groton	46 Rural Home Road
43 Old Groton Road	45 Sandy Pond Road	47 Harvard Road

Special Alarm Signals and their Numbers

34 Blown from Saw Mill, fire nearby.
35 Blown from L. W. Phelps' whistle, fire at Factory or nearby.
36 Fire in the Tannery.
37 Fire in New England Paper & Stationery Co.'s Factory.
2 Blasts after an alarm signifies fire all out.
2 Blasts before an alarm at 7 o'clock A. M. signifies a box test.
10 Blasts for Forest Fire. Line Test **2 P. M.**

All alarms are given Four Times in succession.

No School Signals.—2 blasts of Whistle at 8.05 A. M., or 12.05 P. M., then an interval of one minute and 1 Blast, No Session of Primary Schools. 2 Blasts, an interval of one minute, then 2 more Blasts, No School in Any Grade.

353 REPEATED CALL FOR OUT-OF-TOWN ASSISTANCE

H. S. TURNER, PRINTER, AYER

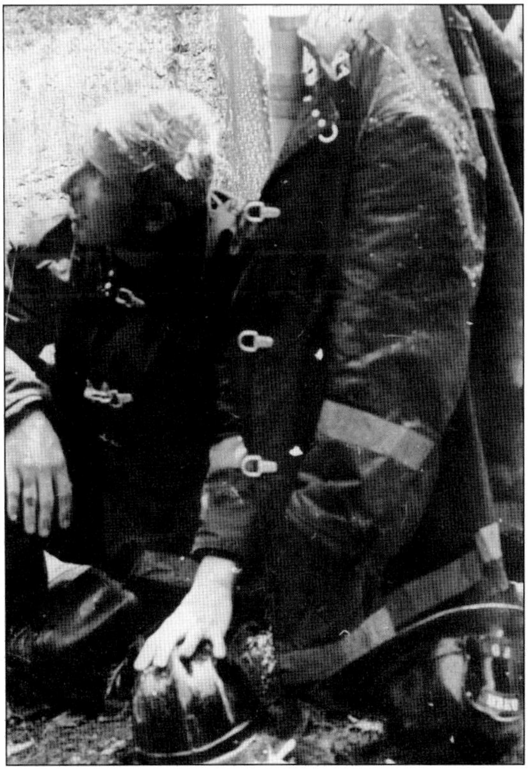

This exhausted fireman has been battling one of Ayer's largest and longest burning fires in June 1961. The Tannery fire burned for almost a week. (Courtesy of the Ayer Fire Department.)

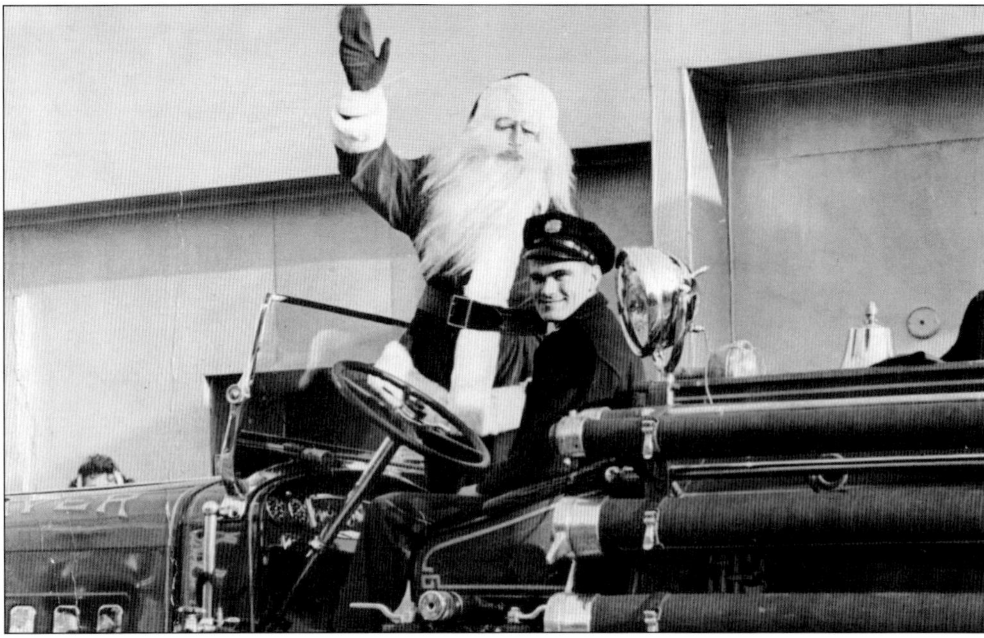

Driver Tex Donahue delivers Santa Claus to the Ayer Playhouse in a 1935 Maxim fire truck on December 22, 1949. The playhouse on Washington Street burned in 1962 and was never rebuilt. The only part that remains today is the lobby. (Courtesy of the Ayer Fire Department.)

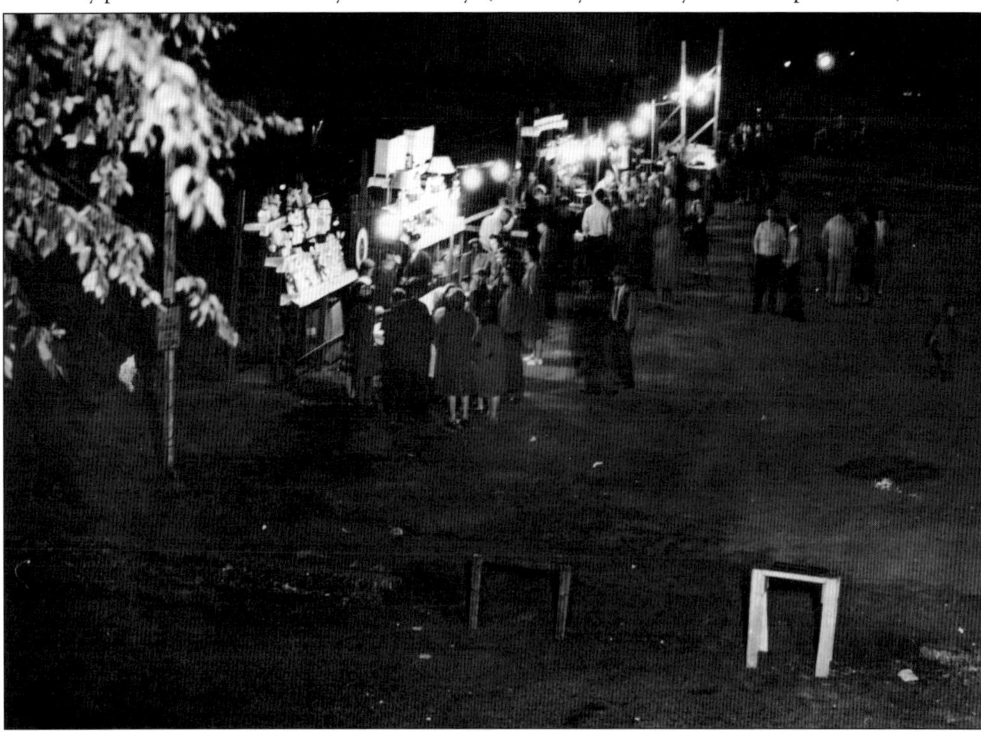

The parking lot across from the fire station is pictured here in the 1940s. There were booths set up for food and games at this Firemen's Field Day. At night, a dance was held in the fire station where the Ayer Firemen's Band would perform. (Courtesy of the Ayer Fire Department.)

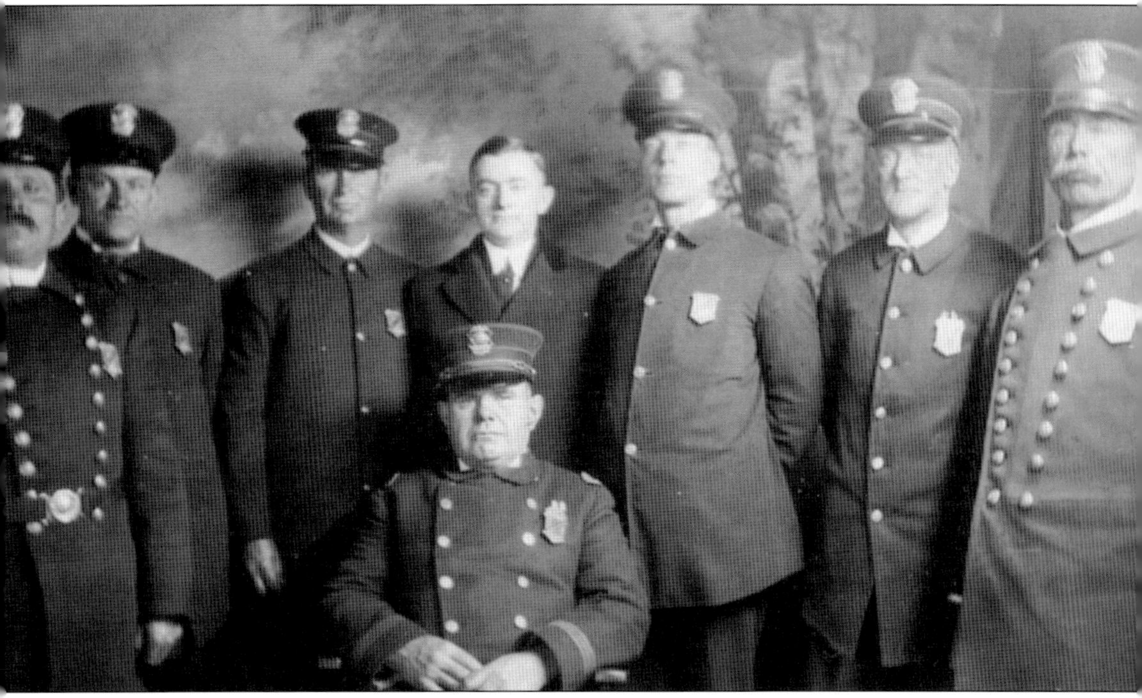

Patrick J. Beatty was chief of the police department from 1909 to 1935. The officers are, from left to right, Jimmy Pirone, unidentified, Donahue, unidentified, Jack Wallace, and two unidentified. The following is taken from the plaque at the entrance to the Ayer Police Station: "Until 1869, the Police Force in the town of Ayer consisted of one or two 'Watchmen,' assisted when necessary by the local Constable. John A. Pingry served as a Watchman from 1886 to 1896. Among Special Policemen during this period were Edwin Saunders, John Hurley, W.E. Hackett and John S. Hartwell. The first Chief of Police of Ayer was Peter A. O'Toole. O'Toole served from 1896 to 1898." (Courtesy of Donald and Josephine Wallace.)

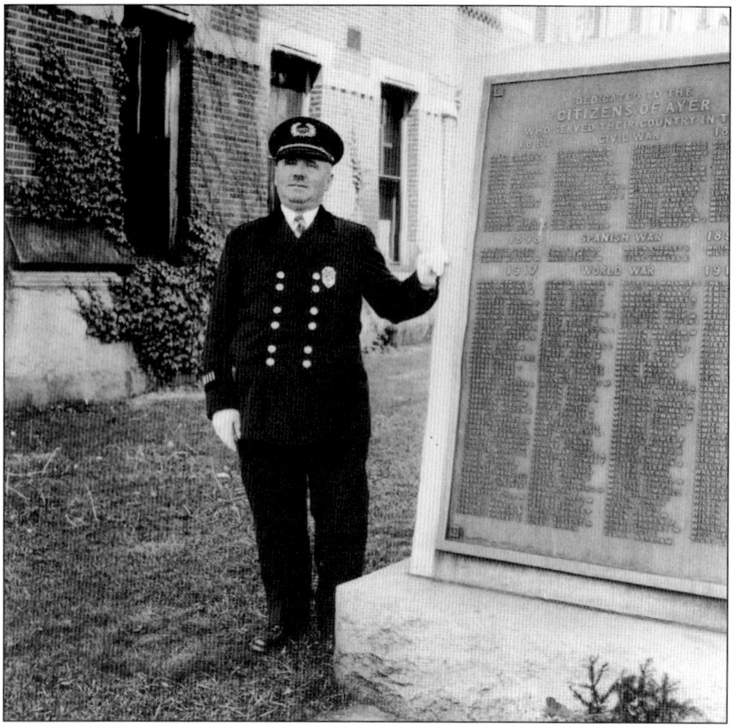

Chief of police Tertulliano "Jimmy" Pirone is seen here at the war memorial at town hall. Pirone served as police chief from 1935 to 1945. During World War II, he would send postcards to the soldiers from Ayer to let them know that people back home were thinking of them. (Courtesy of the Ayer Police Department.)

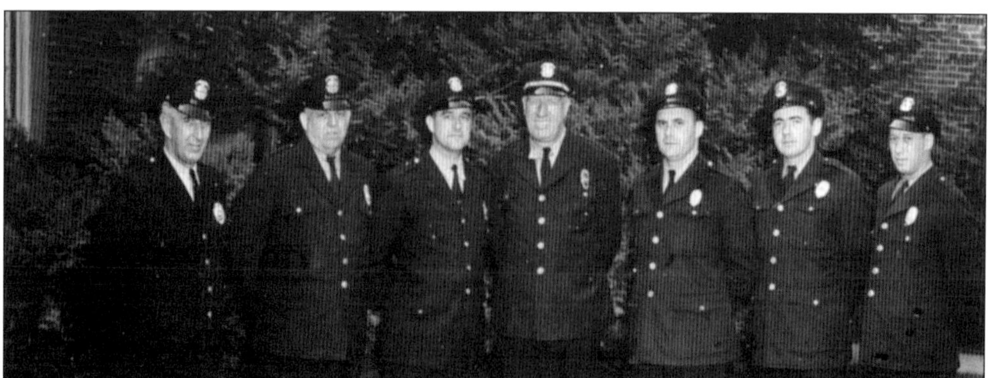

The Ayer Police Department is pictured here in 1946. From left to right are Earl R. Pillman, Newell Robinson, Dell Rockwood, Chief Ernest L. Downing Sr. (1945–1948, 1950–1956), Walter F. Picard, Tom Hurley, and Paul L. Boisseau. The first police station was located in the basement of a school on East Main Street. The fire department was on the first floor, and a school occupied the second floor. That building was destroyed by fire in 1869. (Courtesy of the Ayer Police Department.)

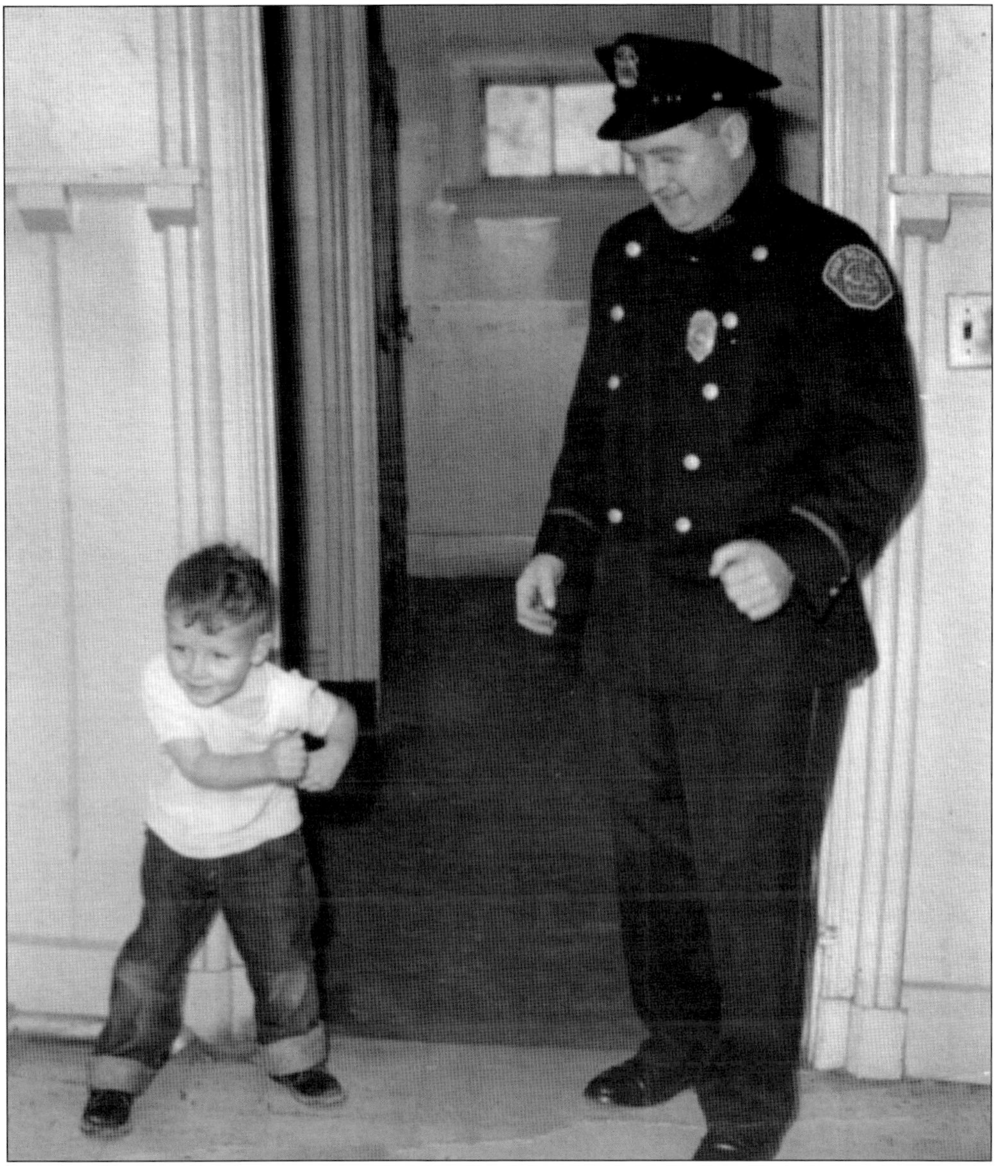

This young boy was lost on Main Street. Officer Robert Rakip looks on as the boy tries to make a quick getaway. The Ayer Police Department, from its beginnings as watchmen, has had a proud tradition of serving and protecting its people and always keeping an eye out for the little ones when they get lost. (Courtesy of the Ayer Police Department.)

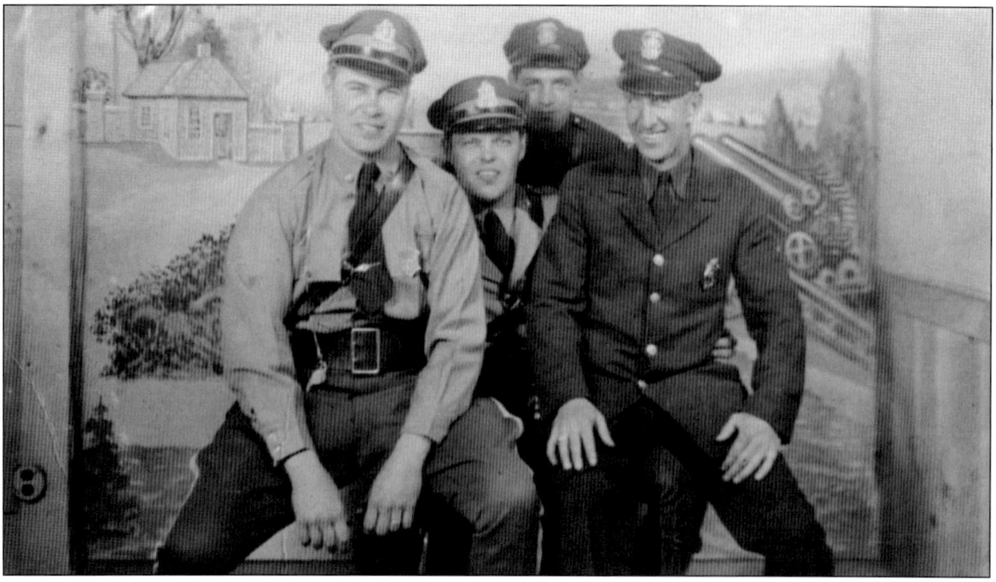

This late 1940s postcard shows two Massachusetts state troopers and two Ayer police officers. Officer Earl R. Pillman on the far right is the only one identified in this postcard. He was also chief of police in 1949, and from 1956 to 1961. (Author's collection.)

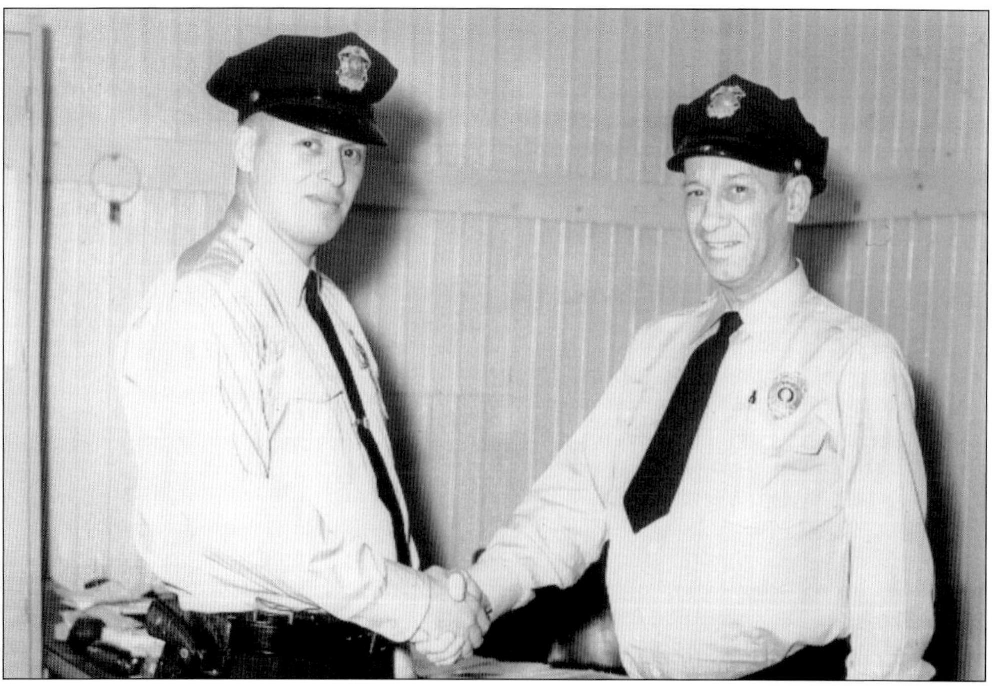

Officer Paul Boisseau welcomes his son Arthur to the Ayer Police Department in 1961. The traditional dark blue shirts were now white. (Courtesy of the Ayer Police Department.)

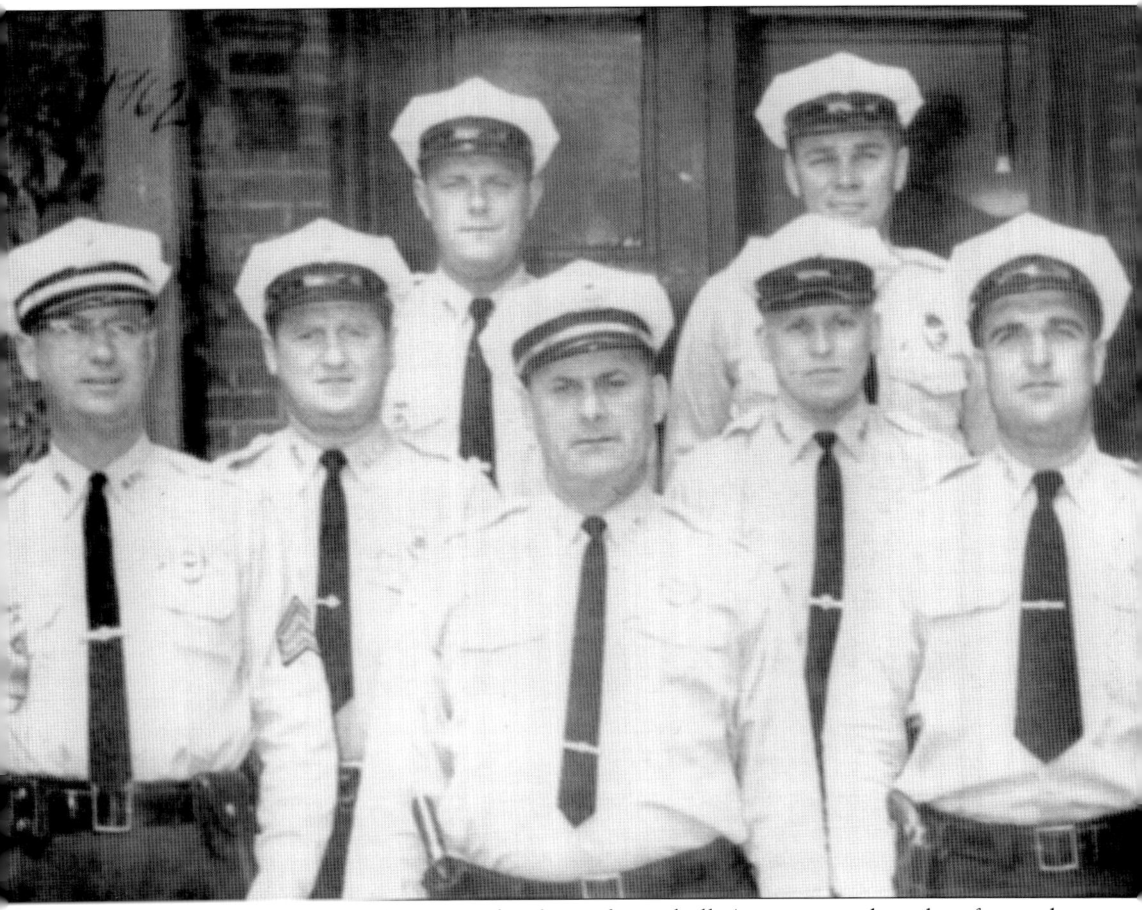

Pictured here in 1962, police officers stand in front of town hall. At one time, the police, fire, and highway departments all occupied the first floor of the town hall. In 1950, the space previously held by the fire department and the highway department was renovated for the police department. A new police station was built in 1997. Note their hats have changed from blue to white. The officers pictured here are (first row) Ernest L. Downing Jr., Chief Walter F. Picard, and Russell D. Rakip; (second row) Robert D. Rakip and Arthur Boisseau; (third row) Wilfred E. Dow and Frank C. Harmon. (Courtesy of the Ayer Police Department.)

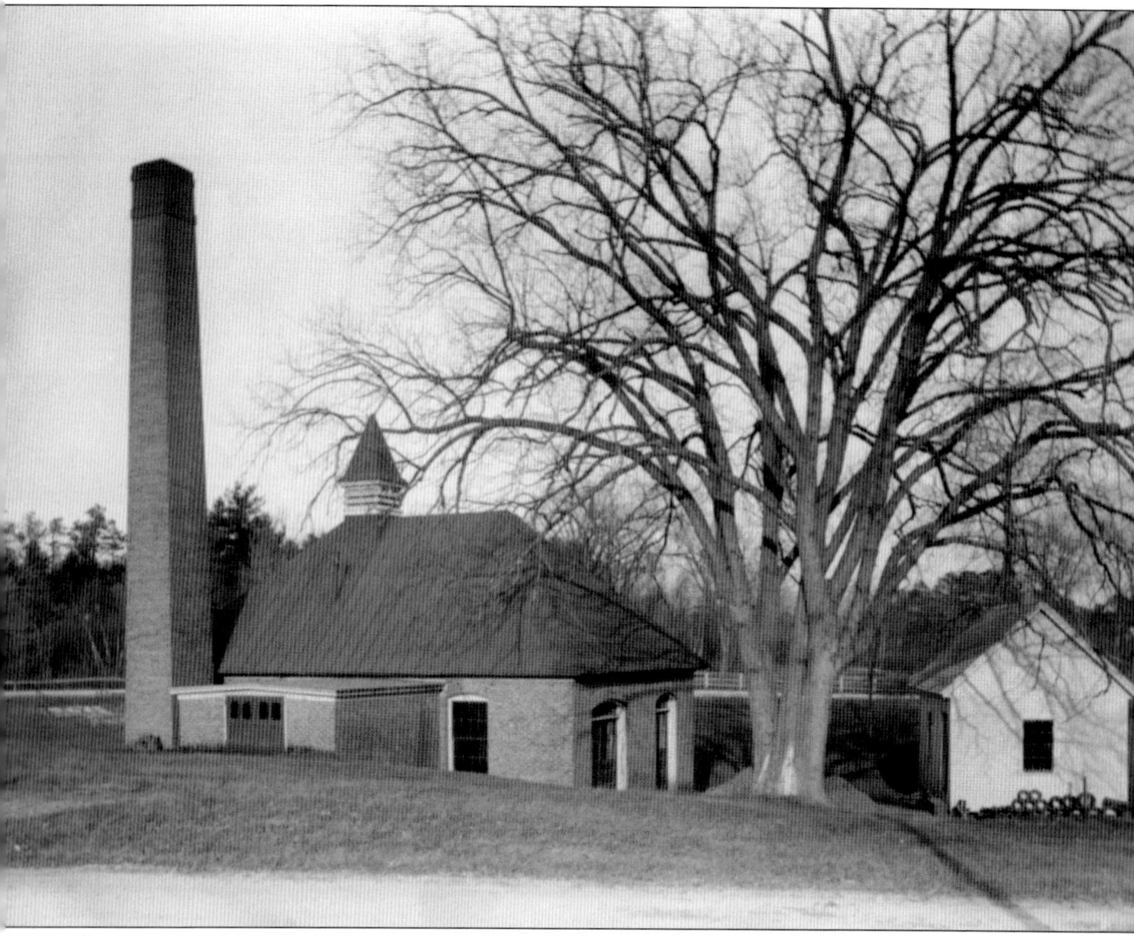

In August 1886, a committee was formed to acquire a contractor to build, manage, and maintain a water system. This would be a private entity and not run by the town of Ayer. This water system would also include the installation of fire hydrants. The committees report recommended that the town hire the contractors to build the water works system and maintain it themselves. The town approved it, and the next step was to seek approval from the state legislature. Approval was granted in April 1887, and construction began soon after. Ayer had more than one water commissioner serving at the same time. Commissioners were Leonard J. Spaulding, James R. Gray, and Andrew Atwood from 1887 to 1901. This photograph of the pumping station was taken on November 10, 1904.

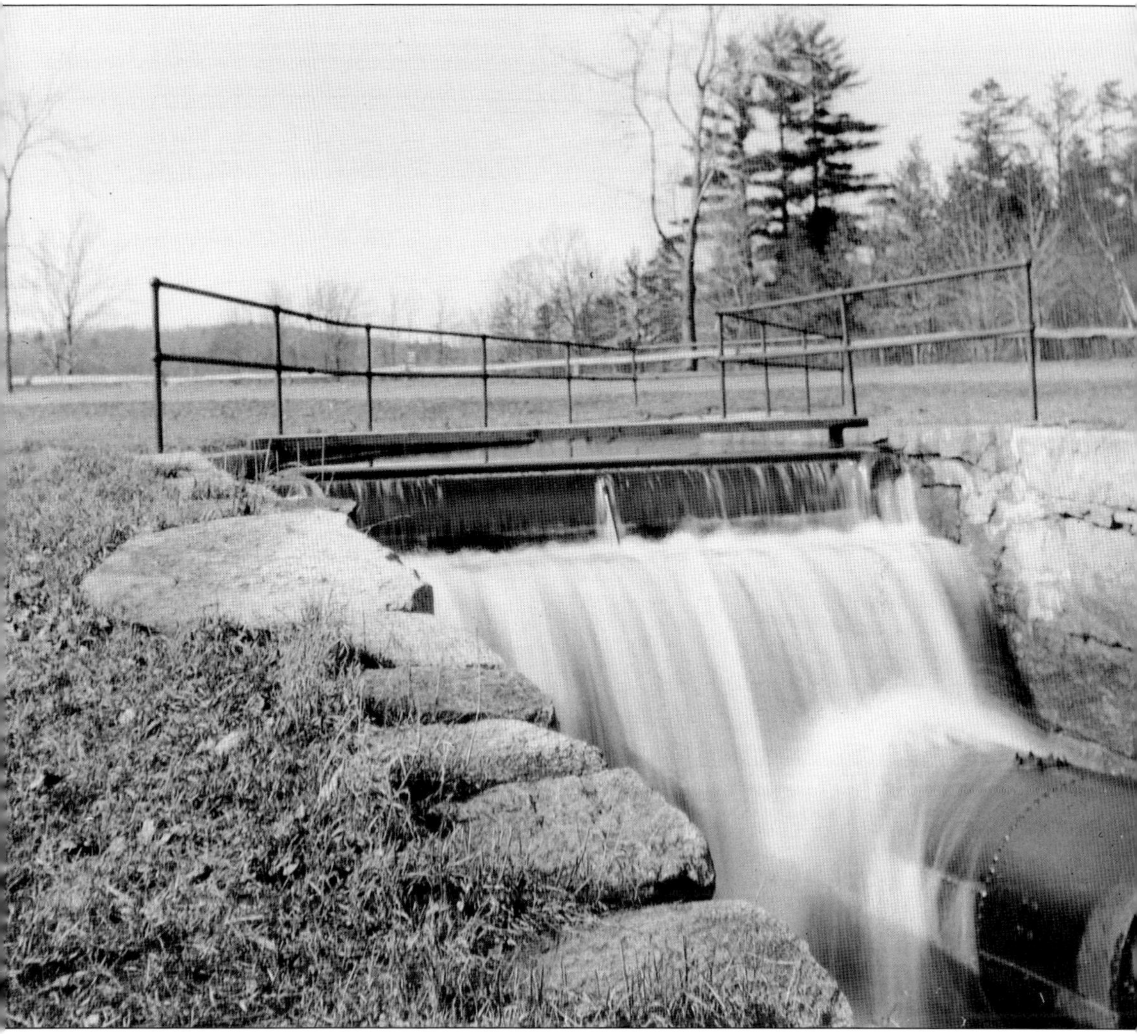

This is the inlet to the pumping station from a pipe underneath East Main Street. The water flowed from Fletcher's Pond to Balch's Pond and then on to the station. The water source for the pumping station was 150 feet above East Main Street. This provided a good flow for the water pumps, with the capability to fire up steam boilers and increase pressure if needed. There was also the third option of a pump engine for additional pressure. In this photograph, the water was running at such a fast pace as to spill over the inlet pipe. This was also the site of the original sawmill built by John Page in 1712, which eventually was bought by Calvin Fletcher. This area was the "Old Common" long before the days of the traffic circle. It was a small village with a few homes and a tavern.

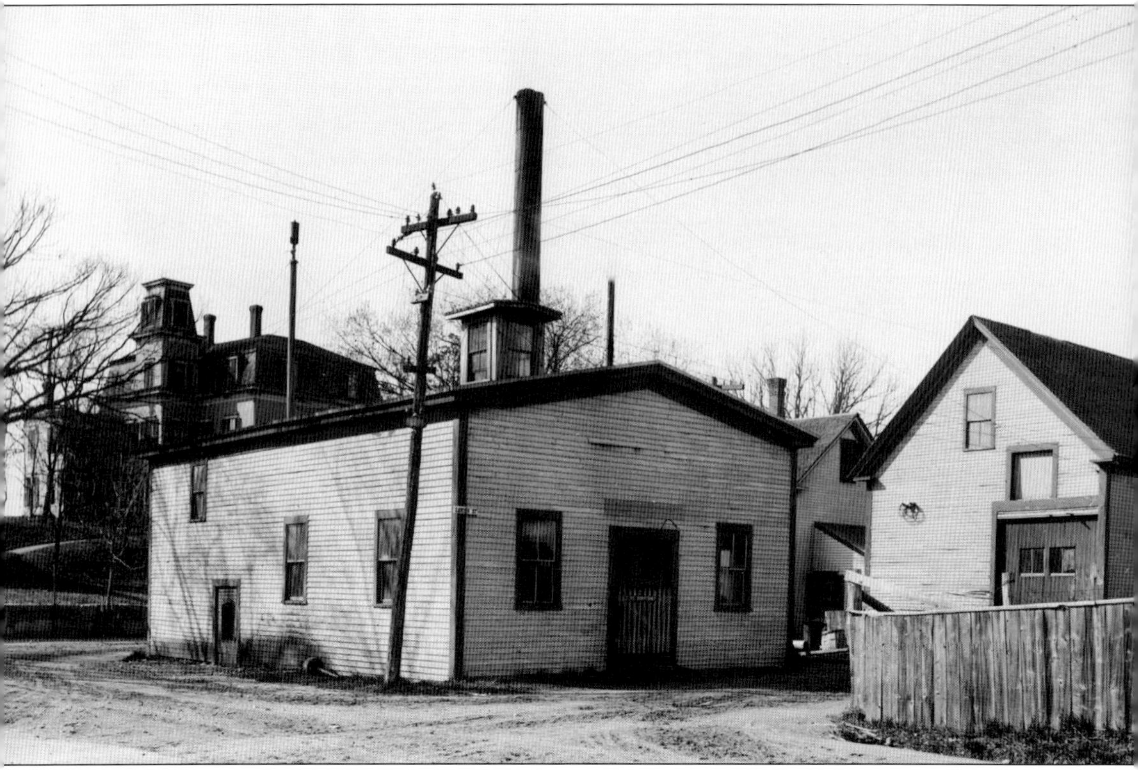

Pictured here on April 15, 1905, the Ayer Electric Light Company was located on the corner of Cambridge and Lawton Street. The chimney stack, for what could be a steam turbine, extends high above the building. At the time of this photograph, mostly all streets in town had streetlights. In 1908, the town believed it was being charged too much for electricity and for one year went back to using gaslights along the streets. In 1906, Ayer was charged $1,991.88 for electricity, and by 1908, it had risen to $2,138.13. In 1909, the total for electricity was $901.25 and the charge from the Globe Gas Light Company was $694.65 for street lighting.

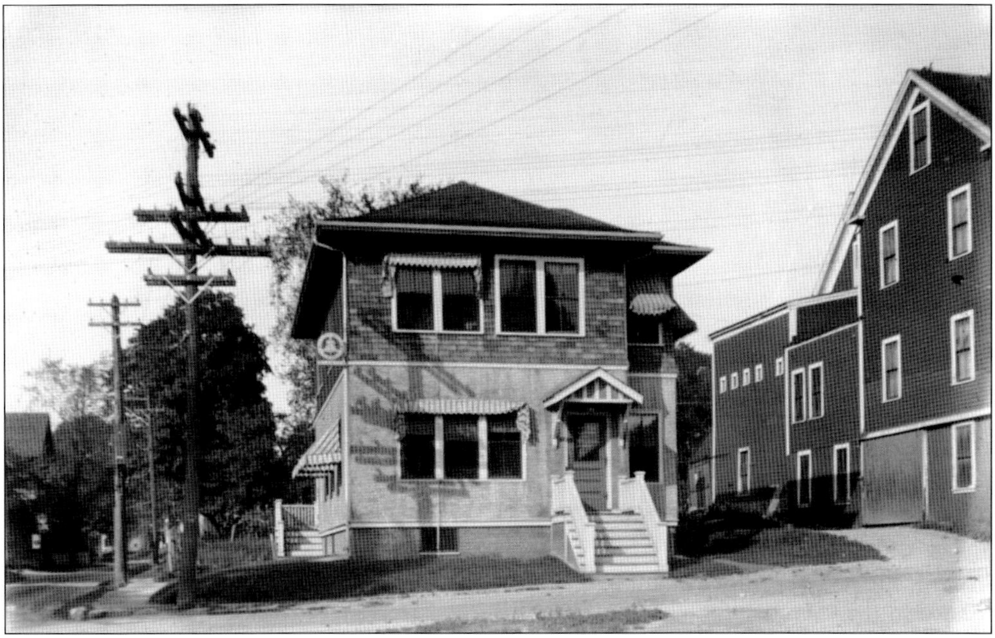

This is the telephone exchange building at 4 Cambridge Street. This was a day and night operation, although it was not likely a 24-hour operation. In 1906, this was a one-story building but it did not take long for the telephone service to expand. This photograph was taken on September 6, 1915. There were eight towns in this telephone exchange district.

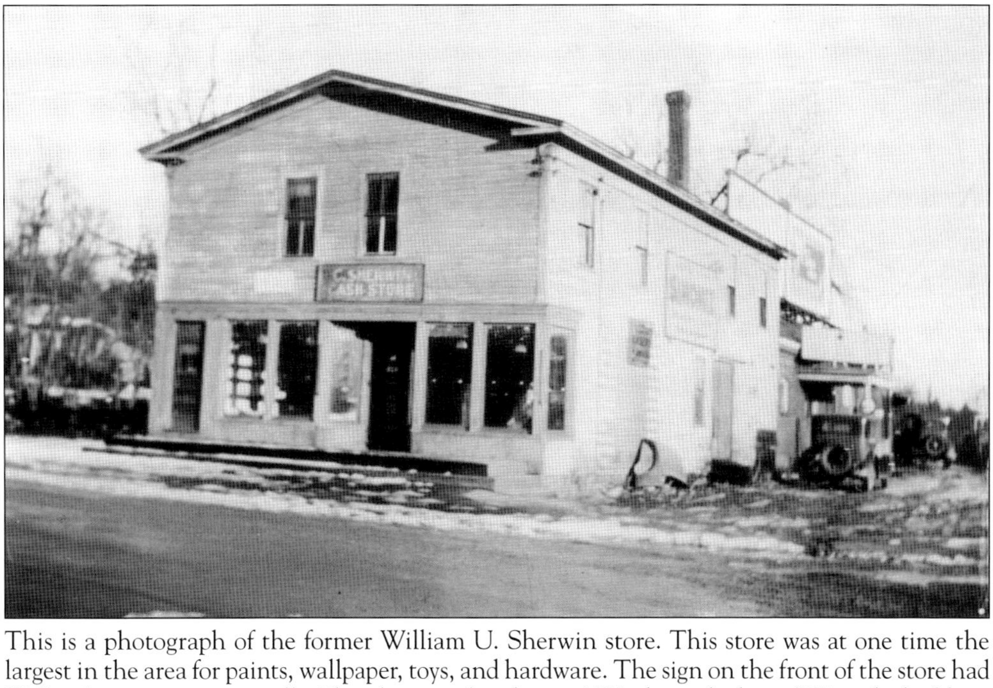

This is a photograph of the former William U. Sherwin store. This store was at one time the largest in the area for paints, wallpaper, toys, and hardware. The sign on the front of the store had William's name on it originally. This photograph, taken in 1933, shows the letter "C" on the building, perhaps indicating William's brother Charles had acquired the store after William passed.

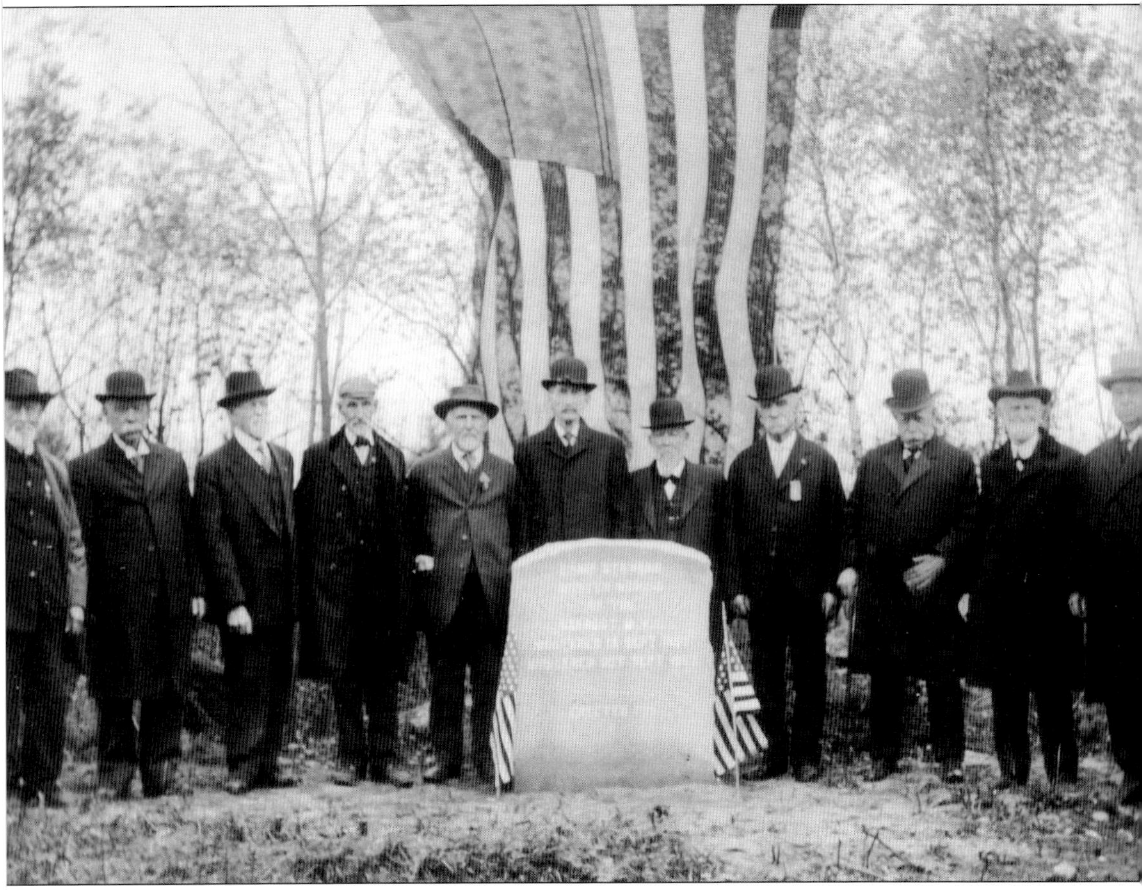

Here are the surviving members of the 53rd Regiment Massachusetts Volunteer Infantry. In 1915, eleven of the soldiers were present at the dedication of the memorial to them and their fellow soldiers. The 53rd Regiment was one of the nine-month troops between October 17 and November 6, 1862. They were then moved by train to New York on November 18, where they remained until January 17, 1863. From New York, they boarded a steamer en route to New Orleans, Louisiana. They were attached to the 3rd Brigade, 3rd Division, 19th Army, Department of the Gulf. After their tour of duty in Louisiana, they headed home and arrived in Fitchburg on August 24, 1863, to an enthusiastic reception. At the dedication are, from left to right, three unidentified, John B. Blood, Samuel G. Humiston, J.C. Ayers, unidentified, William Bush, Henry A. Willis, and William H. Eustis. (Courtesy of Zelda Moore.)

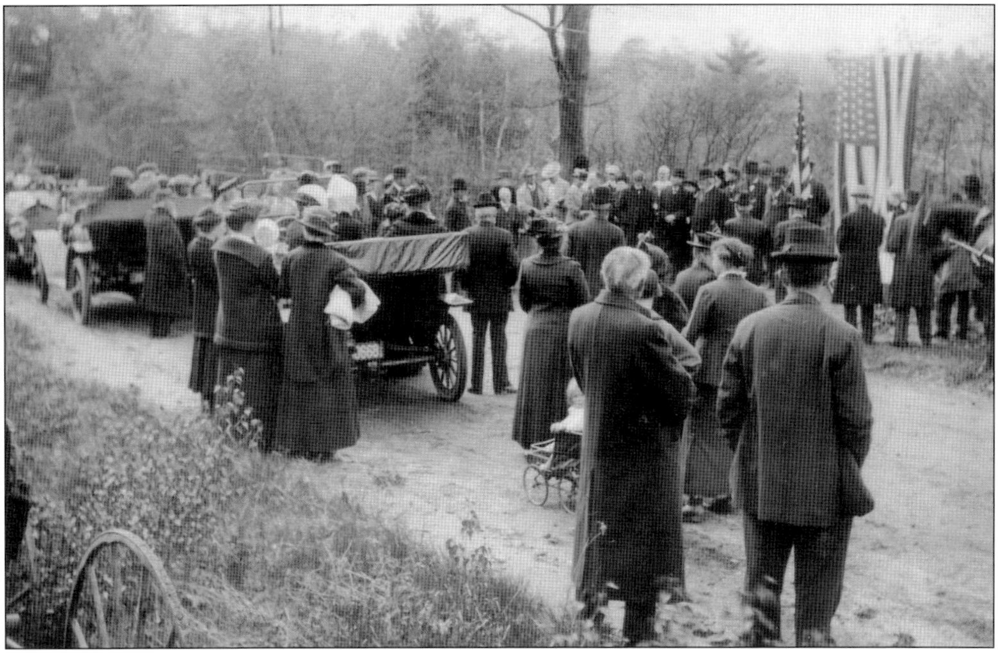

This is the dedication of the Camp Stevens memorial to the soldiers of the Civil War. Camp Stevens was named for Isaac Ingalls Stevens of Andover, a graduate of West Point. He was killed at the battle of Chantilly, Virginia. The monument is still located on a section of road that was once the Fitchburg Road. Fitchburg Road has been rerouted since the time of this photograph. (Courtesy of Zelda Moore.)

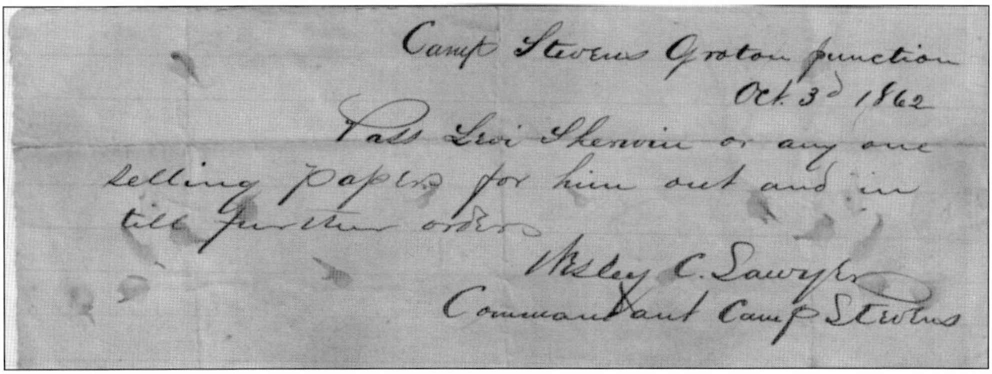

Camp Stevens Groton Junction
Oct 3d 1862
Pass Levi Sherwin or any one selling papers for him out and in till further orders
Wesley C. Sawyer
Commandant Camp Stevens

This is the original pass issued to Levi Sherwin on October 3, 1862. Sherwin's store in South Groton sold periodicals, wallpaper, and toys. This pass allowed him or those working for him to distribute papers inside the camp. The signature of Commandant Wesley C. Sawyer is in the bottom-right corner of the pass.

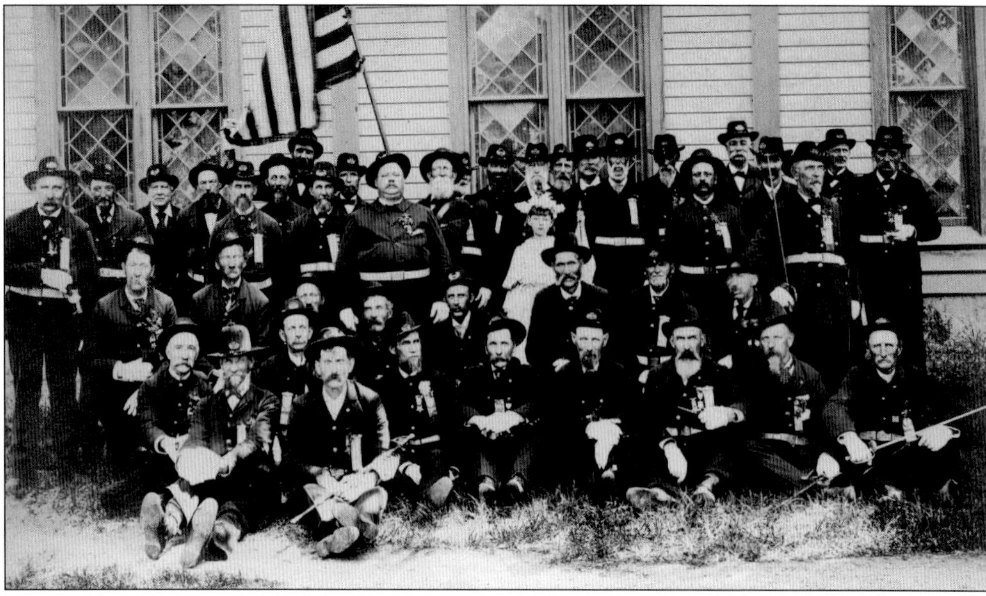

Pictured here are members of the George S. Boutwell Post 48, Grand Army of the Republic in 1895. Initially located in Merchant's Row, the post was destroyed by the fire of 1870. They moved the post to Woods Block where North Middlesex Savings Bank is now. They were burned out again with the fire of April 1872 and relocated to the newly constructed Page Block.

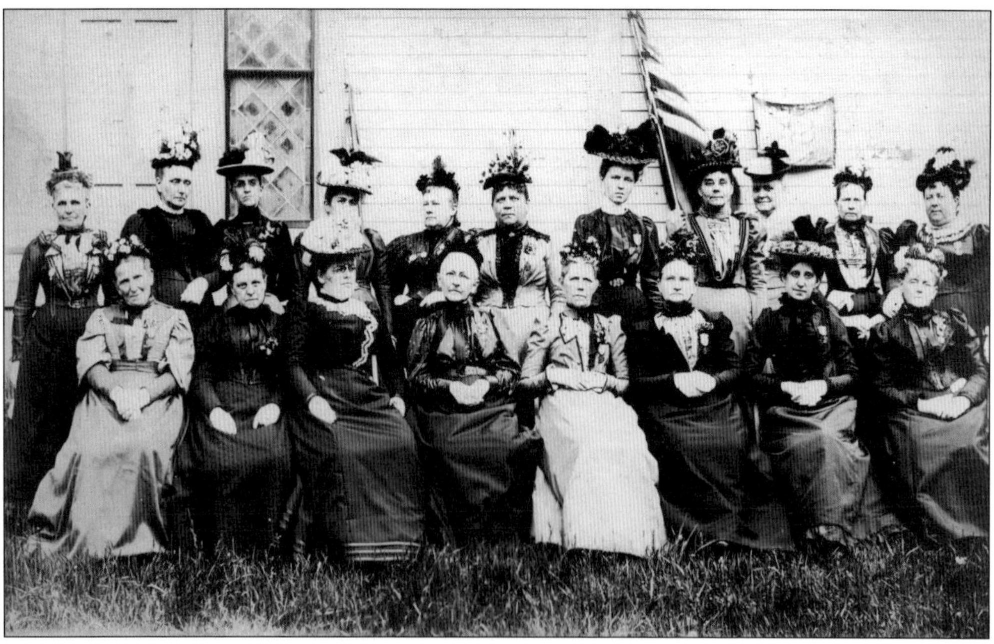

This May 28, 1899, photograph shows the Women's Relief Corps of the George S. Boutwell Post 48 GAR of Ayer. The Women's Relief Corp participated in activities to educate and honor the veterans of the Civil War. Their work included placing wreaths on veteran's graves on Memorial Day, including the Tomb of the Unknown Soldier; encouraging patriotism; and supporting veterans of all wars.

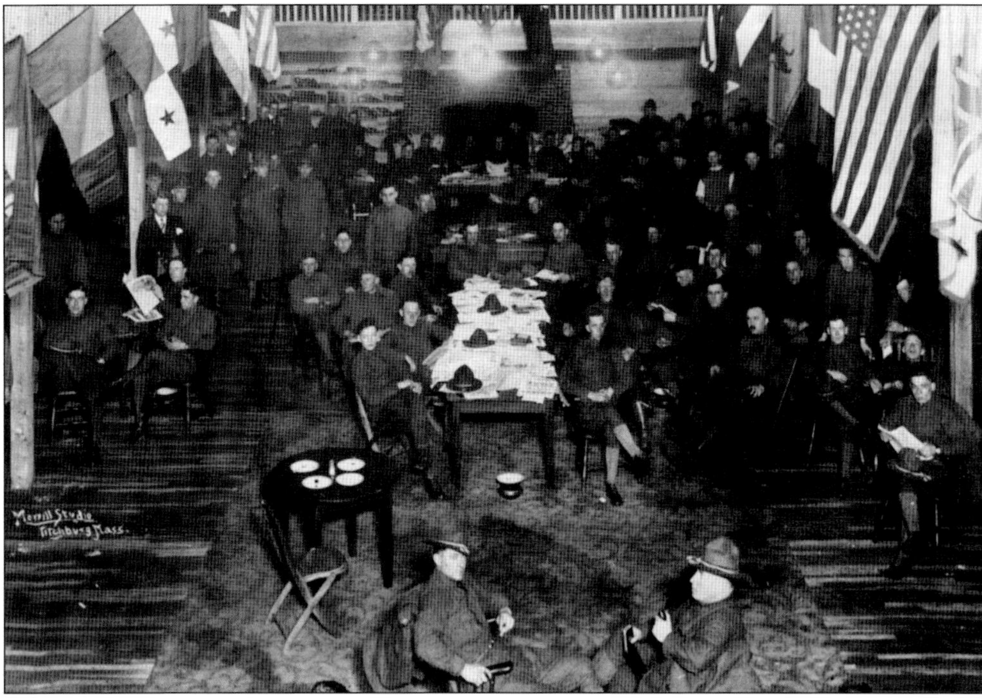

This was the first recreation hall in Ayer for the soldiers during World War I. Located inside the old YMCA building, it provided troops with some rest and relaxation. There was a ring inside to host weekly professional wrestling matches and a stage for the minstrel shows. This building still stands on the corner of Mechanic and West Main Streets. The United Service Organizations (USO) did not formally organize until World War II.

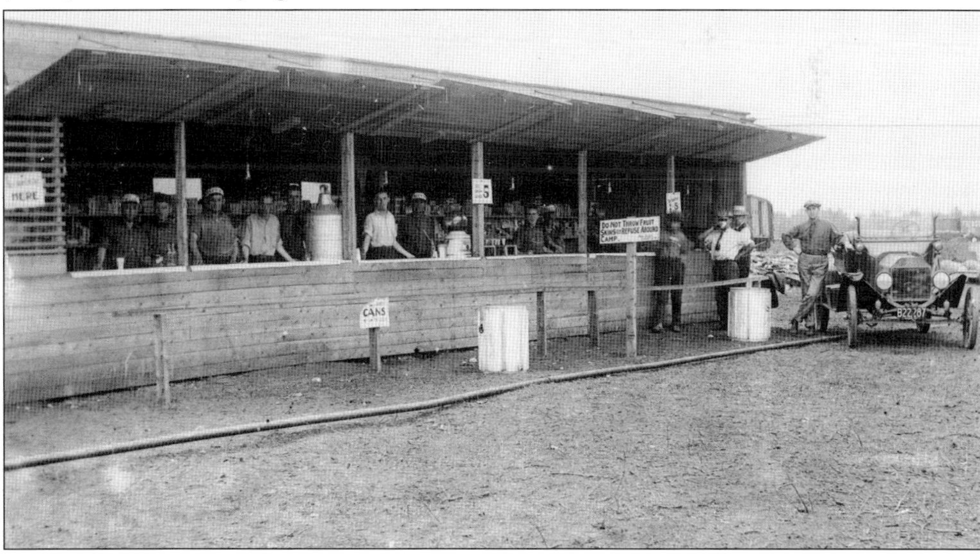

During the construction of Camp Devens, many local civilian workers found jobs at the camp. Some found work as carpenters, others worked in outdoor eating establishments as seen here. One thing was for sure, there were plenty of jobs for anyone who wanted to work. Camp Devens was named after Charles Devens, who came from Worcester and was a general in the Civil War. (Courtesy of Zelda Moore.)

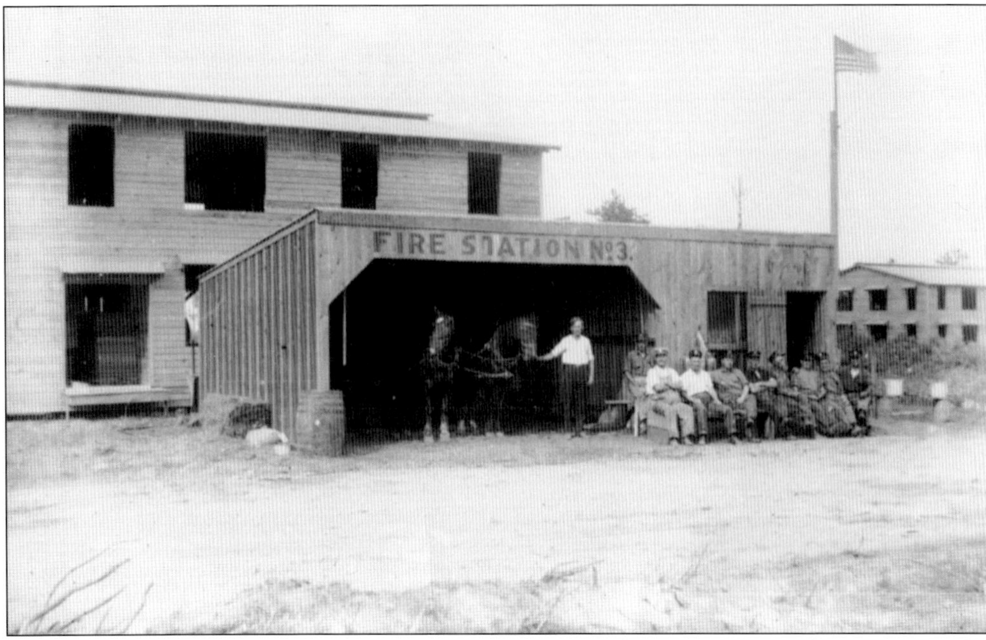

Camp Devens also required its own fire department for the protection of the many wooden barracks. Again, the area townspeople would benefit by the number of workers needed to fill the government jobs. This 1917 photograph shows the No. 3 fire station, and behind it, barracks appear to be under construction. (Courtesy of Zelda Moore.)

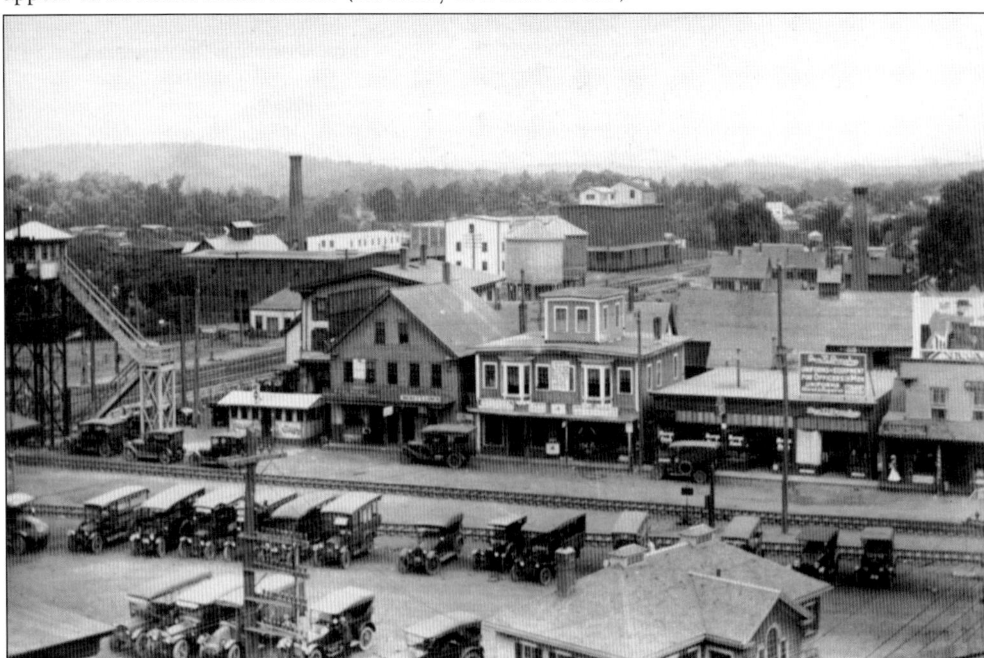

Merchant's Row welcomed the business brought in by Camp Devens. Soda shops, restaurants, and clothiers thrived. Furniture stores did not see an increase in sales, as the soldiers did not need many home furnishings. There is a lot of traffic at the depot in July 1918. The busses at the station may have been used to bring the new recruits to Camp Devens.

In November 1919, a committee was formed to plan a reception and ball for the returning veterans of World War I. The ball and reception took place on Thursday, January 1, 1920. The reception was open to all townspeople to come to the town hall and greet the soldiers and nurses from 2:00 to 4:00 p.m. There were speakers, Civil War veterans, town officials, and representatives of schools and the clergy, all seated on the stage in the great hall. Accompanied by a bugler, a roll call was read of all those present, followed by the names of those who died in service. The names of the fallen were Leon F. Briggs, Joseph M. Connors, Percy J. Fowler, and Robert H. Saunders.

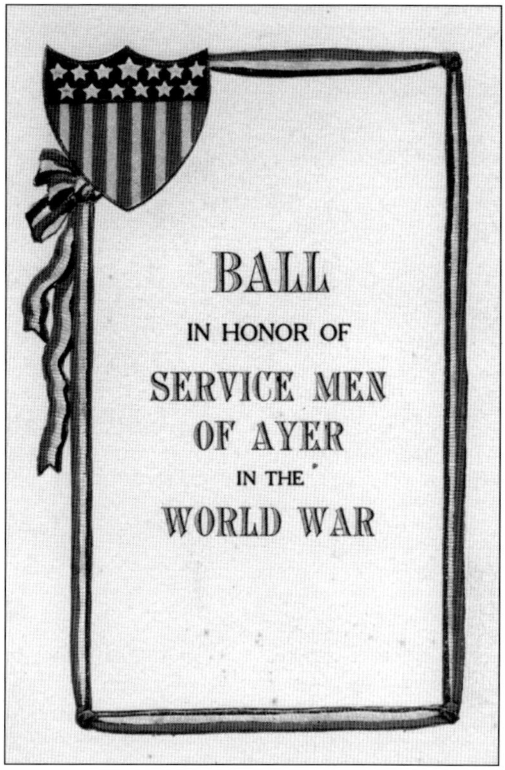

BALL

IN HONOR OF

SERVICE MEN

OF AYER

IN THE

WORLD WAR

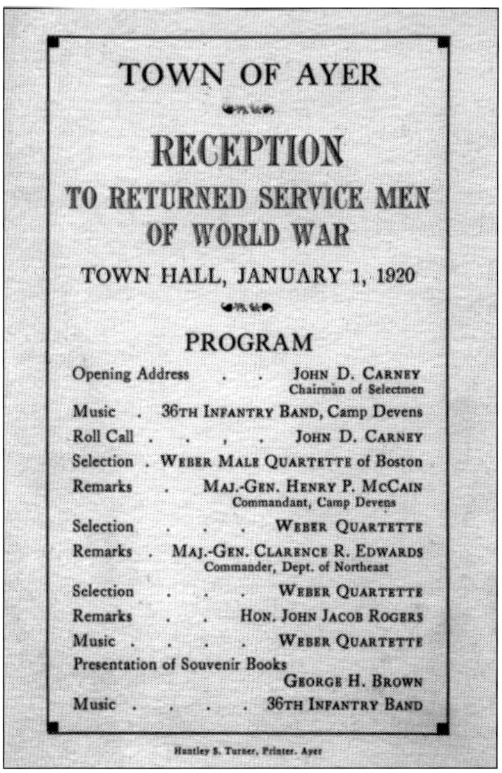

TOWN OF AYER

RECEPTION

TO RETURNED SERVICE MEN

OF WORLD WAR

TOWN HALL, JANUARY 1, 1920

PROGRAM

Opening Address . .	JOHN D. CARNEY Chairman of Selectmen
Music .	36TH INFANTRY BAND, Camp Devens
Roll Call	JOHN D. CARNEY
Selection .	WEBER MALE QUARTETTE of Boston
Remarks .	MAJ.-GEN. HENRY P. McCAIN Commandant, Camp Devens
Selection	WEBER QUARTETTE
Remarks .	MAJ.-GEN. CLARENCE R. EDWARDS Commander, Dept. of Northeast
Selection	WEBER QUARTETTE
Remarks . . .	HON. JOHN JACOB ROGERS
Music	WEBER QUARTETTE
Presentation of Souvenir Books	GEORGE H. BROWN
Music	36TH INFANTRY BAND

Huntley S. Turner, Printer, Ayer

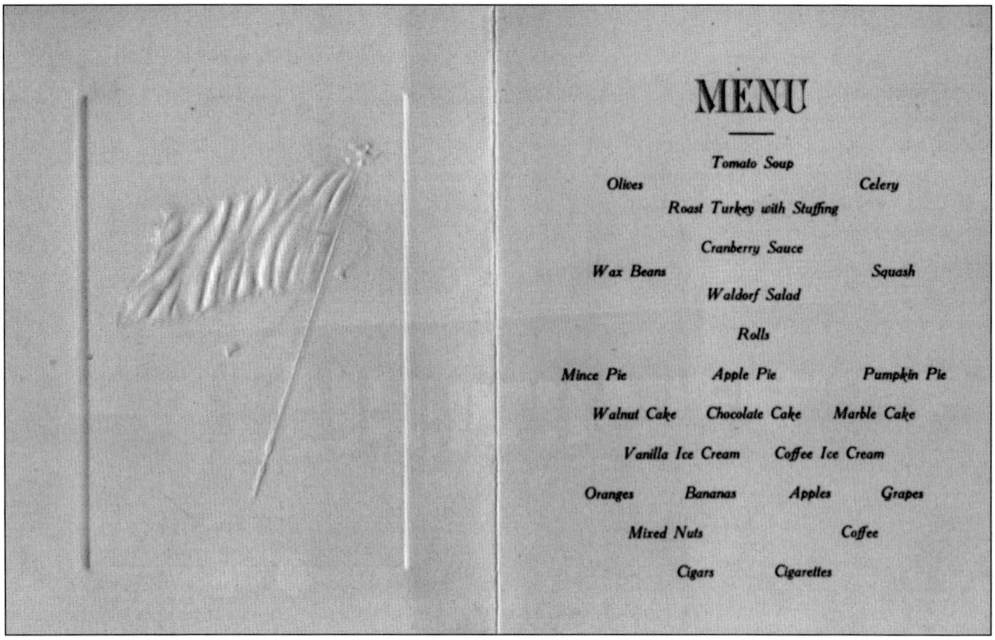

MENU

Tomato Soup

Olives — Celery

Roast Turkey with Stuffing

Cranberry Sauce

Wax Beans — Squash

Waldorf Salad

Rolls

Mince Pie — Apple Pie — Pumpkin Pie

Walnut Cake — Chocolate Cake — Marble Cake

Vanilla Ice Cream — Coffee Ice Cream

Oranges — Bananas — Apples — Grapes

Mixed Nuts — Coffee

Cigars — Cigarettes

The dinner for veterans and their guests was held at the Soldier's Club on January 1, 1920. The Soldier's Club was located on West Street. Federation House, which was the name given to the YMCA building on West Main Street, was still open but a second Soldier's Club was needed to accommodate the increase in the number of troops at that time. The menu included a full Thanksgiving Day meal complete with all the fixings. After the dinner, at 5:00 p.m., the grand ball commenced with music and dancing. The grand ball was open only to those who had tickets, given to the veterans who could then distribute them to family members. The dance card with the order of dances is very rarely seen today.

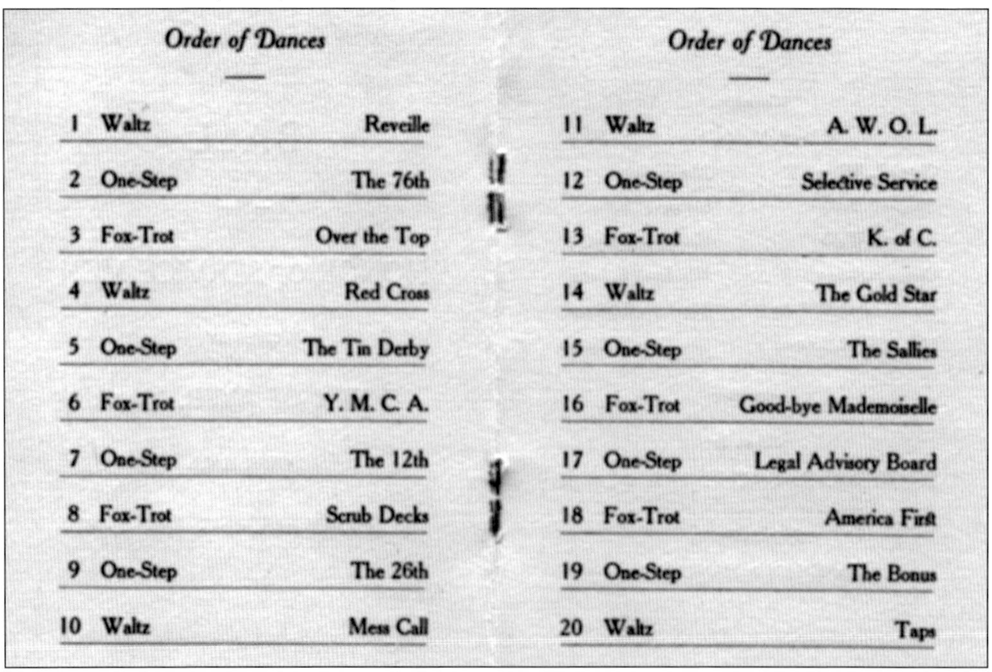

Order of Dances

1	Waltz	Reveille
2	One-Step	The 76th
3	Fox-Trot	Over the Top
4	Waltz	Red Cross
5	One-Step	The Tin Derby
6	Fox-Trot	Y. M. C. A.
7	One-Step	The 12th
8	Fox-Trot	Scrub Decks
9	One-Step	The 26th
10	Waltz	Mess Call

Order of Dances

11	Waltz	A. W. O. L.
12	One-Step	Selective Service
13	Fox-Trot	K. of C.
14	Waltz	The Gold Star
15	One-Step	The Sallies
16	Fox-Trot	Good-bye Mademoiselle
17	One-Step	Legal Advisory Board
18	Fox-Trot	America First
19	One-Step	The Bonus
20	Waltz	Taps

In 1917, thousands of men passed through the gates of Camp Devens on their way to France in World War I. One was a 22-year-old dairy farmer and teamster from Dracut, Massachusetts, Army Pfc. Chester J. Canney, who served as an attendant for horses and mules with veterinary hospital No. 1. His grandson John C. Canney II was elected Ayer's town clerk and tax collector in 2010. (Courtesy of John C. Canney II.)

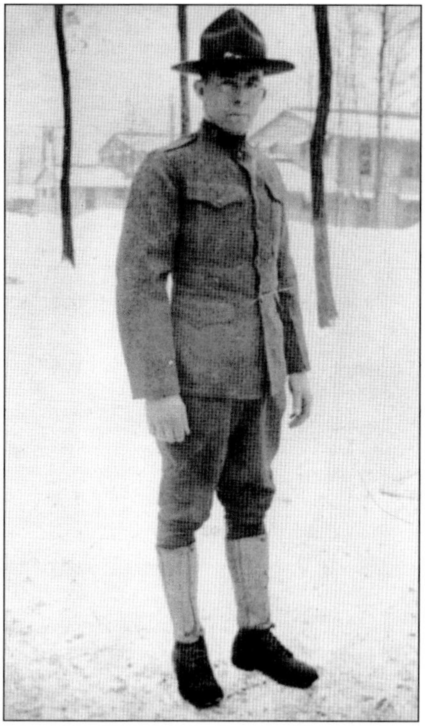

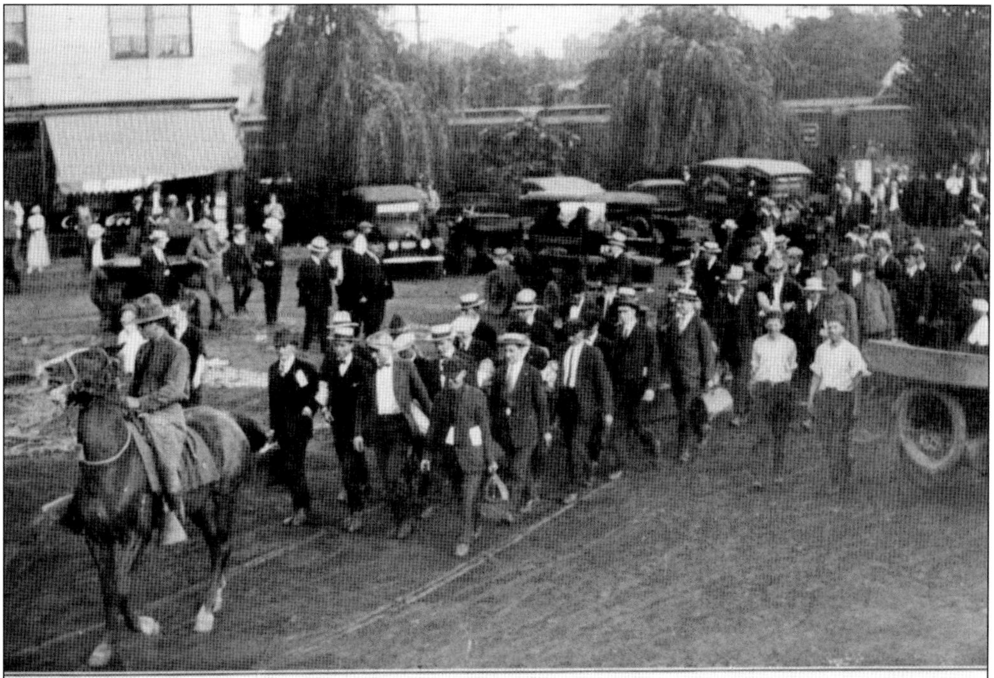

LEAVING THE STATION AT AYER

This postcard shows men arriving at Camp Devens. Upon arriving at the depot, the cavalryman on his US-branded horse would instruct the draftees to fall in line and follow him. This would be the first march of many while in the US Army. (Courtesy of John C. Canney II.)

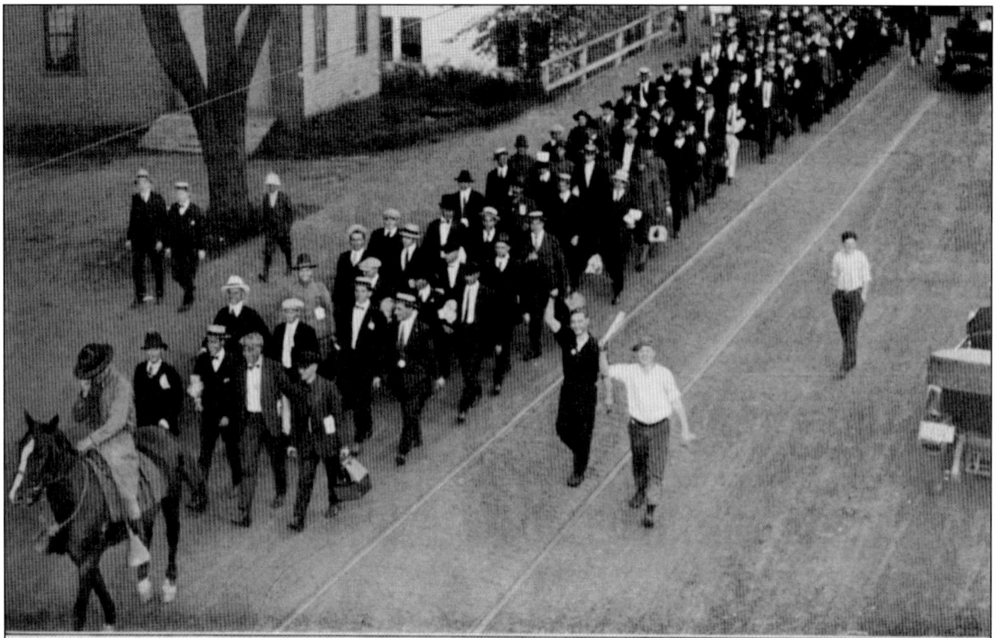

"CAMP DEVENS, NEXT!"

This postcard is showing the new recruits on their one mile march down West Main Street, after arriving at the train station, to the main gate at Camp Devens. To the residents of West Main Street looking on this would be the first of as many as 100,000 soldiers that would make their way to Camp Devens during World War I. (Courtesy of John C. Canney II.)

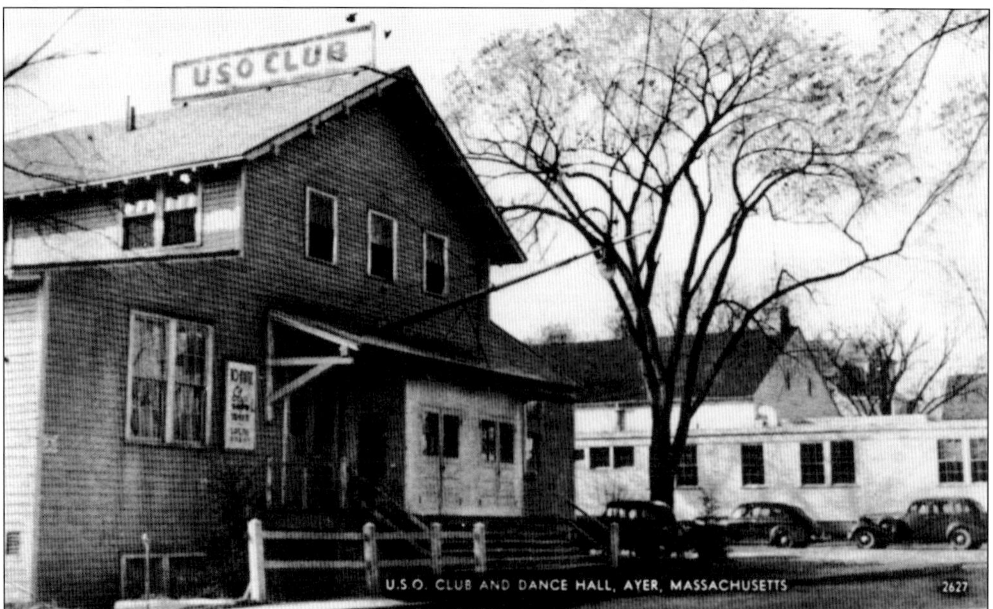

This is a postcard of the USO club on the corner of Mechanic Street and West Main Street in Ayer. During World War I, the building belonged to the YMCA and served the troops as a recreation facility, as did the USO in World War II. As the population of soldiers increased, there was a need for more YMCA recreational facilities and 14 more YMCAs were built at the camp.

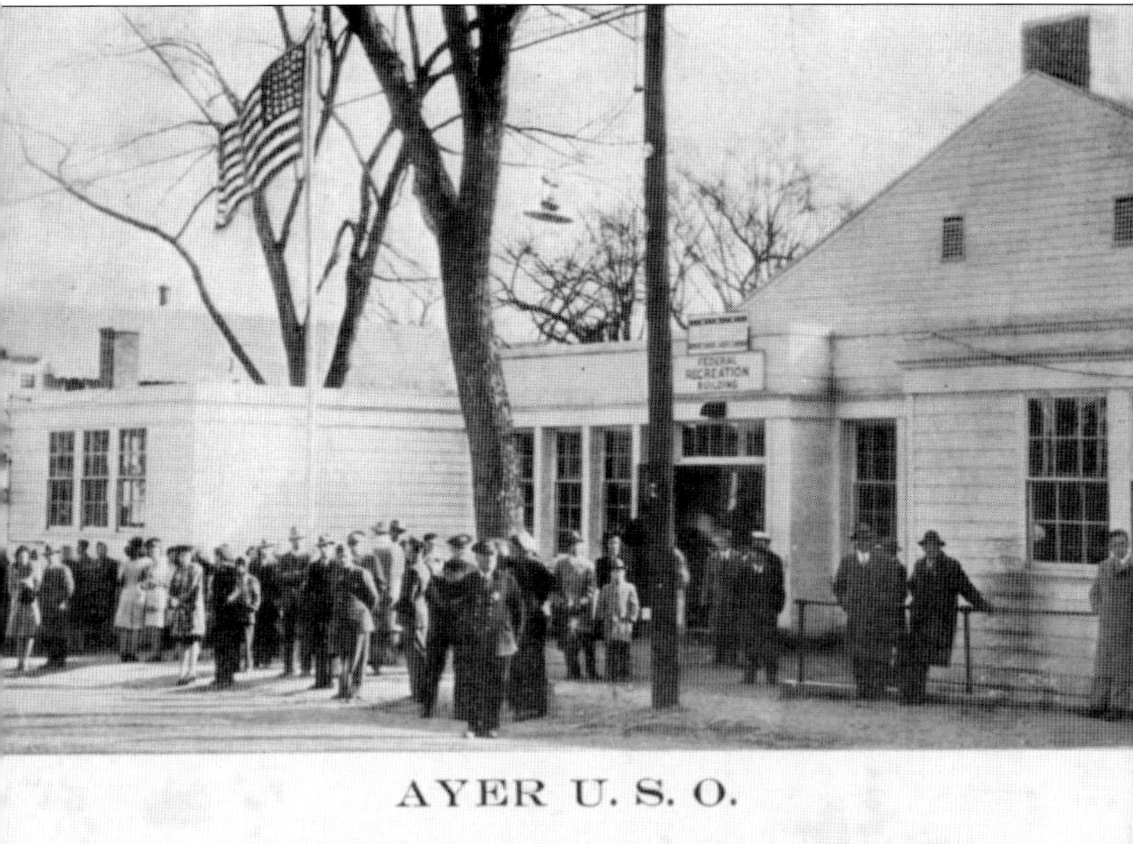

The USO originated in 1941 as a home-away-from-home for soldiers. In this photograph, the USO was located on the opposite corner from the original YMCA building, on the corner of West Main and Mechanic Streets where Parthenon Pizza is today. Both USO buildings had lots of activities, offering music and dancing, snack bars, movies, a location service, and a large game room. It served the enlistees and their parents. This postcard was sent to service men and women from chief of police Tertulliano "Jimmy" Pirone. The chief would personally sign each card.

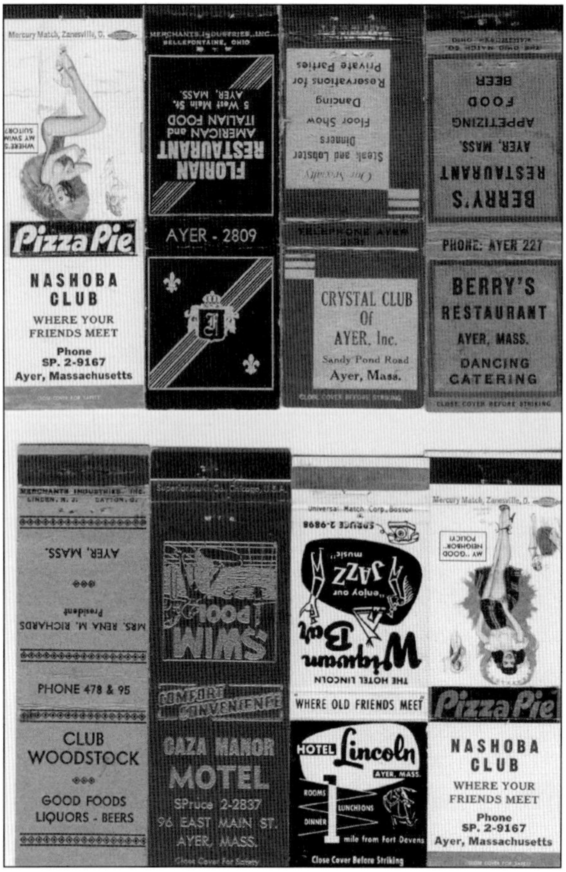

These matchbook covers represent some of the many hospitality businesses that flourished in Ayer because of Fort Devens. They provided entertainment and a place for soldiers to stay, other than their barracks. When soldiers from Fort Devens were able to enjoy a little rest and relaxation, Ayer provided many different outlets in which to unwind.

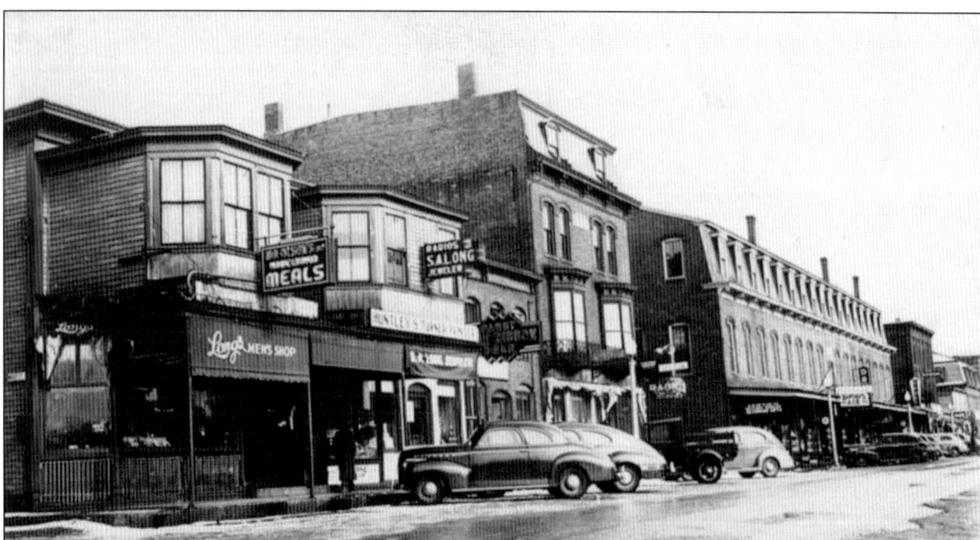

It is a busy day on Main Street in downtown Ayer in the 1940s. Note the angle-in parking. In the foreground is where present-day Kelley's Hallmark Store is located. There were at least three businesses in that one building. There is a men's store and a jewelers on the first floor and a restaurant on the second floor. (Courtesy of Ed Kelley.)

Seven

Education and Worship

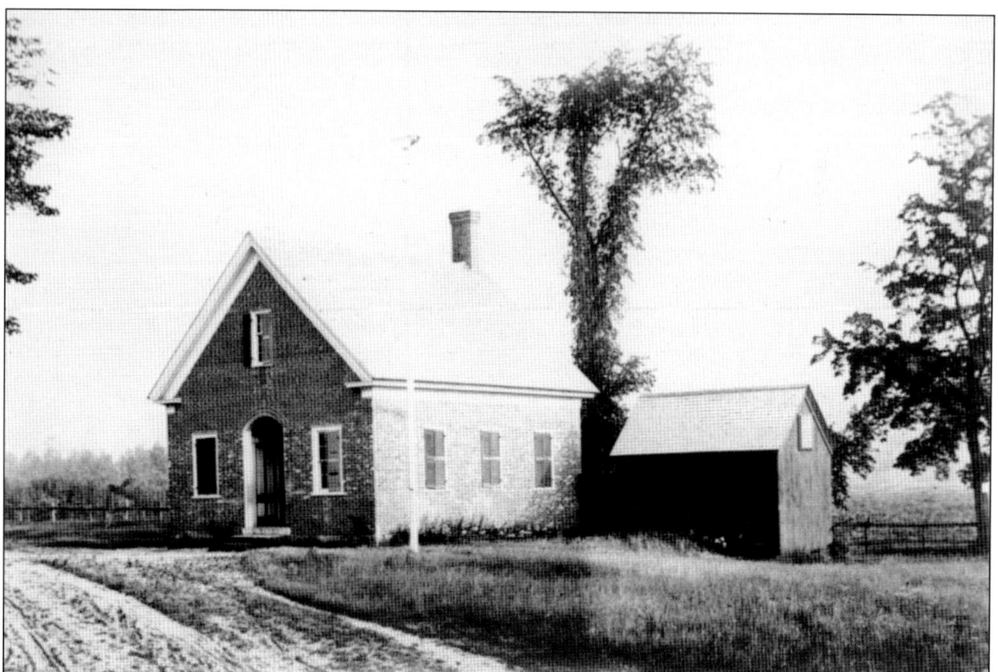

Sandy Pond Schoolhouse appears here on July 27, 1894. It was the District School No. 11 schoolhouse, part of the districts established in 1792 by the town of Groton. There were two previous wooden school buildings at this site. This school building was erected in 1868 at a cost of $1,281.81. It averaged about 18 students in its one room schoolhouse before closing in 1906.

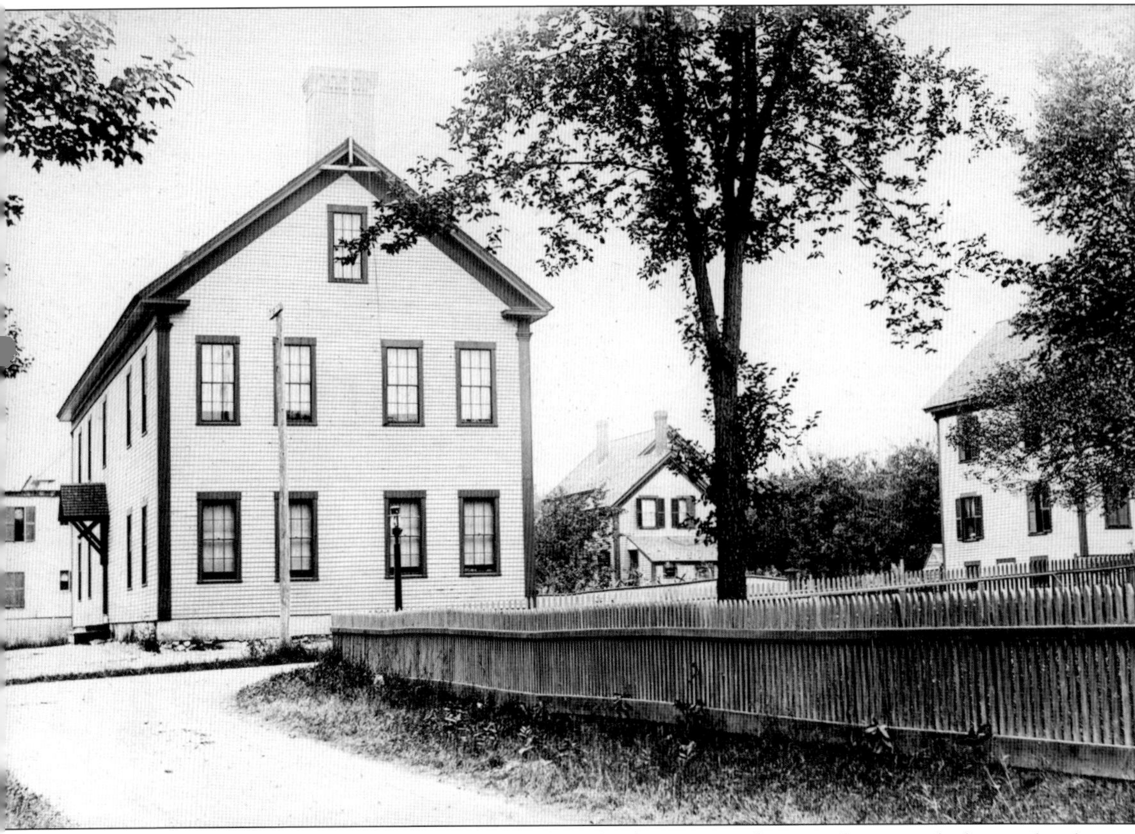

Pictured here, the Washington Street School was built in 1873. This was the second of two schools built on this site. The first school was erected in 1859 and burned in the great fire of 1872. Shown here, it was not until 1873 that a new school was built. It was originally a two-room schoolhouse and in 1883, an addition to the building doubled its size. There were the first and second grades on the first floor and the third and fourth grades on the second. In 1931, the new high school was opened on Pond Street, where students from the high school on Pleasant Street were relocated. At the same time, students from the Washington Street School moved to the old high school, built in 1894. The Washington Street School was demolished in 1933 to make way for the new Central Fire Station erected on that site in 1934.

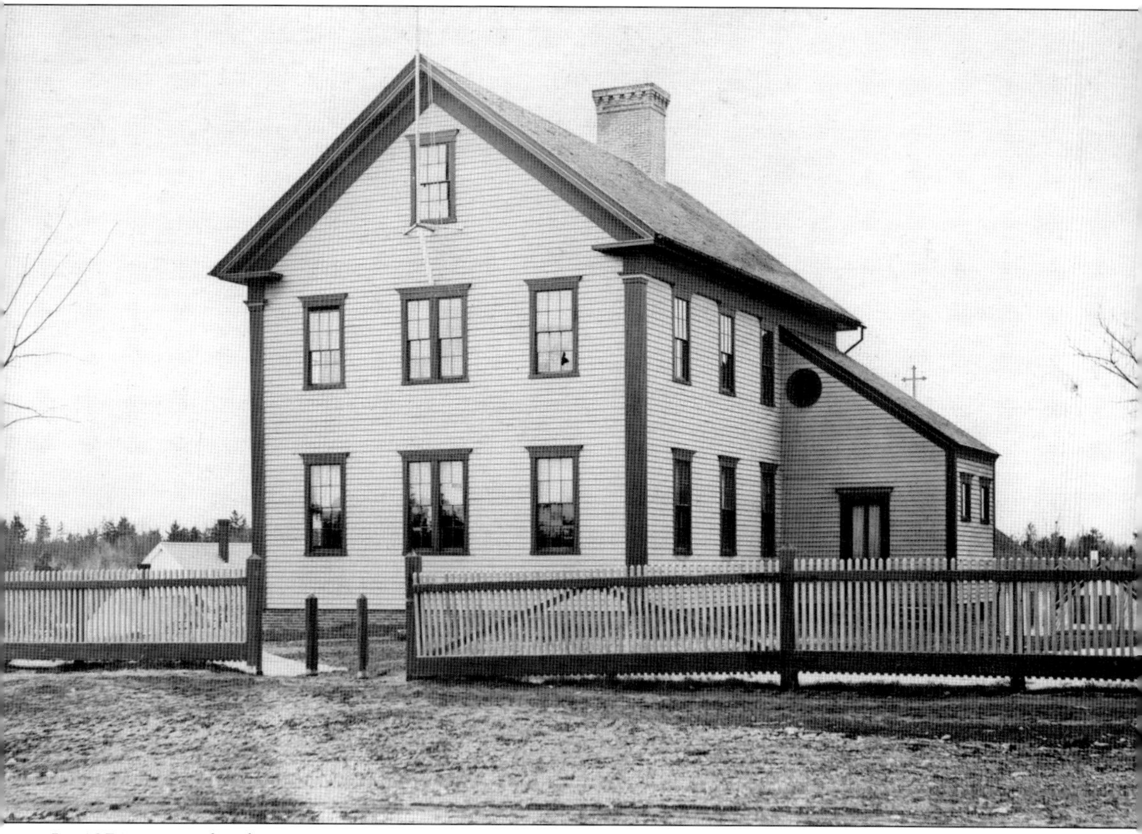

In 1871, soon after becoming a town, Ayer created a new school district called Acre Primary just west of St. Mary's church. At a town meeting held in 1872, a total of $3,200 was allotted for a two-story, two-room, wooden schoolhouse. The Shirley Street School was built in that same year at a final cost of $4,500. The pastor of St. Mary's was not in favor of the school being built so close to the church. He was concerned that the noise from the schoolchildren would interfere with the church services. In 1950, St. Mary's Church set up a parochial school in the same building they had objected to 78 years earlier. The school still stands today.

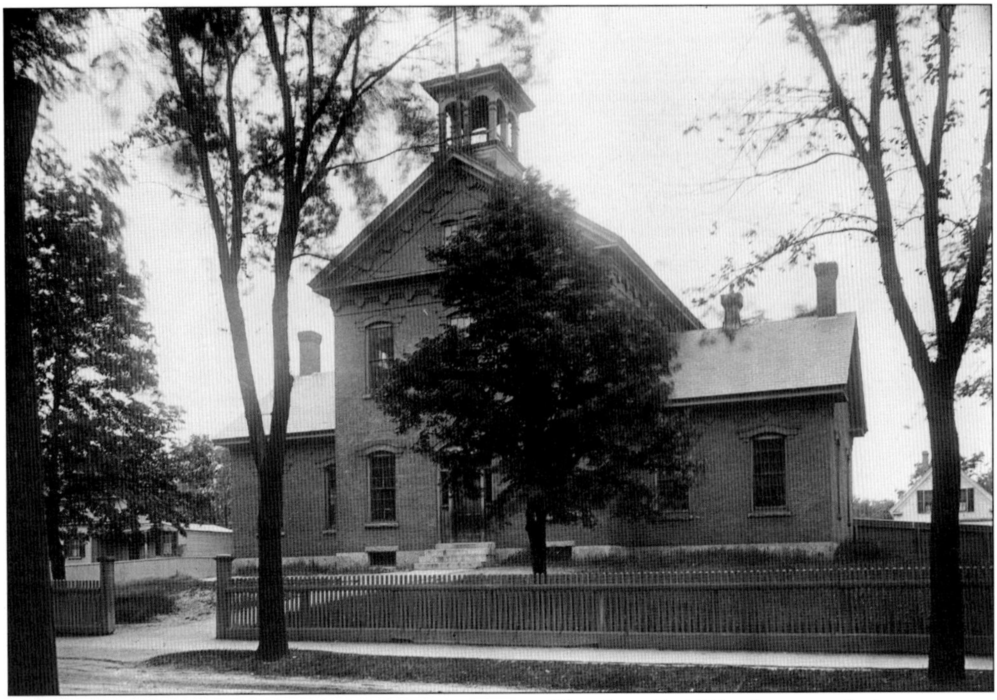

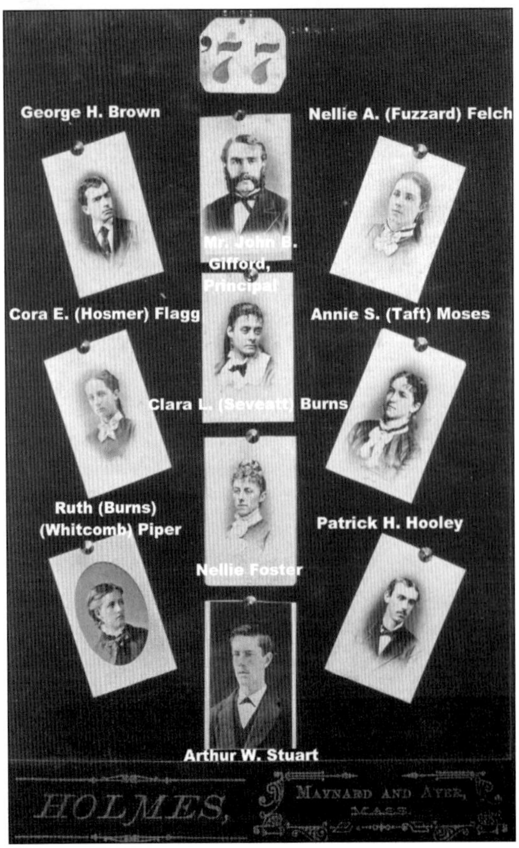

This June 7, 1913, photograph shows East Main Street School. Originally, it was a one-story schoolhouse when it was built in 1868 at a cost of $7,234.89. When Ayer first became a town in 1871, it wasted no time in adding a second floor. This became the new and long-awaited high school. In 1894, a new high school was built on Pleasant Street, and the students from East Main Street moved up to the Pleasant Street School. In 1968, the school was demolished to make way for a courthouse. At the time, the East Main Street School was one of the oldest municipal buildings in Ayer. It was demolished exactly 100 years after it was built.

The Pleasant Street School was completed in 1894 at a cost of $10,000. Classes began the next day, and all East Main Street school students were moved to the new building. Dr. John G. Park of Groton, whose family had owned land in that vicinity since 1783, donated the land. In 1906, an addition to the high school building doubled the size of the school.

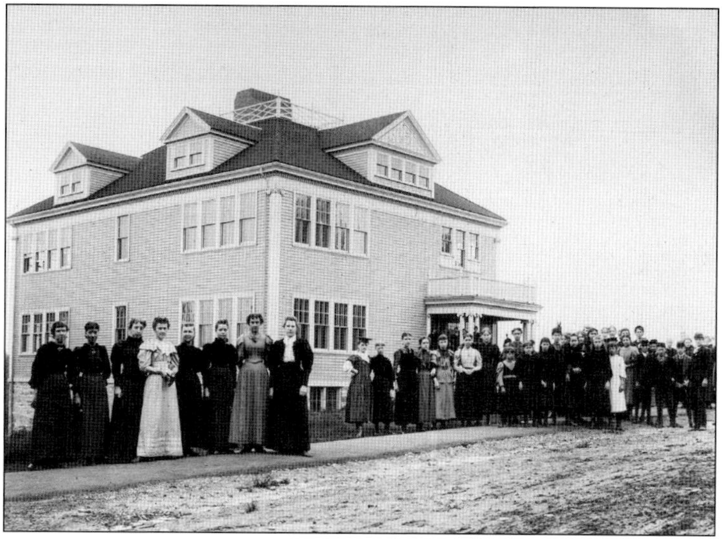

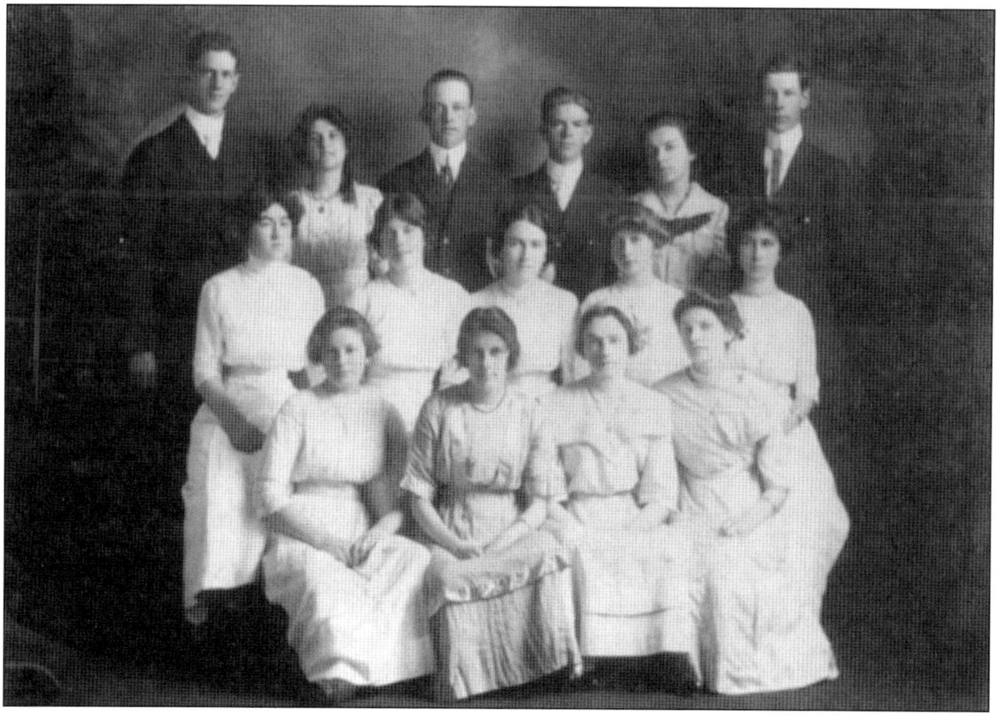

This is the graduating class from Ayer High School in 1913. From left to right are (first row) Pauline M. Sherwin, Margaret E. Hume, Alice R. McCarthy, and Gertrude I. Carrigan; (second row) Mary E. Leahy, Helen M. Moore, Madeline D. O'Neil, Flora I. Cole, and Anna J. Taylor; (third row) Victor L. Fillebrown, Evelyn M. Sanderson, Roger C. Lawrence, Frank E. Brown, Lillian E. McMahon, and Charles T. Mullin.

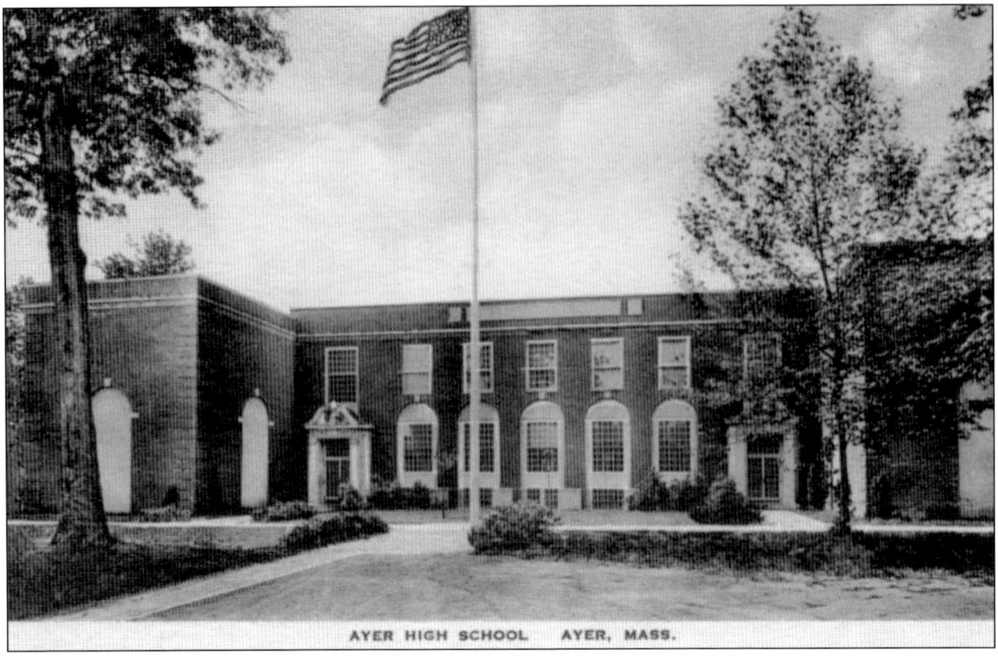

The brick high school, which was built in 1931 on Pond Street, appears in this postcard. Its first graduating class was in the spring of 1932. The school was closed in 1963 when the new high school and middle school were built. The old high school was demolished, and a new senior center and senior housing units were erected on the site.

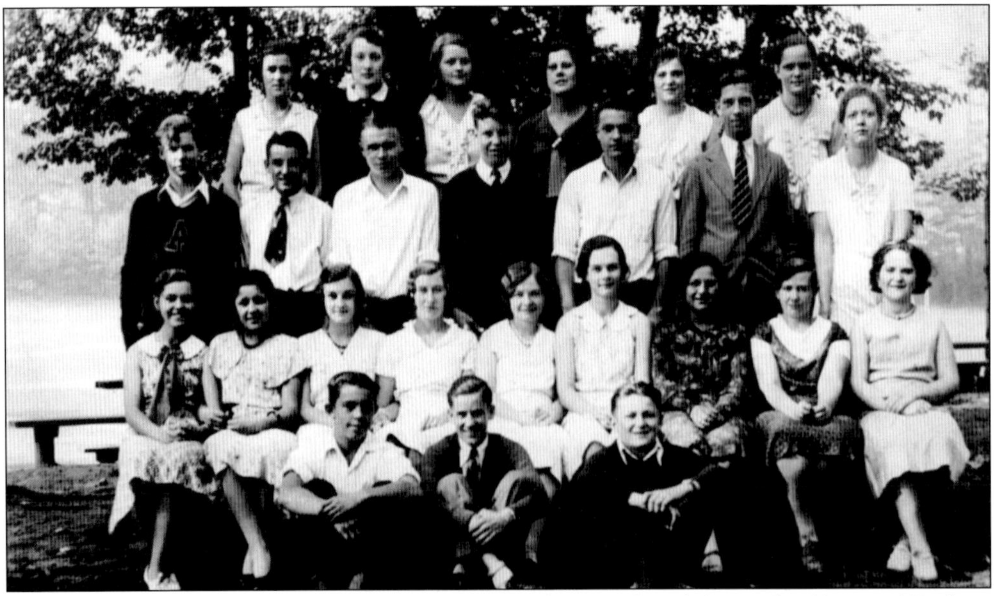

Members of the 1932 Pond Street School graduating class are, from left to right, (first row) Rodney Kidder, William Lambert, and Richard Pillman; (second row) Bernice Gravel, Marguerite Pirone, Josephine Auld, Louise Belisle, Elizabeth MacClellan, Geraldine Moore, Ida Kozlov, Eleanor Bean, and Olive Fletcher; (third row) Kenneth Wood, Lloyd Burdell, Wescott Winchester, John Guthrie, Frank Balcom, Williard Noddin, and Janet Sherwin; (fourth row) Mae Jenkins, Helen Curran, Pauline Wilker, Phyllis Reech, Pearl Fletcher, and Inda Winslow. Effie Little was absent.

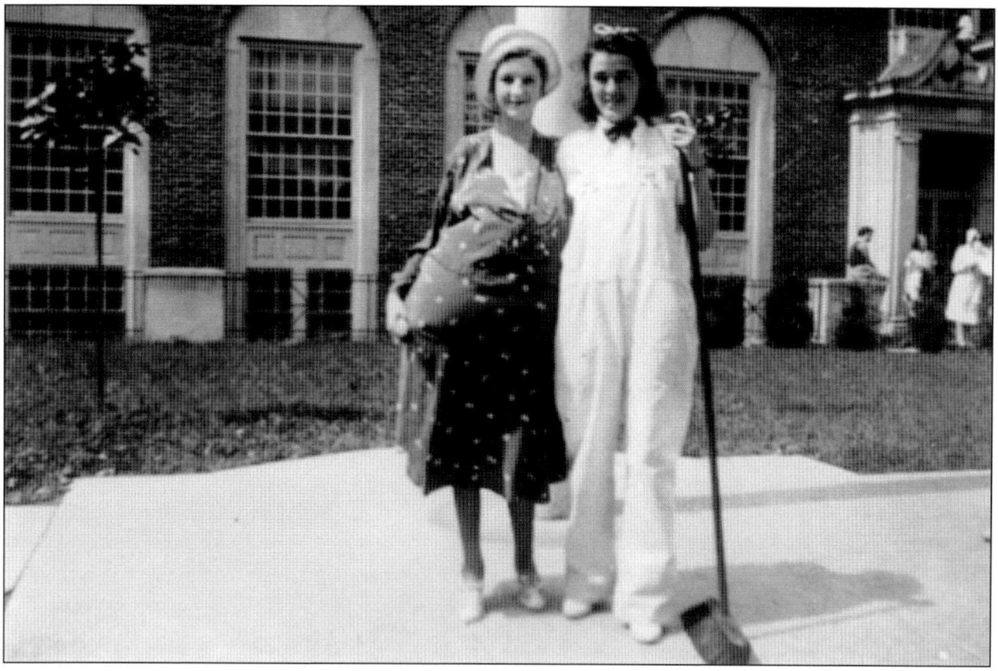

Effie Little (left) and Mae Jenkins are members of the first graduating class of the new Ayer High School on Pond Street in 1932. This may be a seniors' day at the high school; the costumes may be a part of the festivities.

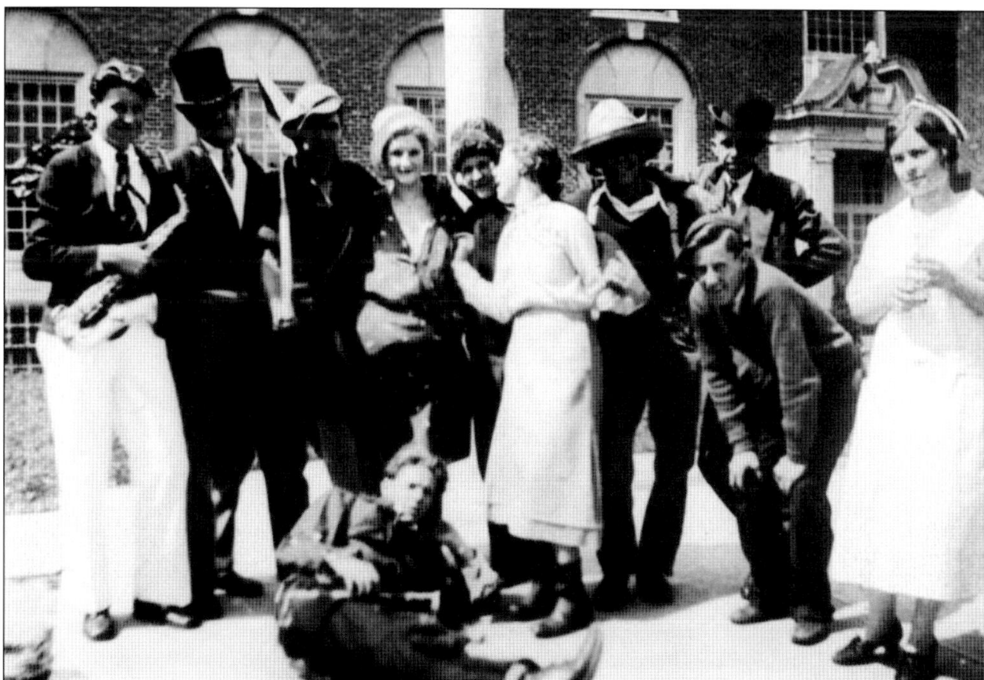

These are the students of the class of 1932. From left to right are John Guthrie, Frank Balcom, Joe Rutherford, Effie Little, Richard Pillman, Bunny Gravel, Rodney Kidder, Wilmot Bailey, Bill Lambert, and Elizabeth MacClellan. Kenny Woods is on the ground.

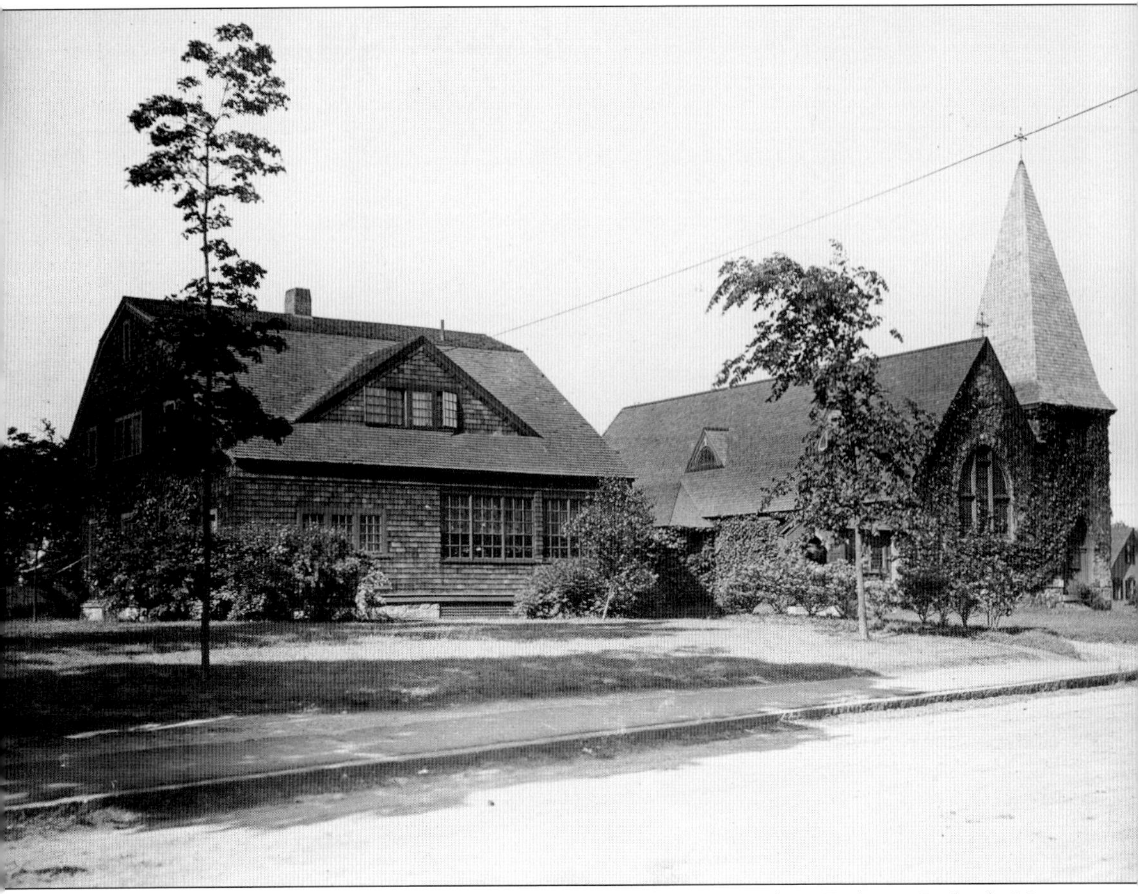

St. Andrews Episcopal Church began as a mission by the Reverend Dr. Endicott Peabody. He was headmaster of the Groton School and organized the church in 1889. The services were initially held in the town hall for three years. Ground was broken for the church on August 29, 1892, and the cornerstone was placed in September 1892. St. Andrews was completed on December 25, 1892, and the first services were also conducted on that day. In 1895, upon leaving the parish, another master from the Groton School, Rev. Charles L. Slattery, had the church debt fully paid. St. Andrews continued to be affiliated with the Groton School until 1950. In 1953, Parish Hall was built, which was used for Christian education classes and for the parish social affairs and projects.

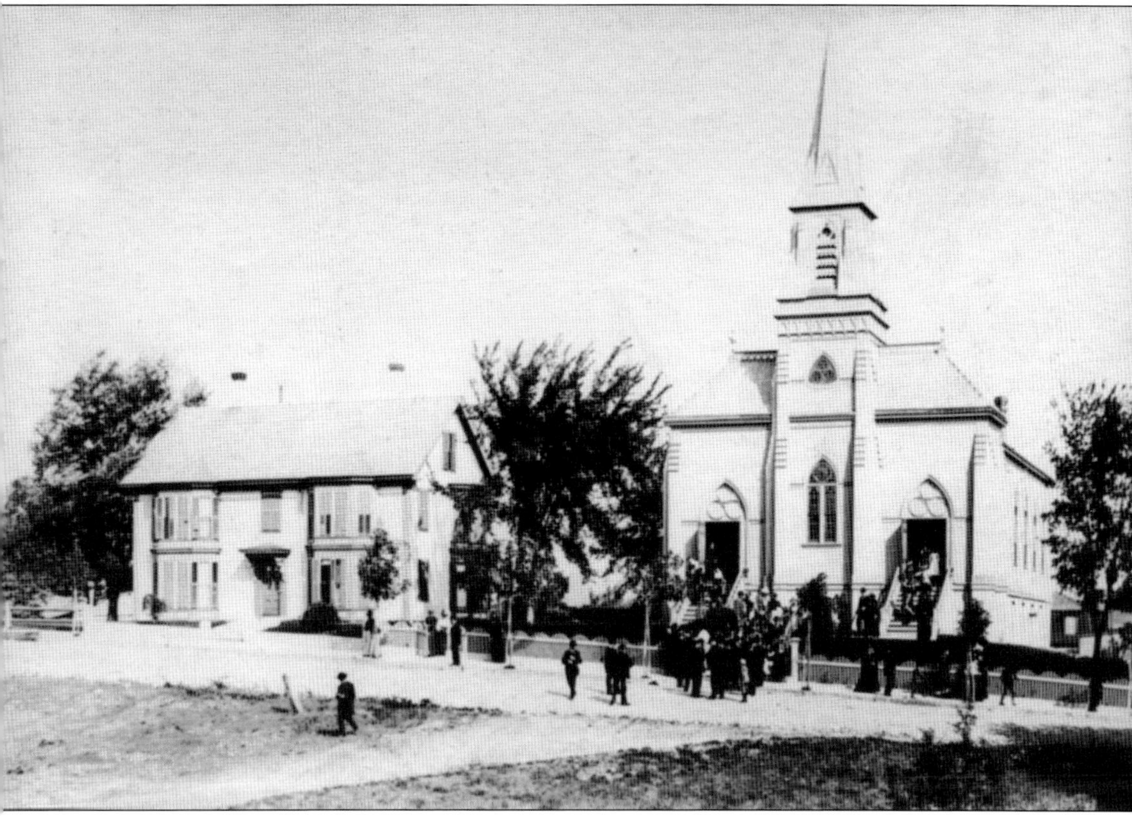

St. Mary's church and parsonage were dedicated on December 4, 1870. The church was originally formed in 1855. Services were held in private homes and then in the Union House, which was formerly Pingry Hall. It was the second church for St. Mary's; the first was built on West Main Street in 1858 by Alfred and Thomas Page. St. Mary's parish originally included Groton, Pepperell, Shirley, Townsend, Harvard, and Littleton. During World War I, the soldiers at Camp Devens received their spiritual needs from St. Mary's priests. In 1948, the pastor, Rev. William J. McCarthy, was interested in reopening the Shirley Street School as a parochial school. He was given permission to purchase the school and soon after began renovating and furnishing it. The school was dedicated on October 8, 1950. This photograph was taken on September 20, 1894.

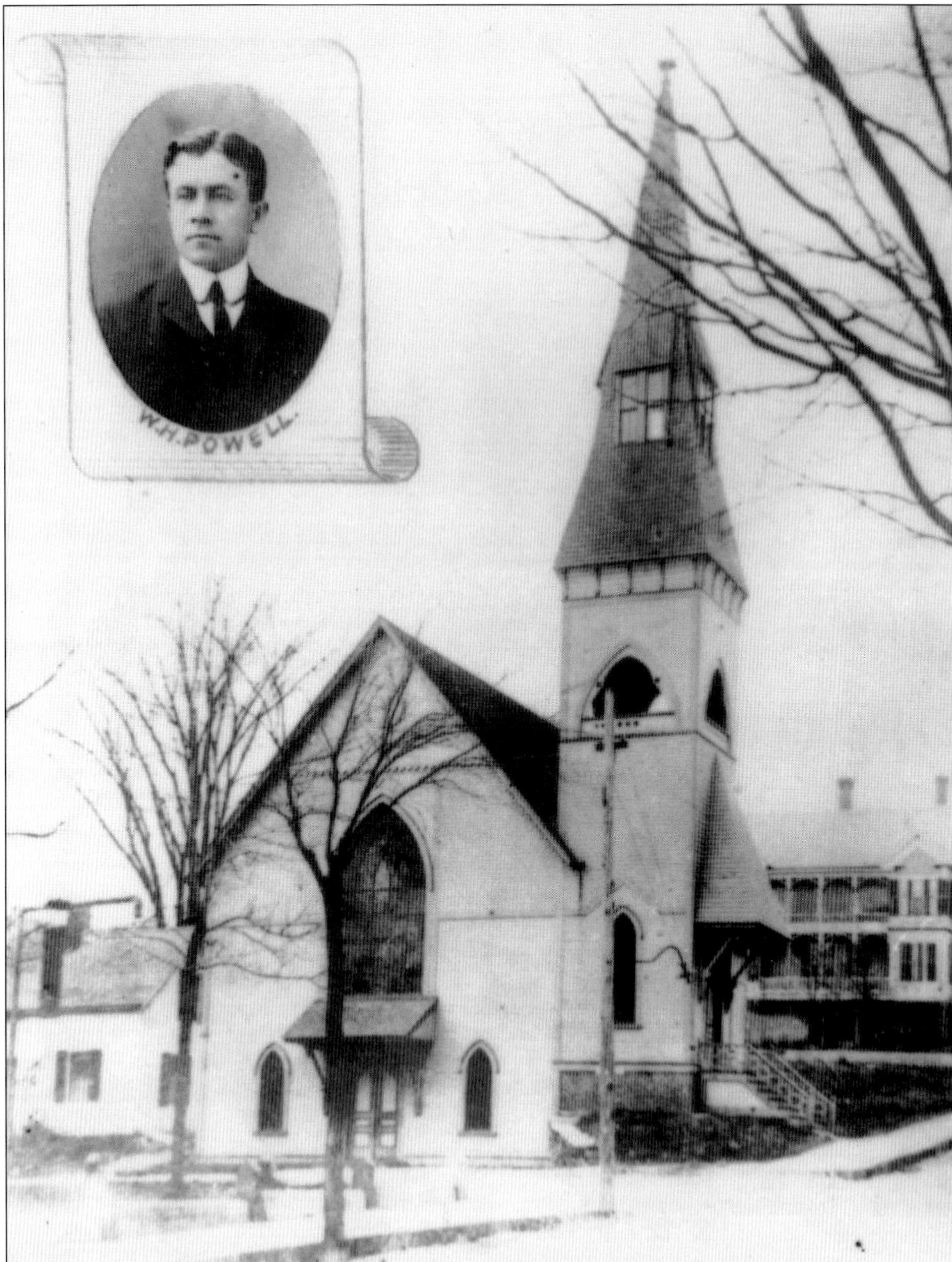

This church was originally built in 1887 as the Methodist Episcopal Church. Formed in 1869, Methodists would gather in members' homes, and as the congregation grew, they were able to meet in various halls. Just prior to erecting this church, they were meeting in the lower town hall. During World War I, the church, no longer active, rented to the Robert Burns Lodge No. 159 of the Independent Order of Odd Fellows (IOOF). The IOOF opened their doors to the soldiers at Camp Devens as a place to socialize. In 1938, the steeple was toppled and the large stained-glass window on Newton Street was destroyed during the hurricane. Webster H. Powell, shown here, was the pastor of this church at the turn of the 20th century. Today, the church is the home to the Apple Valley Baptist Church.

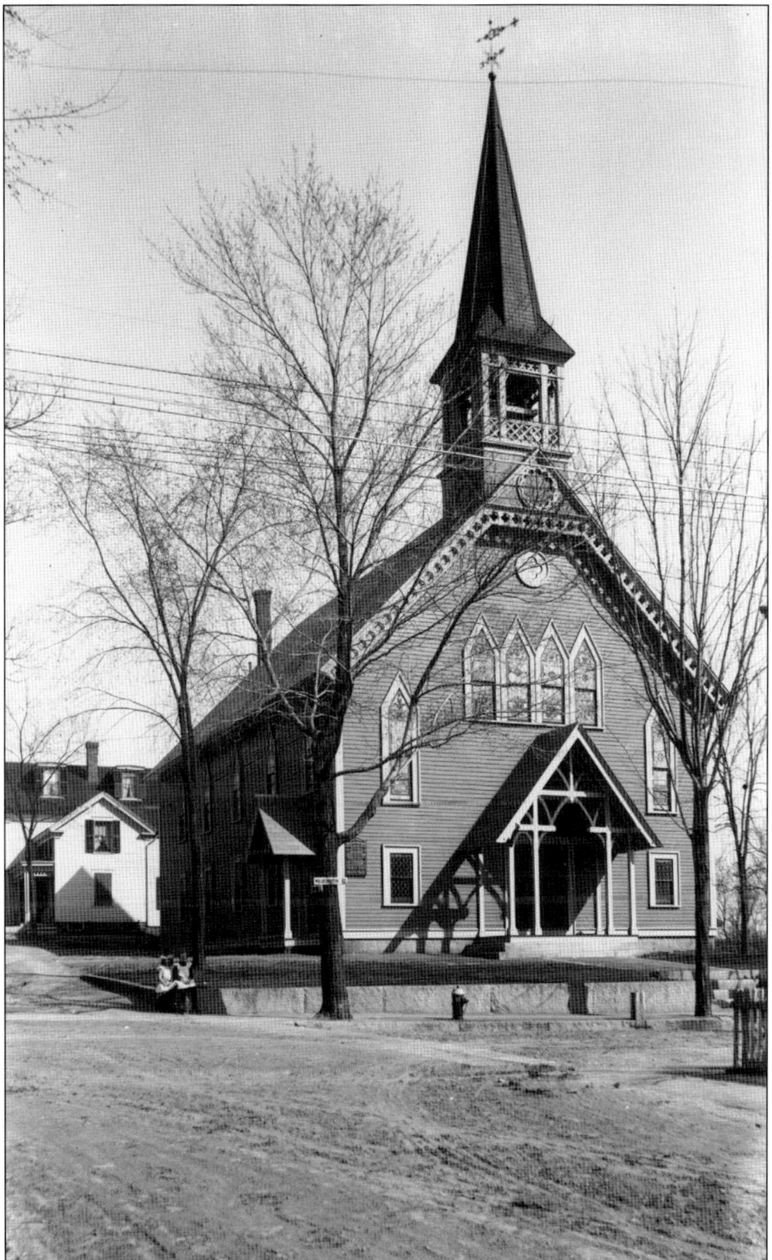

Pictured here in 1904, this church was known as the First Congregational. The church was built in 1867 by Daniel G. Waters of Ayer, four years before the town of Ayer was incorporated, and is located at 21 Washington Street. Donations from 50 other churches helped to finance the project. Those soliciting for donations were given a free rail pass from the railroad to travel to and from their church. One interest-free grant of $500 was repaid in 1966, ninety-nine years later. In 1915, the Methodist Episcopal Church joined with the Congregational Church. This federation of the two churches worked so well that by July 1931 this federation was dissolved and a new one was formed with the Congregational, Methodist, and Baptist Churches. The first service of the new federation was held on September 13, 1931, in the present building.

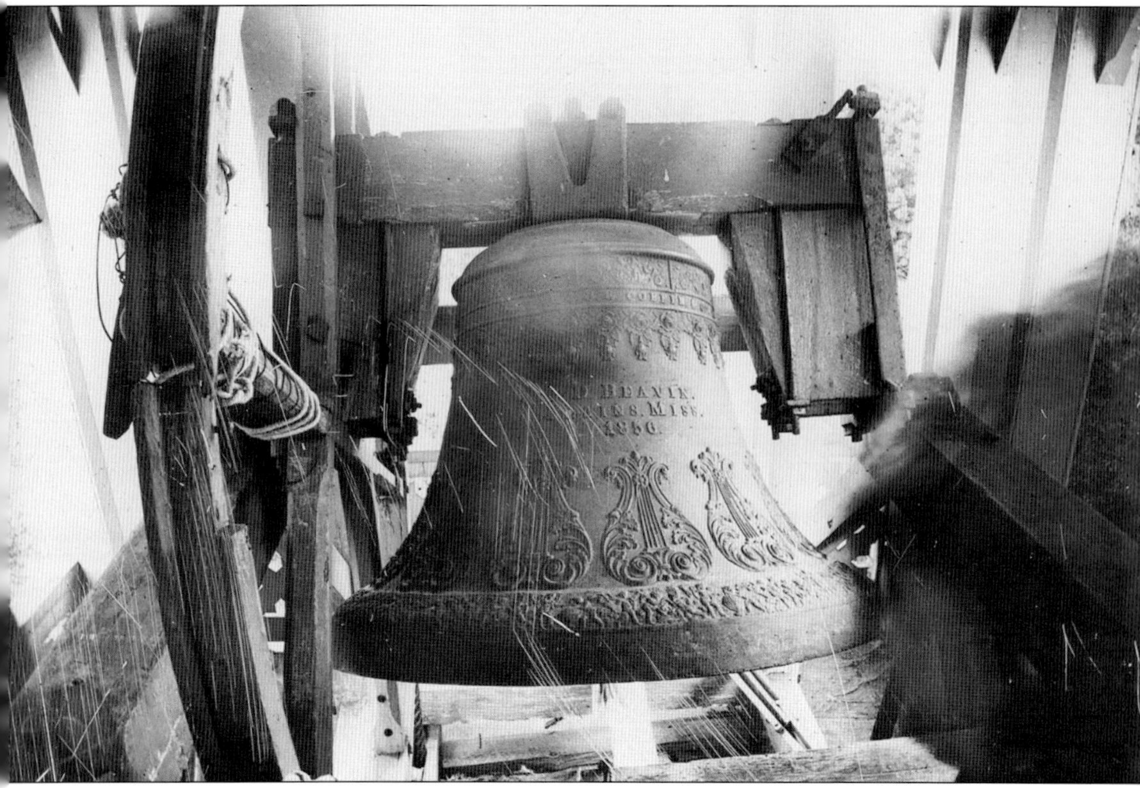

This bell hangs in the tower of the Federated Church on Washington Street in Ayer. During the Civil War in New Orleans, Gen. Benjamin F. Butler seized this 800-pound bell, along with others. The bells were sent to Boston and sold at an auction. Most of the junk dealers sent the bells to be melted down. For some reason, three bells were spared from that process. One went to Canton, Massachusetts, another to Morrisville, Vermont, and one was bought by Dr. Benjamin Snow of Fitchburg and given to the Unitarian Society there. In 1872, the bell was bought from the Unitarians and placed in the tower of the Federated Church in Ayer. When the bell was seized by General Butler, it was on its way to New Orleans to be melted down to make cannons for the Confederacy.

Eight

Town Life

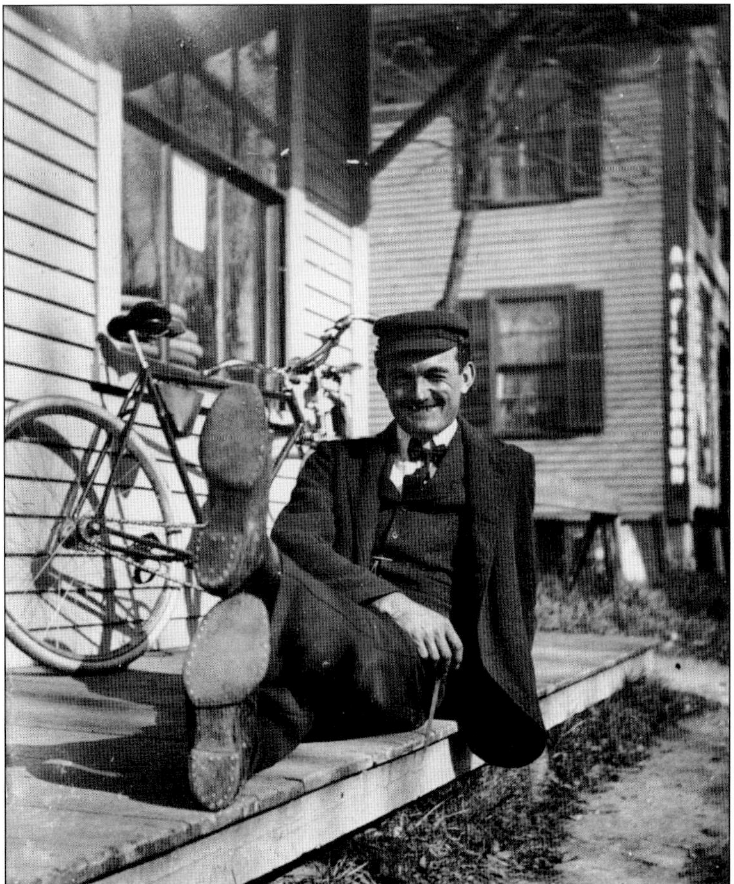

Pictured here on October 10, 1902, Aaron Slocomb sits on the front porch of his shop. Slocomb owned a bicycle sales and repair business on East Main Street. His store was next door to photographer Charles Kennison's home. Albert A. Fillebrown's store is behind Slocomb.

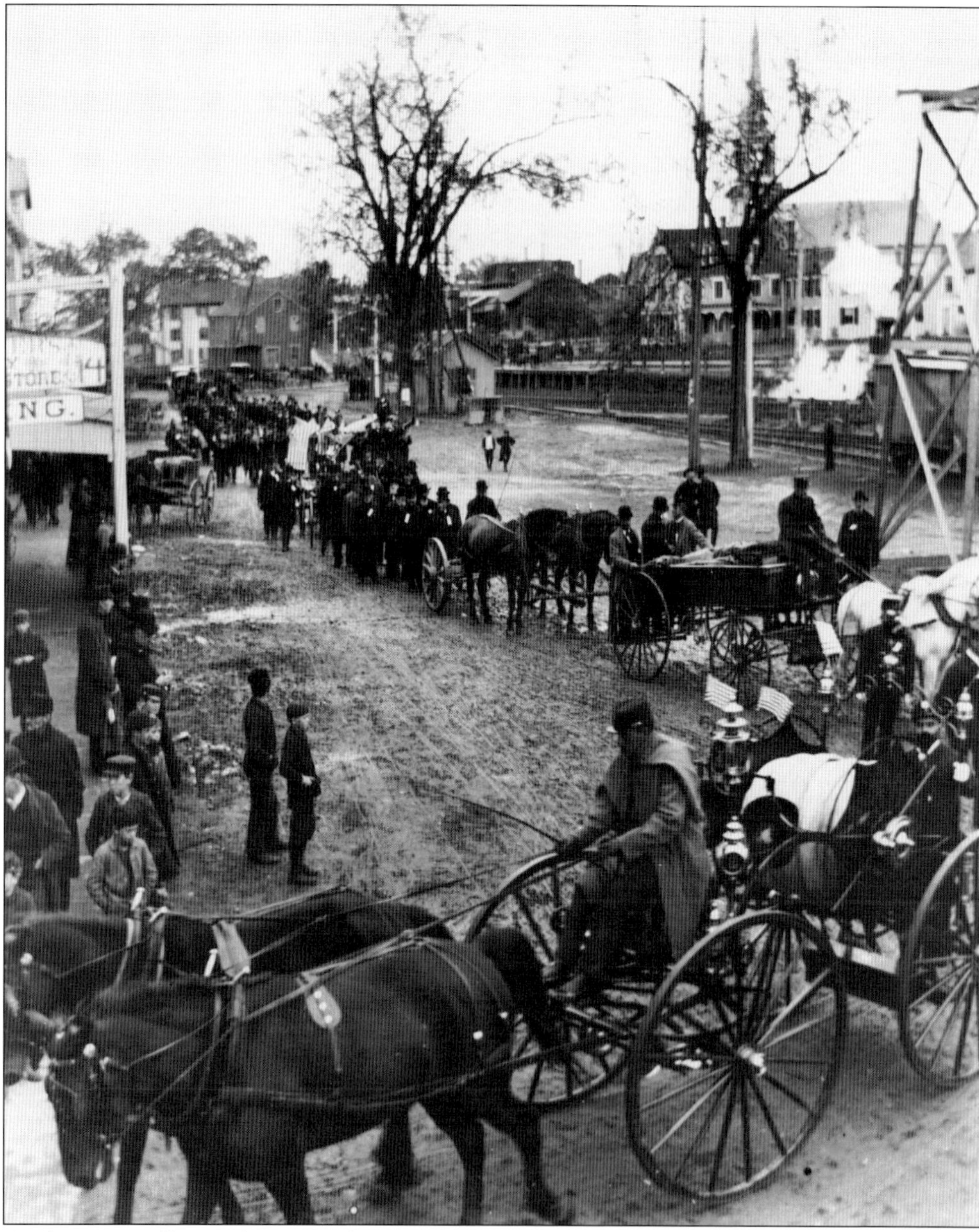

As there are still some leaves on the trees, this parade was probably held in the fall. The horses and wagons belong to the hook and ladder and hose companies. At the time, there was also the Alert Hook and Ladder Company and the Page Hose Company and Hartwell Hose Company. The parade route goes from East Main Street, over the Main Street rail crossing, and eventually onto Washington Street. One of the hoses can be seen on a roll on the top and inside of the first wagon. Just at the turn, at the left of the photograph, Fletcher's Clothing Store is visible. Owned by Daniel W. Fletcher, the store was located in the Spaulding Building at that time. Shown here in 1892, this parade was most likely a Firemen's Muster.

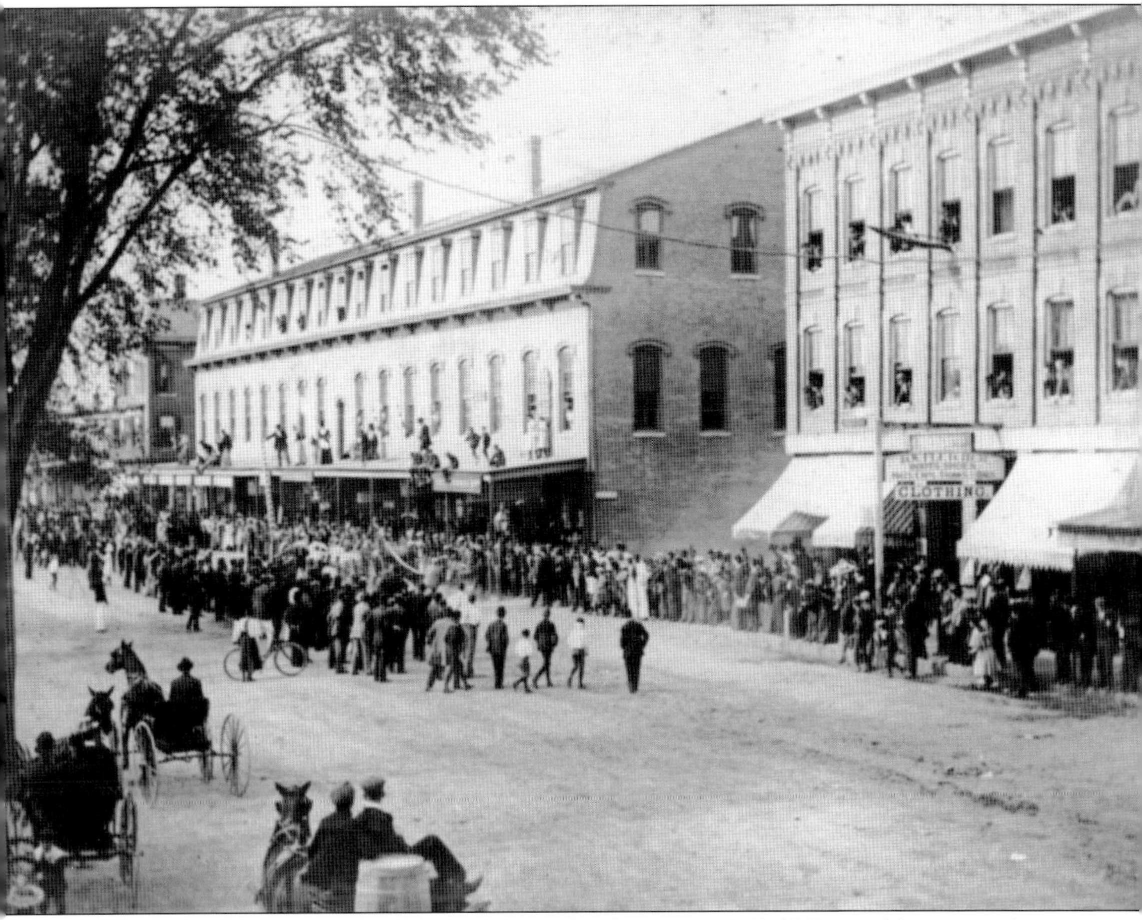

On October 6, 1897, the town of Ayer prepares for the Firemen's Field Day or Muster parade to make its way down Main Street. There are people in the center of the street watching a hose wagon. This is actually one of the hose company's firemen pulling the hose off the reel. There are people in the windows and on the roof over the sidewalk at the Page Building. The people standing on the sidewalk roof appear to have their cameras ready to film the event. Note that men, women, and children are on the roof. Today, for safety reasons, they would not be permitted to stroll freely on an unsecured roof.

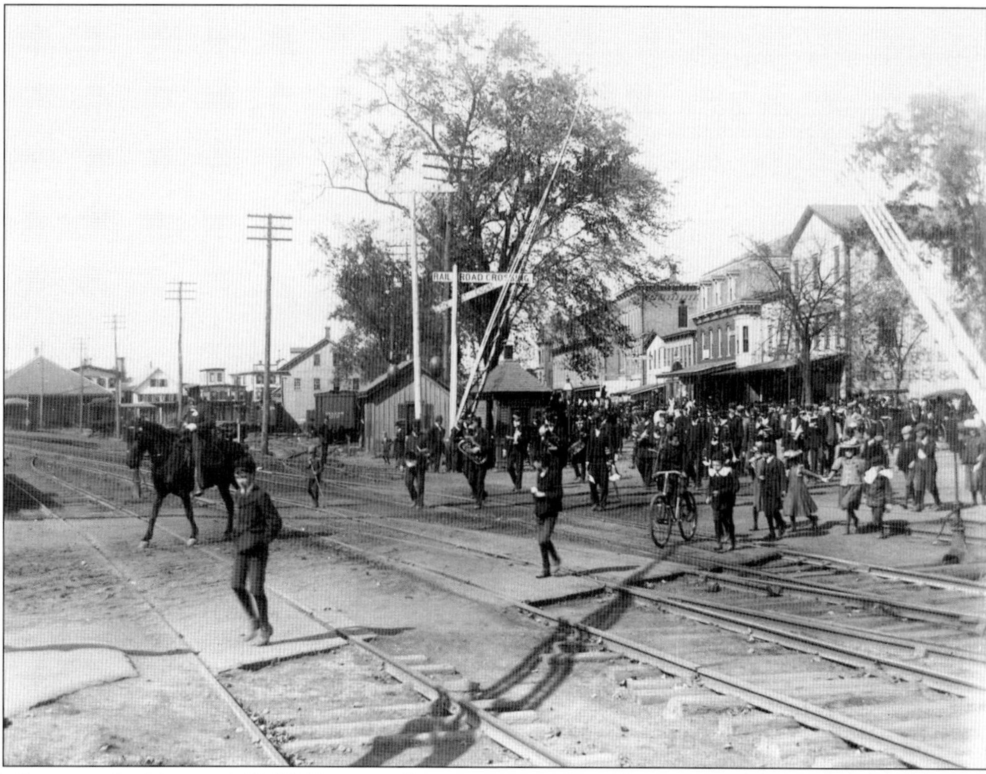

This was the Firemen's Field Day parade as it passes through Main Street and onto East Main Street. These parades are also sometimes referred to as Firemen's Musters. Some towns have a tradition of 100 years of musters. They are usually held between the middle of summer to October. This particular muster parade took place on October 6, 1897, with Chief Parsons leading on his horse.

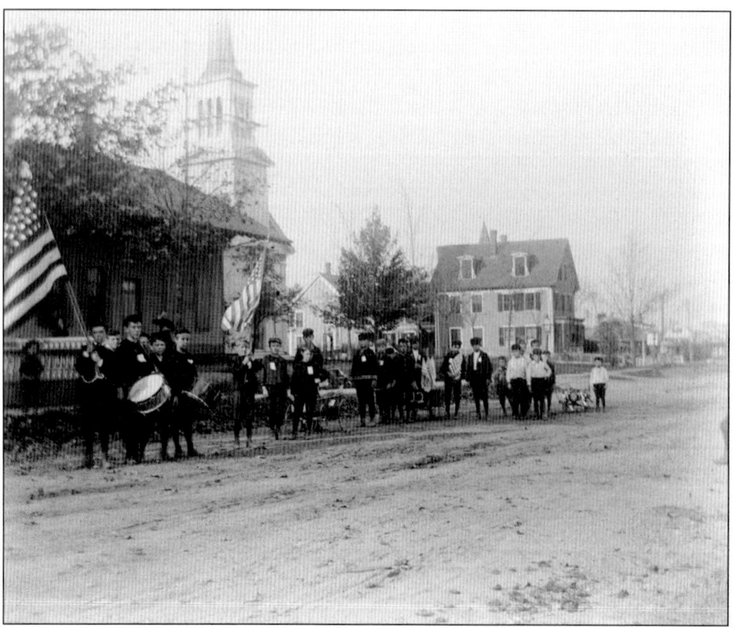

On October 6, 1897, these boys are dressed up for the Firemen's Field Day parade. They are standing on East Main Street not far from the Baptist church, which can be seen behind the building on the left in the photograph. The image is labeled "Kid Firemen."

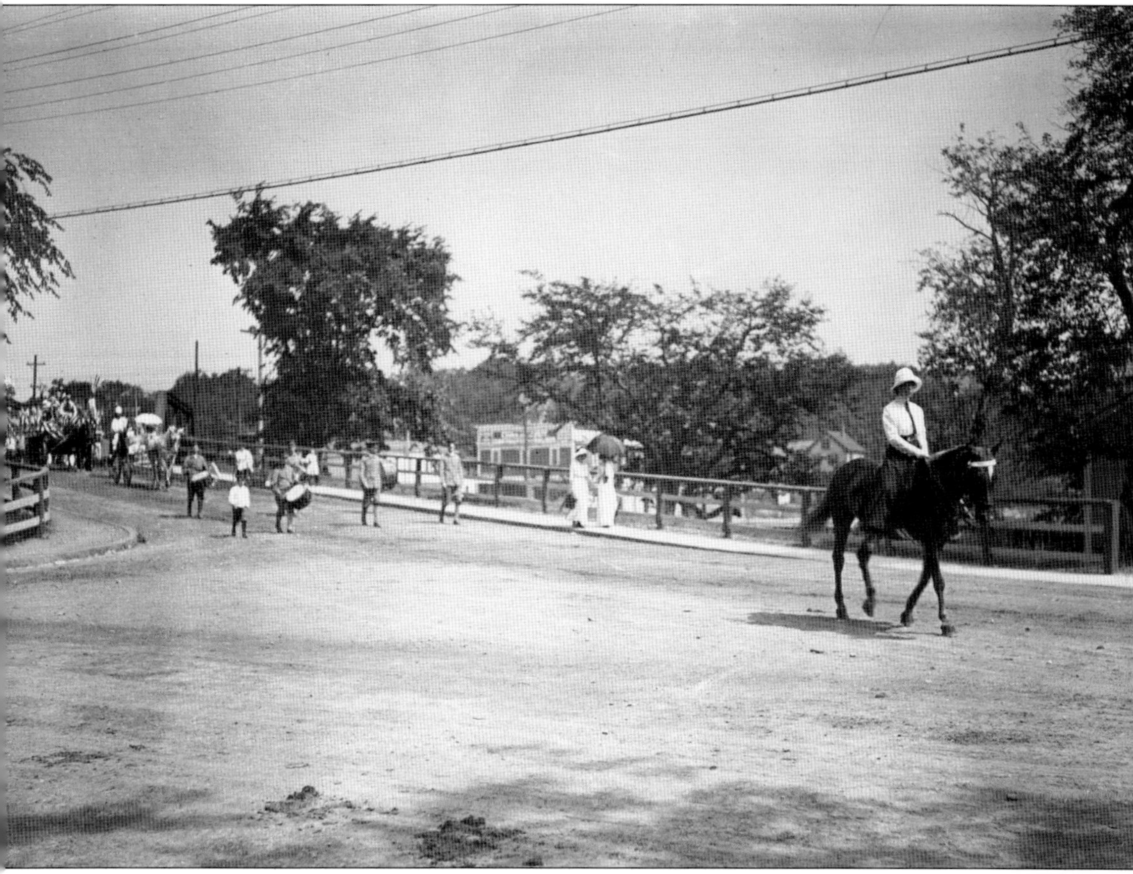

This is the 1912 Fourth of July parade. The parade marshal, Madeline Whitney, is on her horse leading the Shirley Cornet Band. The parade is marching over the bridge on East Main Street on its way to the town park, now Pirone Park. At the park, concerts were held in the afternoon and evening. In the morning, there were baseball games between the businessmen and professionals. In the afternoon, there were sports events for young boys and girls. Events included sack races, shoe races, and the 100-yard dash. At night, the celebration ended with fireworks at 8:00 p.m. It must have been a hot, sunny day, as the ladies on the sidewalk carry an umbrella. At the time, the cost of the parade was $200.

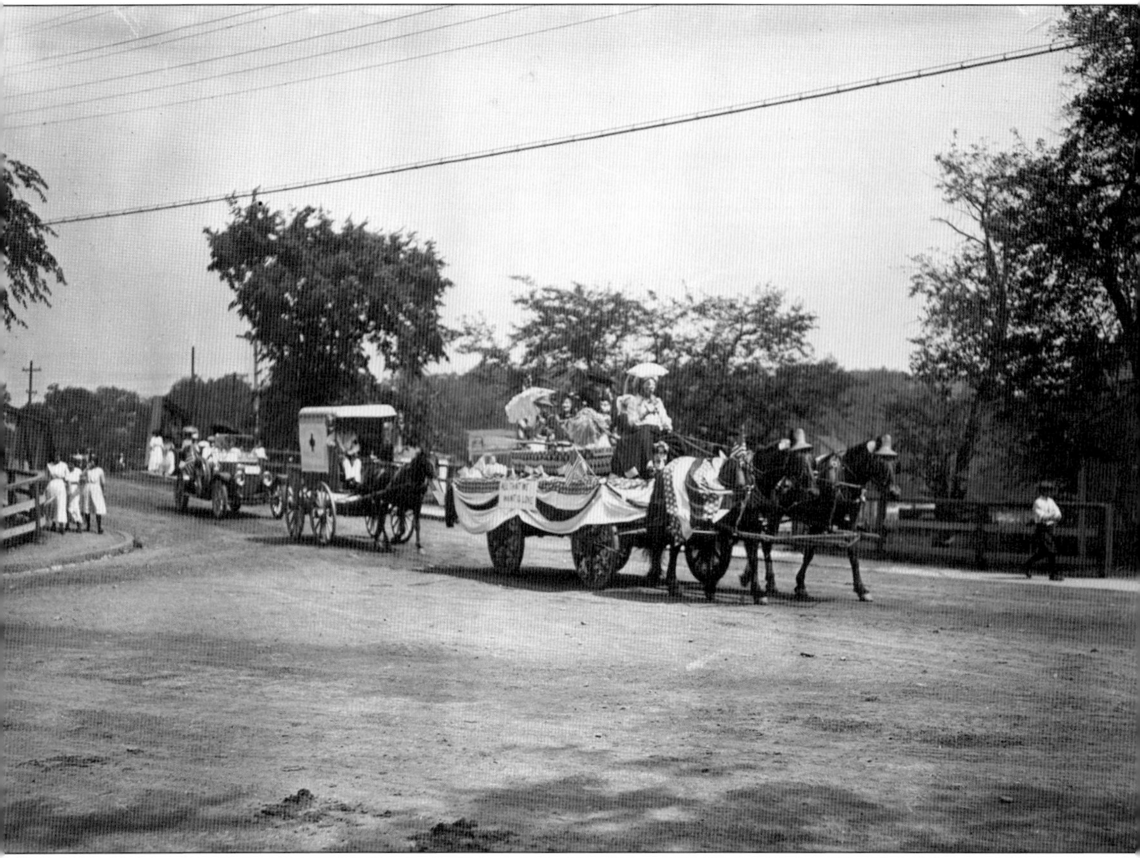

This 1912 photograph of the Fourth of July parade was made from one of Charles Kennison's glass negatives. The Red Cross float and the Belles of Ayer float are visible. Upon close inspection, the Belles of Ayer either wear masks or white makeup. The sign on the side of their float reads, "All that we want is love." These are just two of what would be many floats in the parade. Parades would usually begin early in the morning, followed by celebrations on the eve of the Fourth of July. The Ayer police kept a watch for any celebration that was a bit more jovial than allowed. The Fourth of July parades have always been a favorite in Ayer.

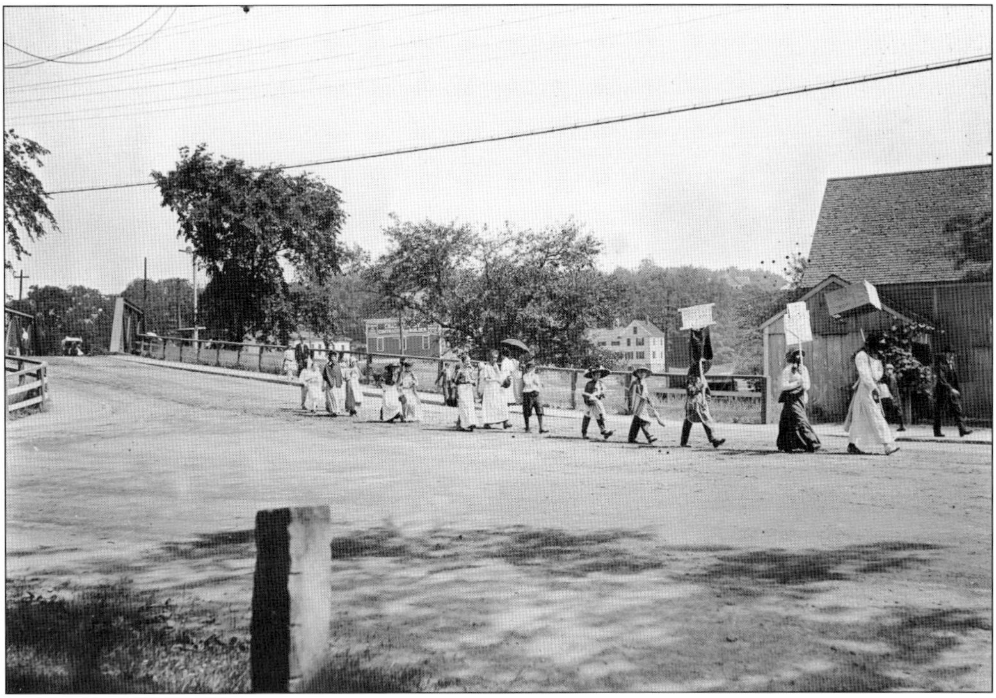

This is the 1913 Fourth of July parade. These suffragists are members of the Ayer Women's Club. It is almost hard to believe that at one time all Americans were not allowed to vote.

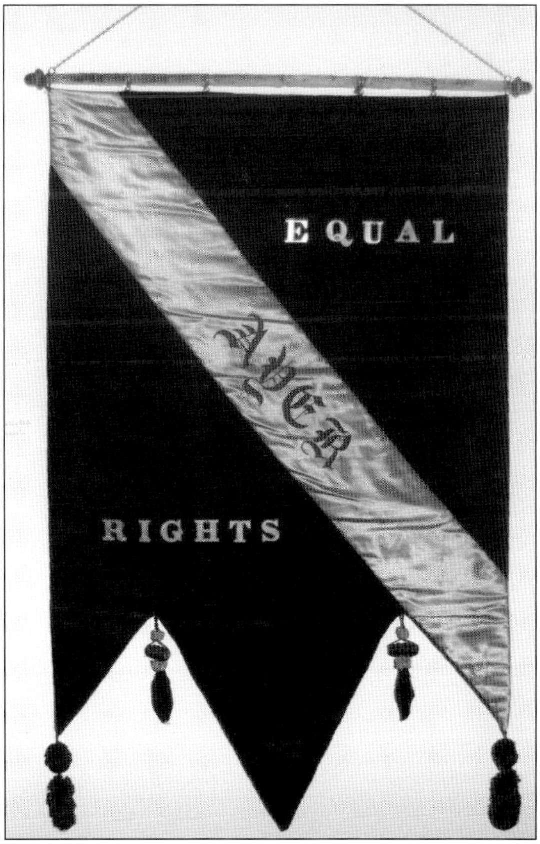

This is the banner used by the Ayer Women's Club in the 1913 Fourth of July parade. The Ayer Women's Club donated it to the Ayer Library. It hangs on the wall of the Nutting Historical Room.

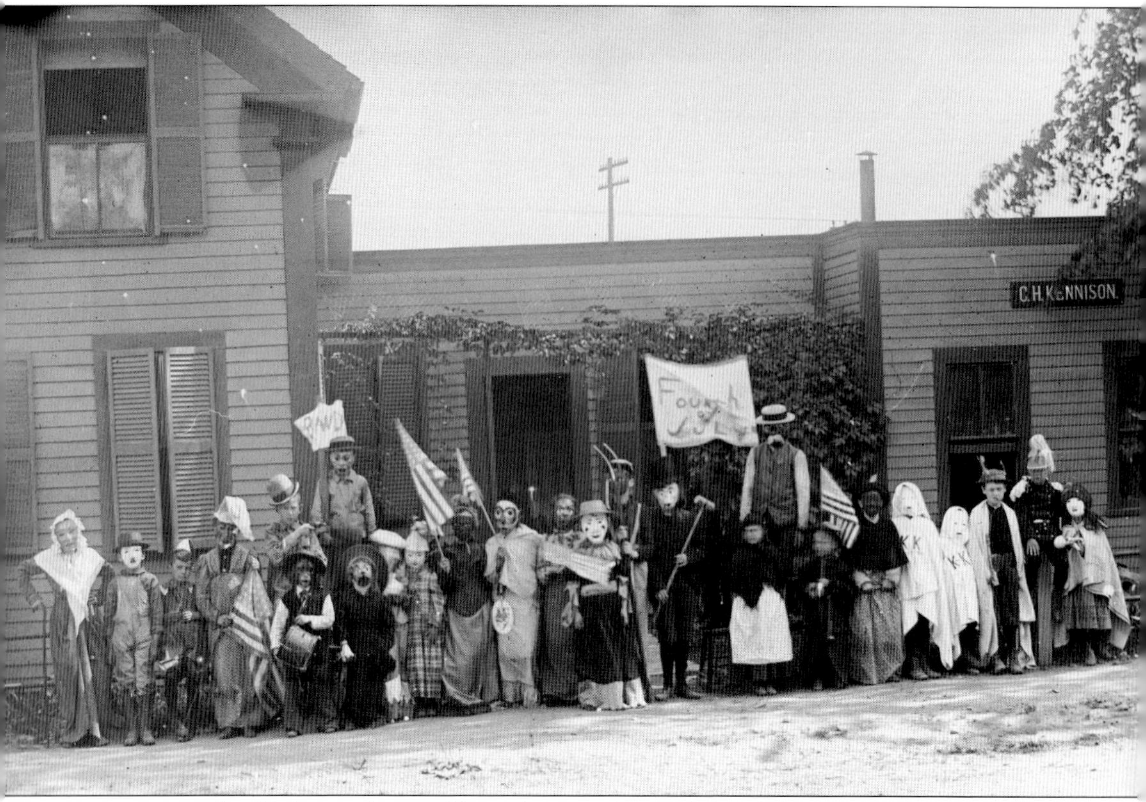

Ayer's Fourth of July parades would not be complete without the "Horribles." The Horribles would dress in burlesque costumes, which were usually comic or something grotesque. Pictured here in 1893, the Horribles were still a part of the parade in 1913. The events for the day would start with those who were marching in the parade being required to assemble at 7:30 a.m. The parade would most usually commence at 8:00 a.m. at the town hall, proceed from Main Street to Washington Street, and eventually make its way to the town park.

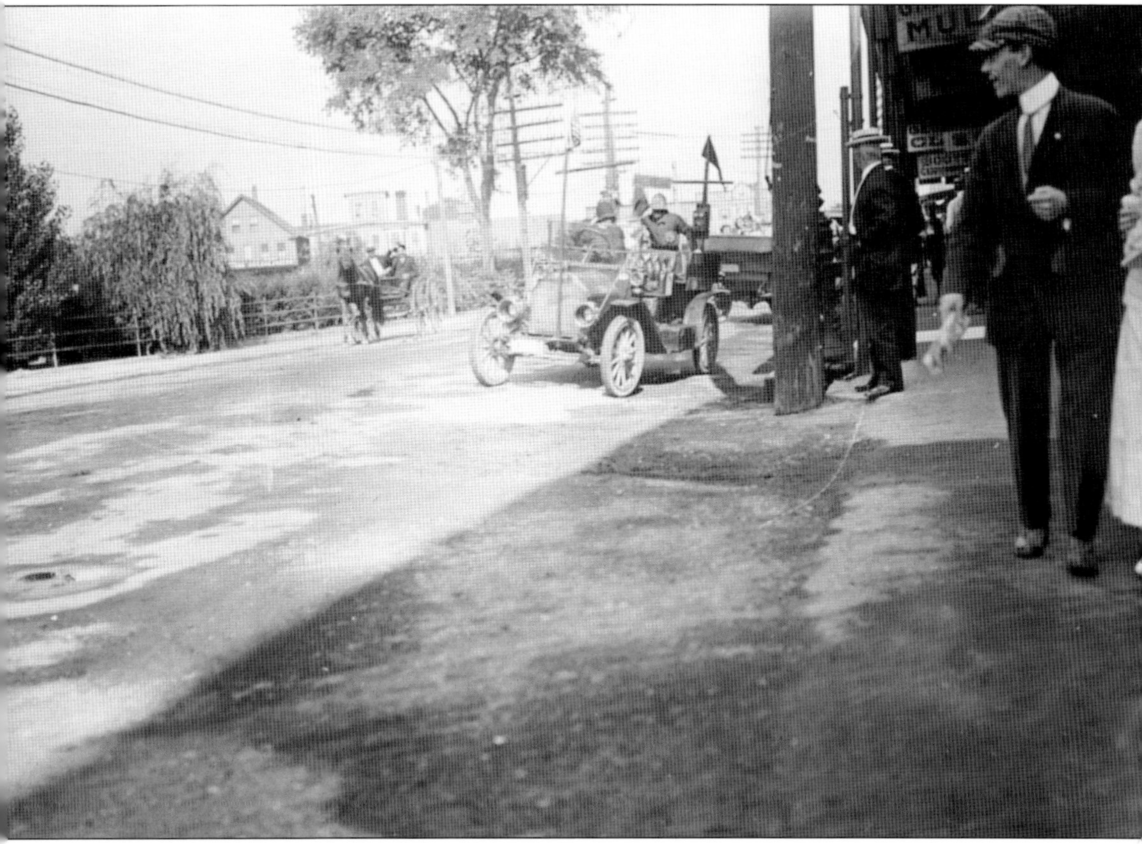

This was the police entry in the 1913 Fourth of July Parade. The caption on the back of the photograph describes this scene as "wireless police patrol." Note the telephone mounted on a pole in the back of the police car. Little did they know, phones would one day become so small and portable and that they would have the wireless in their patrol cars. The two police officers are Jack Mandescheid and Arthur G. Hazzard. In this event, the police car led the parade. And at the sound of a bell, a person created a disturbance causing the police car to spring into action. The culprit would then be "arrested." The night before, festivities began with a bonfire in Depot Square, which, in 1913, was reported by the police to be reasonably quiet.

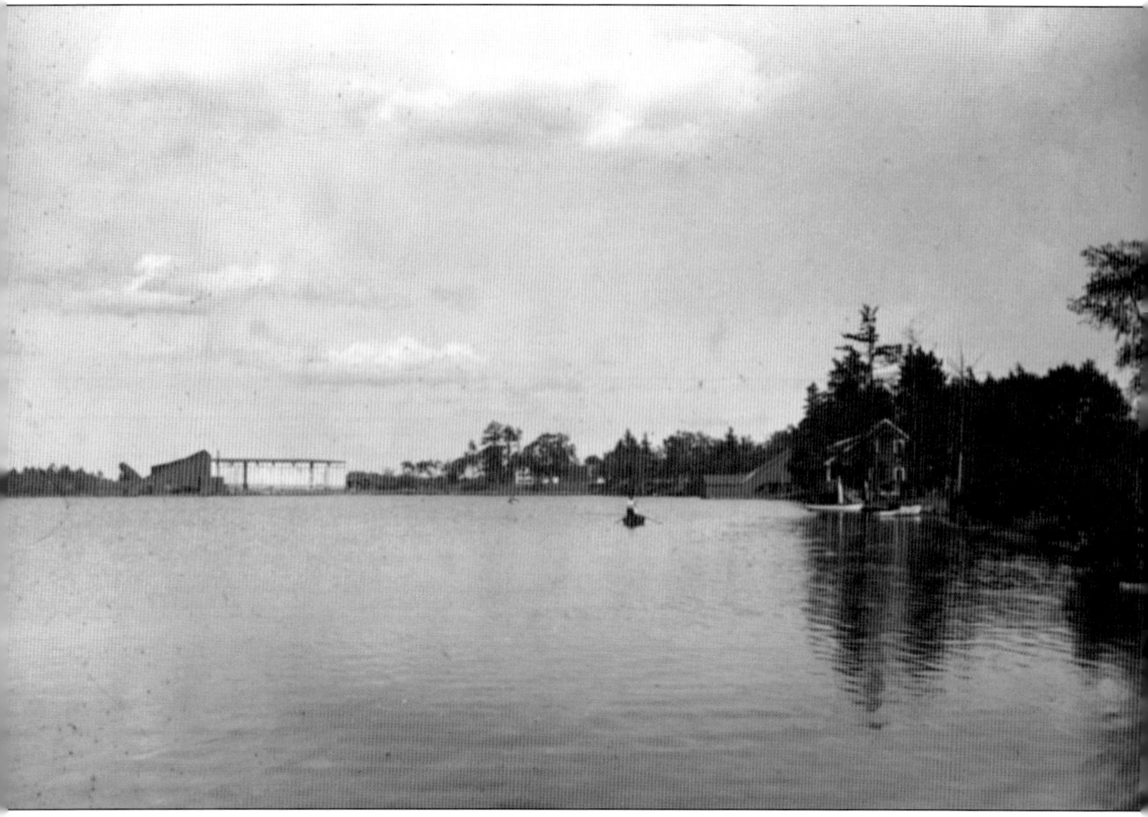

It is a nice day on Sandy Pond on July 18, 1915. Note the two people in the rowboat. It is barely visible, but one is standing with a fishing pole, while the other person rows. Originally, Sandy Pond was a secluded area with only four homes or cottages along its banks. When Central Avenue was built and the trolley rail installed, this changed the access to Sandy Pond. Now, with a trolley line going right by Sandy Pond, it became appealing to those looking to build a summer home on the beachfront. In the distance, the Boston Ice Company is to the left of the center, while the Ayer Ice Company is to the right of center. Originally owned by Oliver K. Pierce, the Ayer Ice Company was sold to Michael Horgan in 1919.

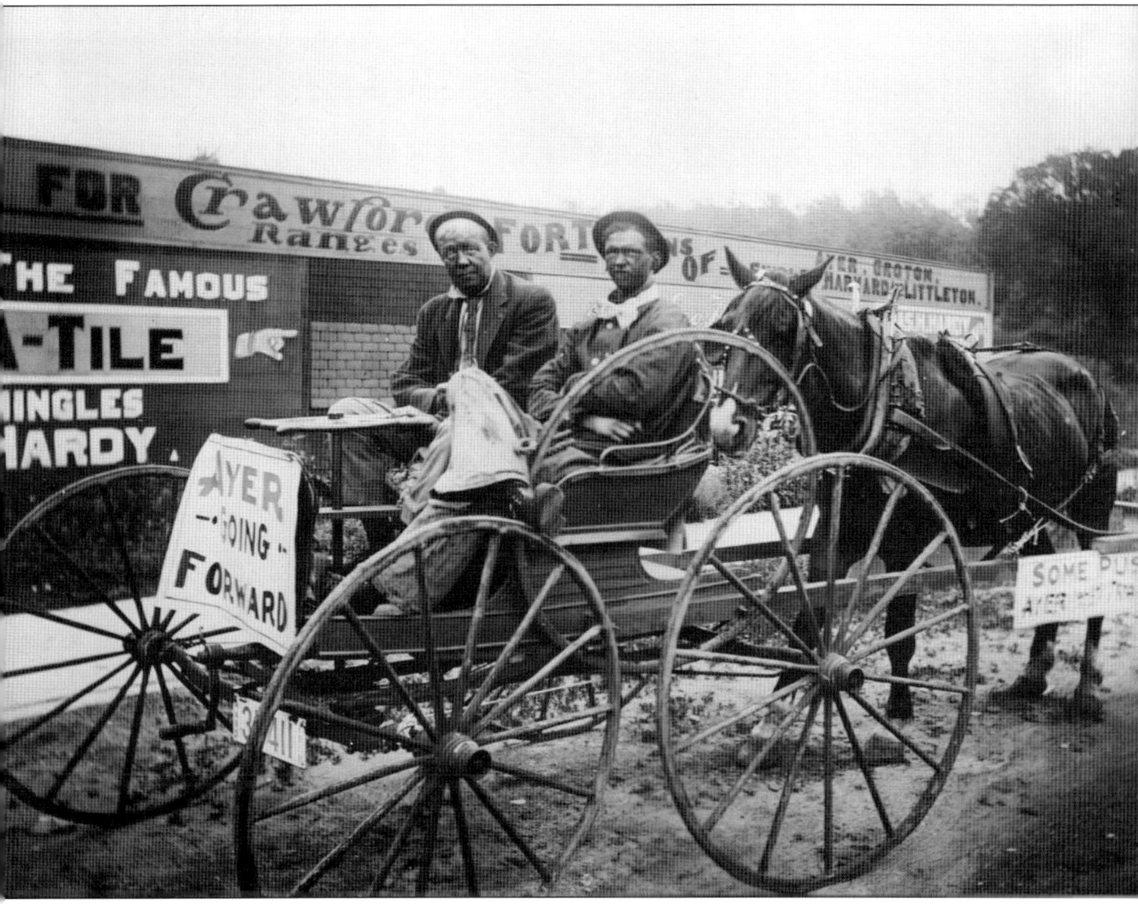

In preparation for a Fourth of July parade, this cart literally comes before the horse. The signs on the carriage reads, "Ayer Going Forward" on the front and "Some Push (for) Ayer Free Trade" on the side. Two men show their displeasure because more out of town tradesmen were being contracted for town construction projects than the local tradesmen at that time. This photograph was taken in front of Charles H. Hardy's building and business, which today is the home of Nashoba Restaurant on Central Avenue. His building was also home to the Ayer Board of Trade. The two men in the wagon are Barney McGovern on the left and Paul K. McGuane Sr. on the right. Note that the wagon is actually being steered from the large wheel shown between the two men. (Courtesy of Donald and Josephine Wallace.)

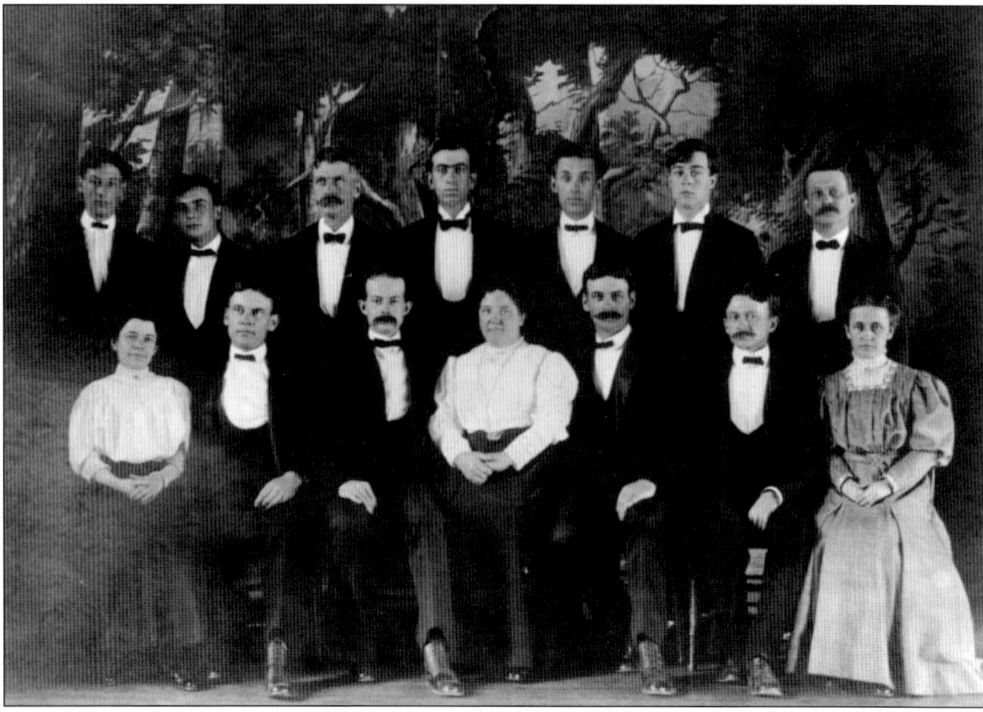

This is the cast from the play *Up Vermont*, performed on May 28, 1906, in Page Hall. The names of the cast members are not known. Page Hall was host to many types of activities. From plays to auto shows, the hall had been an active place for entertainment. Today, Page Hall is still a great place for entertainment, offering billiards, music, and beverages.

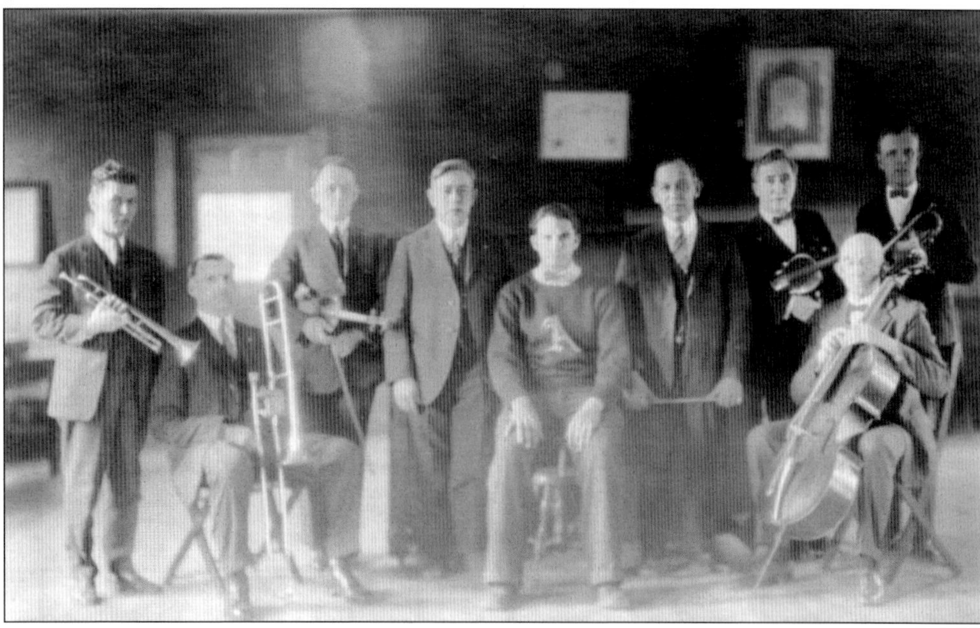

This is a brass and string musical group in Ayer. From left to right are McLean Woodbury, Raymond Handfield, George Barrows, Herbert Hardy, Donald Martin, director Frank Harmon, George A. Andrew, Walter Lougee, and Ralph Livingston.

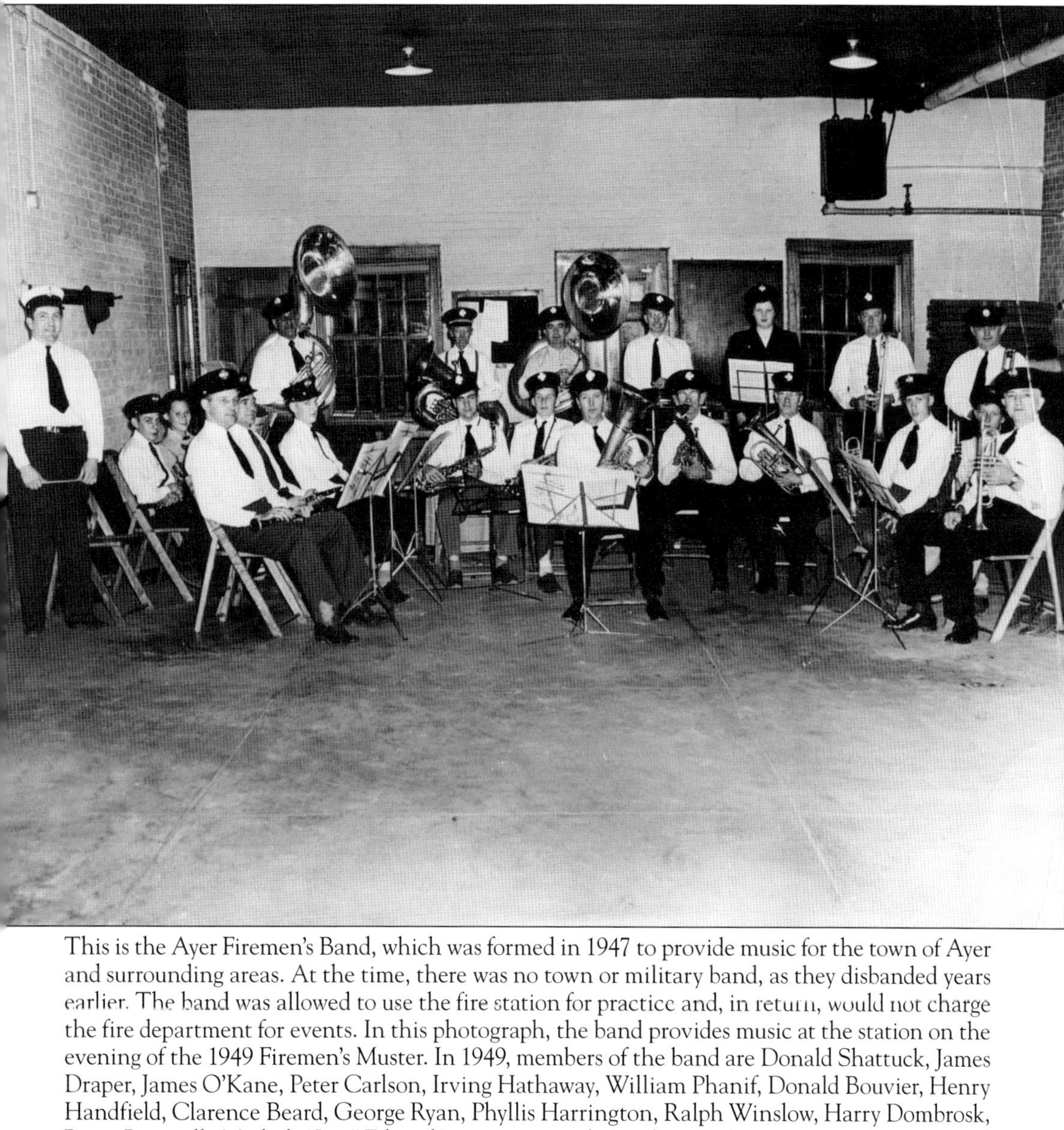

This is the Ayer Firemen's Band, which was formed in 1947 to provide music for the town of Ayer and surrounding areas. At the time, there was no town or military band, as they disbanded years earlier. The band was allowed to use the fire station for practice and, in return, would not charge the fire department for events. In this photograph, the band provides music at the station on the evening of the 1949 Firemen's Muster. In 1949, members of the band are Donald Shattuck, James Draper, James O'Kane, Peter Carlson, Irving Hathaway, William Phanif, Donald Bouvier, Henry Handfield, Clarence Beard, George Ryan, Phyllis Harrington, Ralph Winslow, Harry Dombrosk, Roger Pascarelli, Markula "Leo" Edward Linstrom, Woodsie Wilson, Robert Swain, Edward Carlson, Patsy Delebro, Fred Dubois, Chester Shattuck, Ralph Livingston, Raymond Handfield, Maclean Woodbury Sr., Walter Lund, Newell Warner, John McNulty, and Ruth Mullin. (Courtesy of the Ayer Fire Department.)

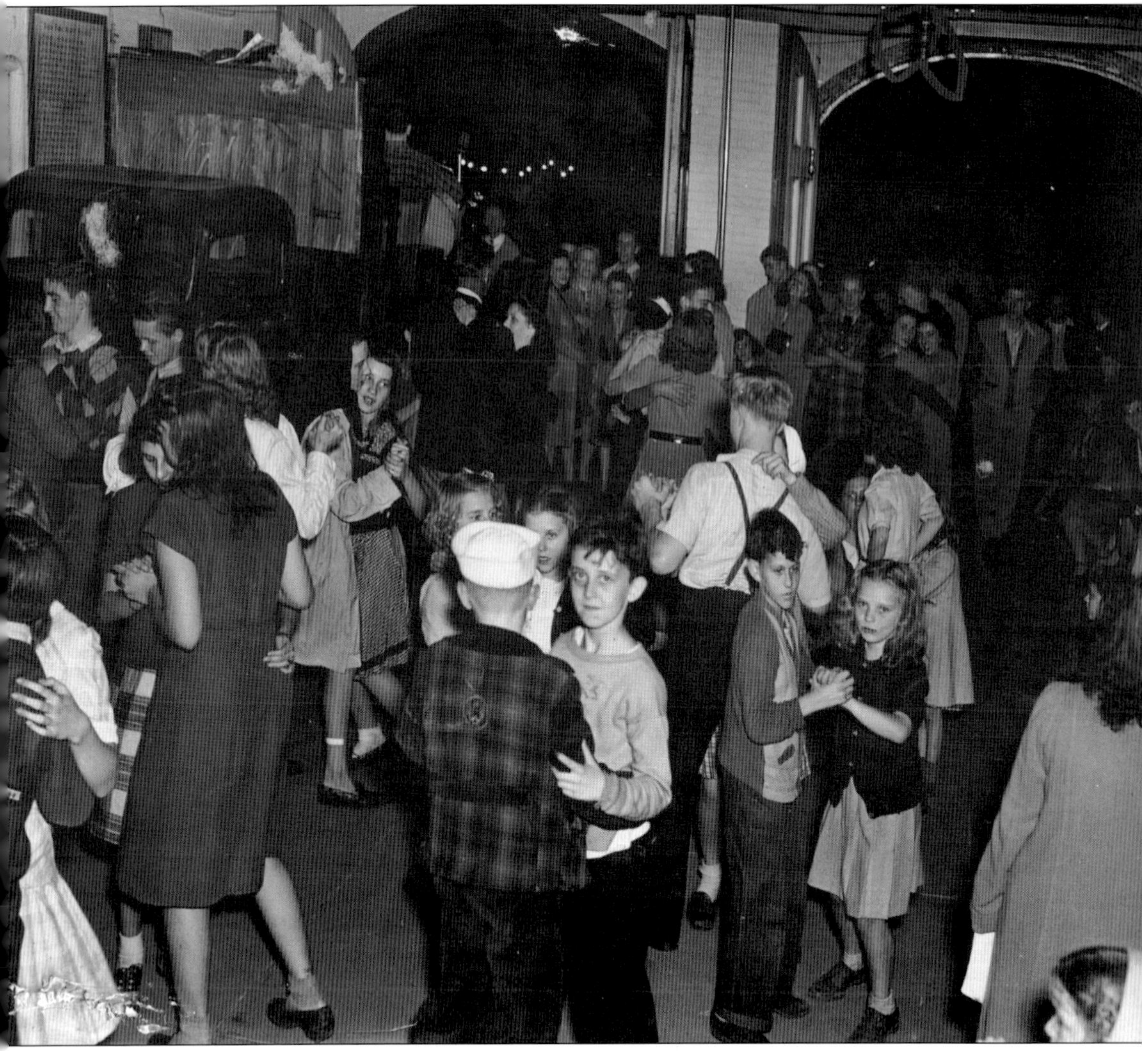

In this late 1940s photograph, people are dancing at the fire station during the annual Firemen's Muster. The parking lot across the street from the station was used for food, games, and muster events. During the day, a contest was held to determine who could get the longest stream of water to shoot out of the hand pumpers. This competition, among others, demonstrated a fireman's firefighting capabilities. In the early 1900s, the Colonel Needham would be polished up and used for the town musters. At night, there were outside lights for the booths, which extended the festivities. (Courtesy of the Ayer Fire Department.)

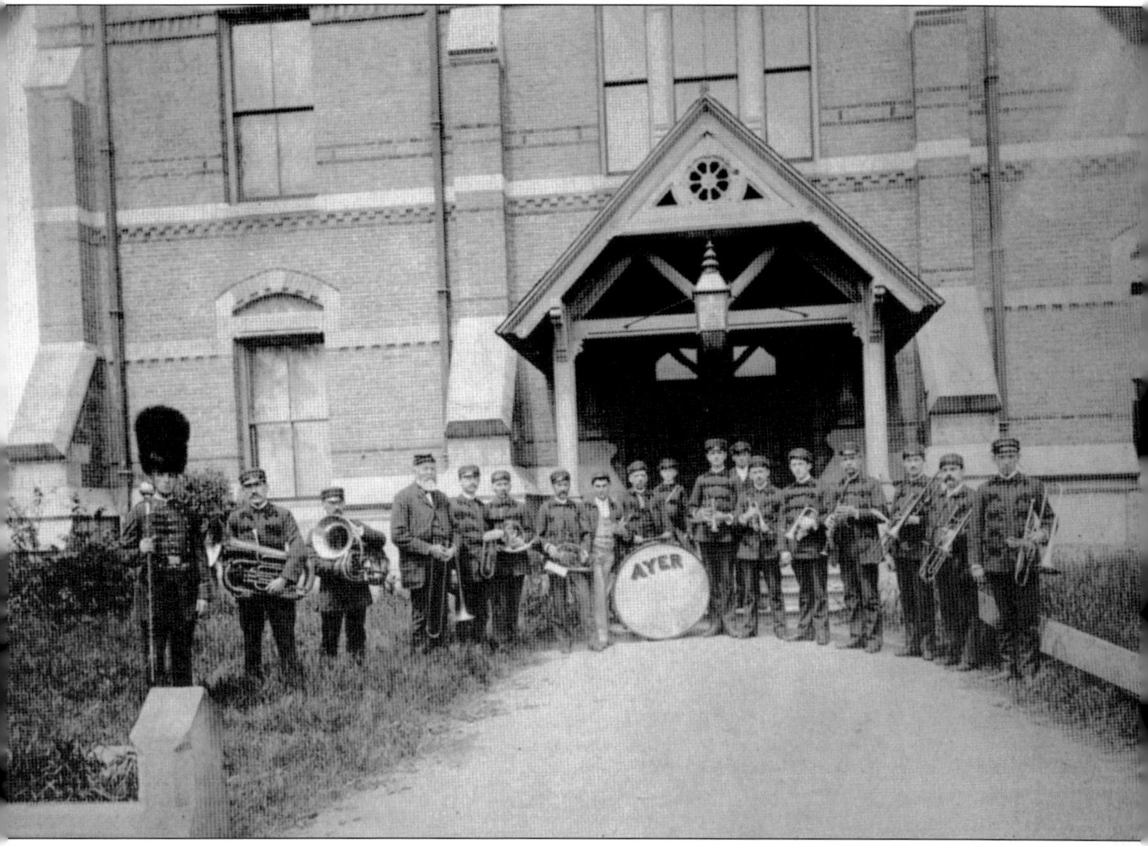

The Ayer Cadet Band poses in front of the town hall on May 30, 1890. The band was made up of mostly local residents and musicians and would play for private or public concerts, including Independence Day celebrations. The military bands were self-supporting in that they had to raise their own money for uniforms, music, and instruments. As seen in this photograph, the grounds at the town hall were not as meticulously maintained as they are today. At the time, Ayer did not have a town park or bandstand. There was only an area referred to as the "Old Common." It was located near the old pumping station on East Main Street and was more of a pasture than a park. It was not until later that a bandstand would be erected at depot square and in 1910 at the newly acquired town park, which was formerly Nuttings Grove.

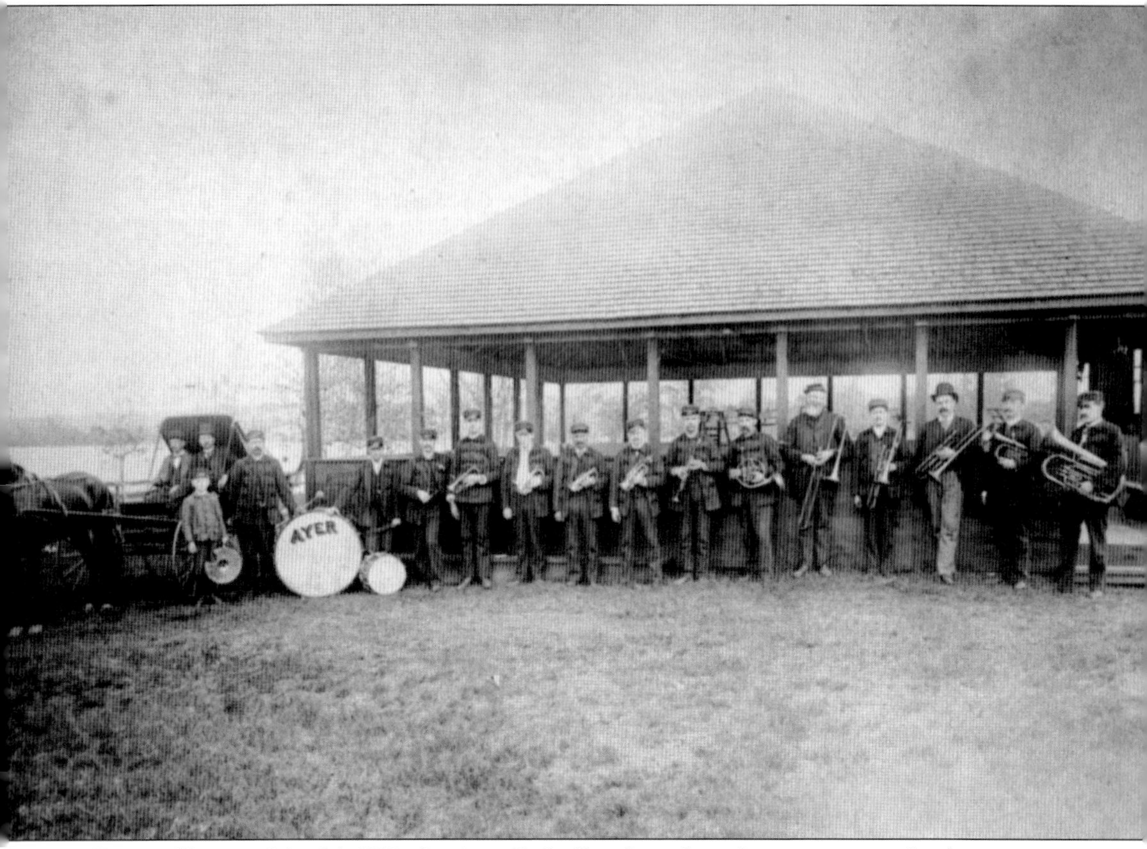

Pictured here on May 24, 1890, the Ayer Cadet Band may have been practicing for the upcoming Memorial Day at the pavilion at Sandy Pond. It is believed that the pavilion was owned by the Ayer Cadet Band. During the summer of 1890, the band performed a concert at this pavilion every Wednesday, drawing large crowds from Ayer and the surrounding towns. The concerts were a boon to the soda and ice-cream business. In 1890, Sandy Pond was on Littleton-Lunenburg County Road. This was the main road from Littleton, which would pass by Sandy Pond and wind its way through Ayer by way of Harvard Road, Groton Harvard Road, onto East Main Street, over the crossing, and out through Park Street.

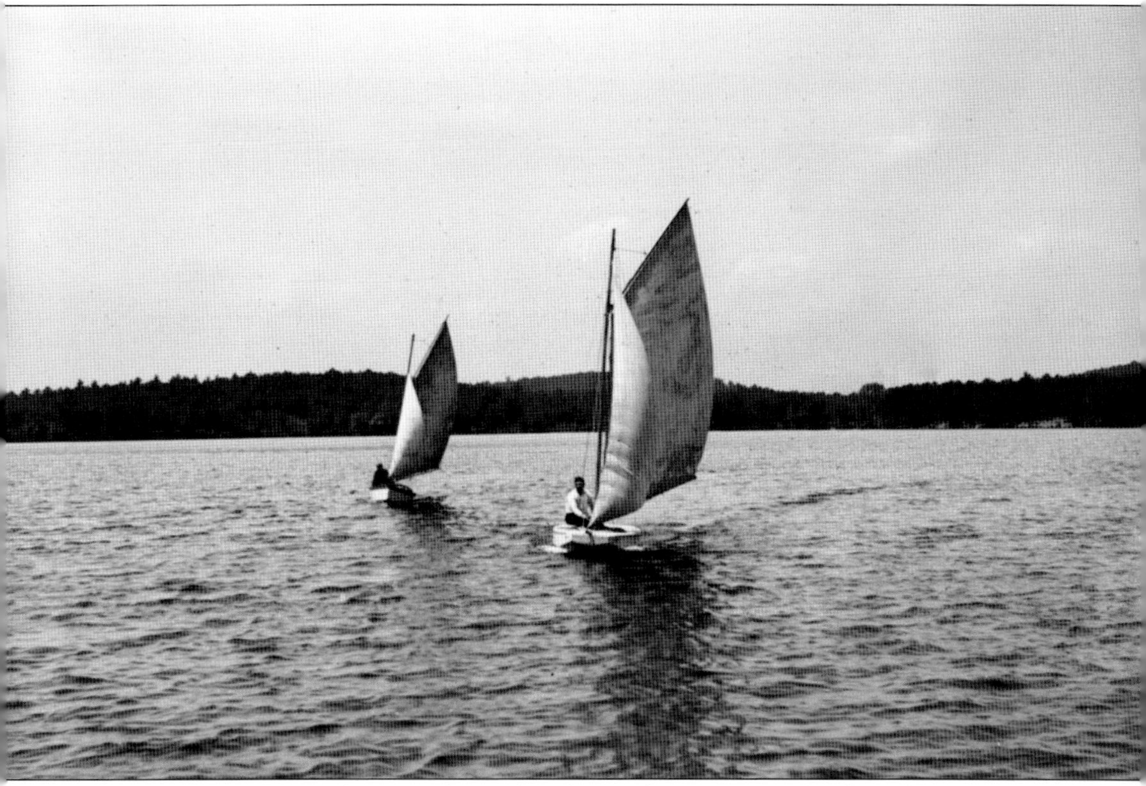

Ayer has been fortunate to have Sandy Pond so close and easy to get to for all residents. There is fishing in the summer and ice-skating in the winter. Sandy Pond was also home to two icehouses—the Boston Ice House and the Ayer Ice Company. The icehouses operated year-round and would ship the ice to Brookline, New Hampshire, and to Boston. At one time, there was a third, purely local icehouse on Fletcher's Pond, destroyed by fire in 1885. Some years later, a clubhouse was built on the site of the former icehouse. It offered dinner, dancing, and a steam launch. The launch departed from the dock that was behind John Flanagan's house. It would cruise up Fletcher's Pond, cross under the hand-cranked drawbridge at Snake Hill Road, cruise around Sandy Pond, then return to the clubhouse.

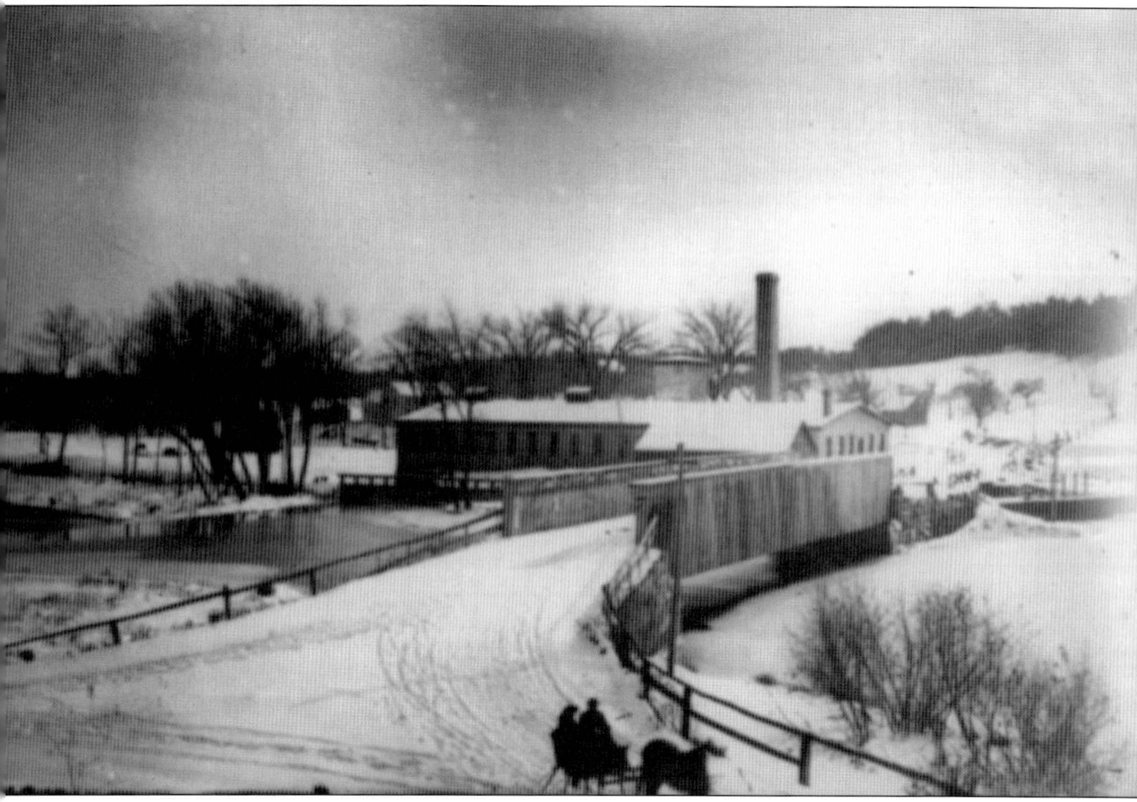

This postcard shows a one-horse open sleigh crossing over the Nashua River Bridge at Mitchellville in the winter. The photograph shows one of the many water-powered mills that have operated on this site since 1790 when the area was still part of Shirley. It must have been taken before 1906 due to the fact that when the Fitchburg and Leominster Street Railway Company erected their power station, they replaced the wooden bridge seen in this photograph with a new one built on concrete piers. In 1933, the property was acquired by Michael J. Horgan who had been successfully operating the Ice Company on Sandy Pond. Once the Ayer Ice Company occupied this site, it generated its own electric power to manufacture ice. Extra power would be sold to the town.

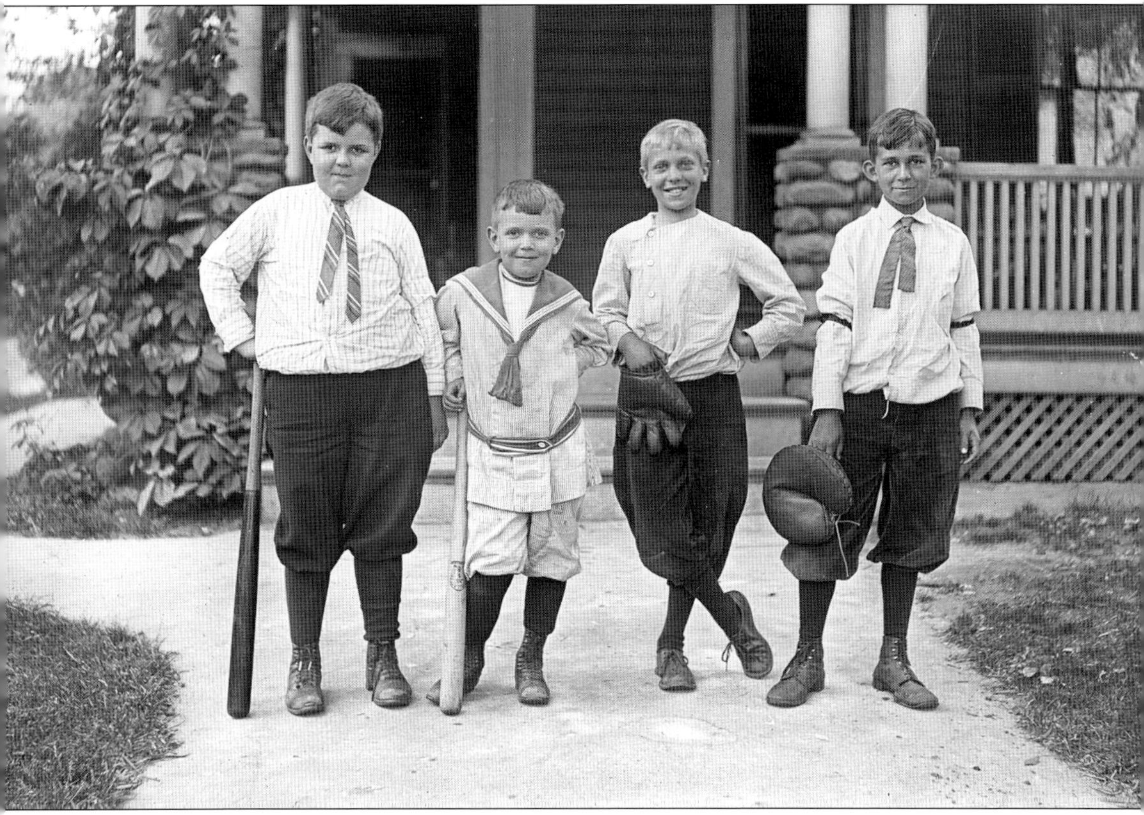

These boys gather outside the Sanderson home for baseball in the early 1910s. The boys are, from left to right, R. and G. Sanderson, L. Sprague, and D. Whitney. Children of that age would do homework, chores, and most often played outside. In the absence of television and video games, boys and girls during this era would invent games or play pickup games of such sports as baseball or football. Girls would generally play with dolls, hopscotch, jump rope, and make up rhyming songs. Boys would generally play chasing games like tag or kick the can and play with erector sets or tinker toys.

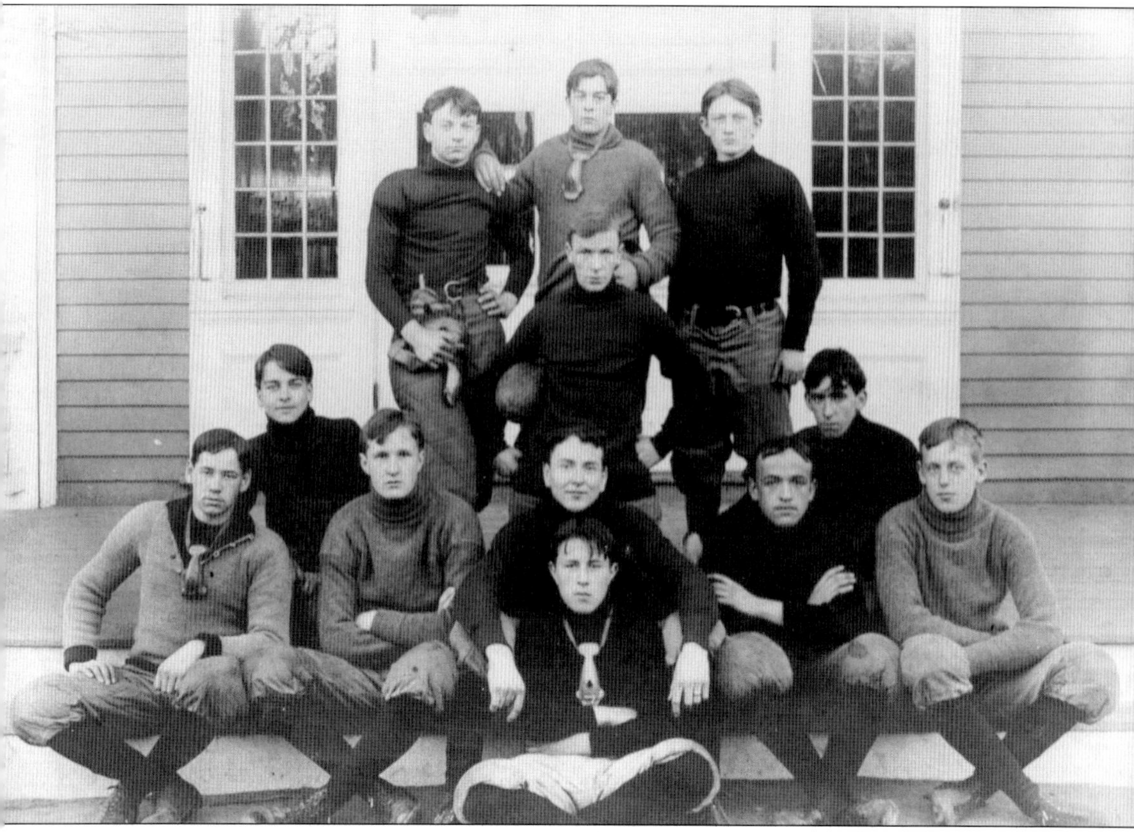

This is the 1904 Pleasant Street High School football team. They are, from left to right, (first row) Walter Sullivan; (second row) Lewis A. Sargent, Walter M. Fillebrown, Selah Holbrook, Francis T. Ryan, and Alfred P. Richardson; (third row) Arthur W. Carley, John McGuane, and John H. Hooley; (fourth row) John M. Carrigan, E. Hartwell Bigelow, and George Barrows. In 1904, high school football was played with much less safety equipment. This photograph does show the use of some padding, leather helmets, and leather nose guards, which hang from some of their necks. Football in high school was new, and usually it was difficult to have enough players to form a team. It was considered quite an accomplishment to graduate from high school, and the classes were quite small. There were not many boys in the class to field a team.

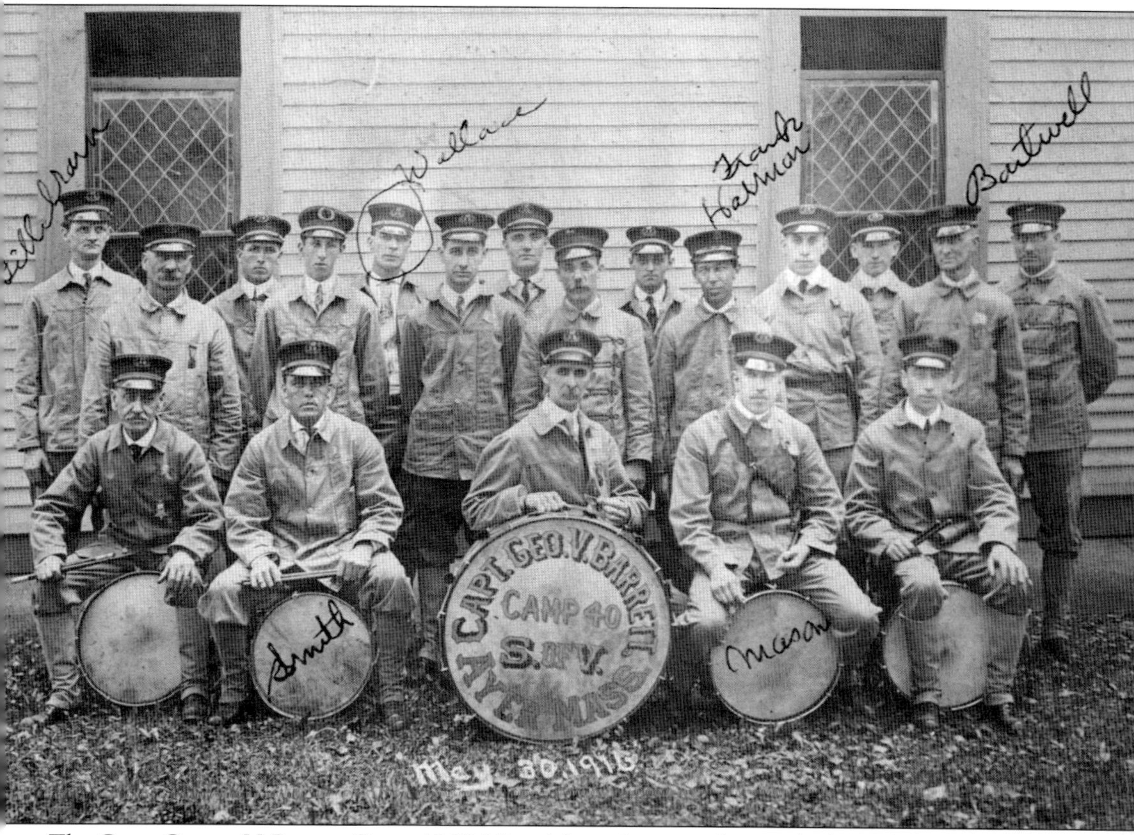

The Capt. George V. Barrett Camp 40 S.V. Band from Ayer stands outside the Federated church on Washington Street in 1916. Capt. George Varnum Barrett was born in Boston in 1839. He enlisted in the 6th Regiment Massachusetts Volunteer Infantry for three months in 1861. He reenlisted in September with the 23rd Regiment in Lynnfield. He then served in many different companies and in several campaigns, eventually becoming first lieutenant. At the end of the Civil War, he received the rank of captain. He then returned to Groton Junction, where he worked as a ticket agent for the Fitchburg Railroad. From left to right are (first row) unidentified, a Mr. Smith, Capt. George V. Barrett sitting behind the bass drum, a Mr. Mason, and unidentified; (second row) Albert A. Fillebrown, three unidentified, Jack Wallace, four unidentified, Frank Harmon, two unidentified, Rex Boutwell, and unidentified. (Courtesy of Donald and Josephine Wallace.)

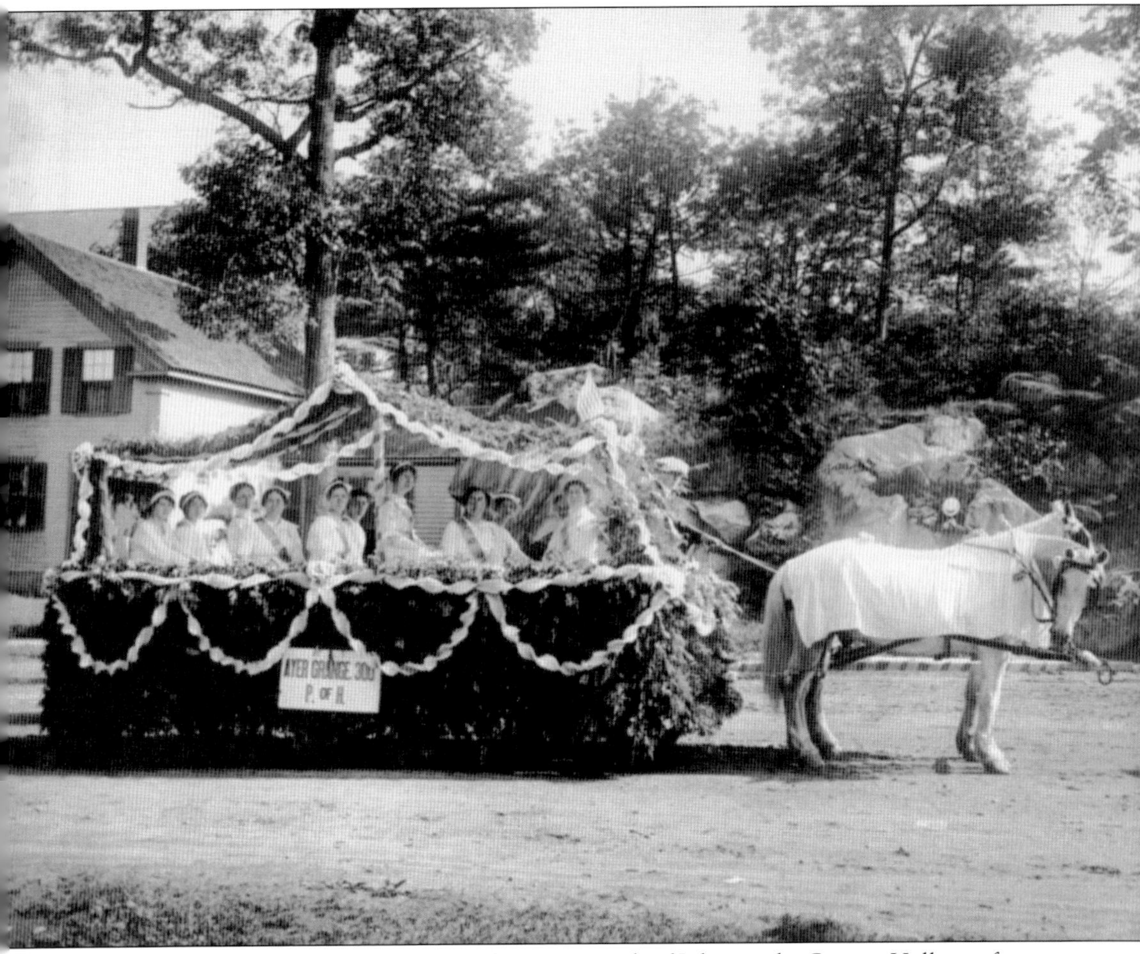

This is the Ayer Grange 300 float at the 1914 Fourth of July parade. Grange Hall was, for a time, located at Hardy's Hall on Central Avenue. Founded in the 1860s after the Civil War, the Grange promotes patriotism, service, and agriculture. Its focus was to unite private citizens in improving the economic and social position of the farming community. The letters P and H on the sign refer to the fraternal order of the Patrons of Husbandry. It was one of the first formal groups to admit women on an equal basis with men. When the headquarters opened in Washington, DC, in 1957, Pres. Dwight D. Eisenhower was asked to dedicate it.

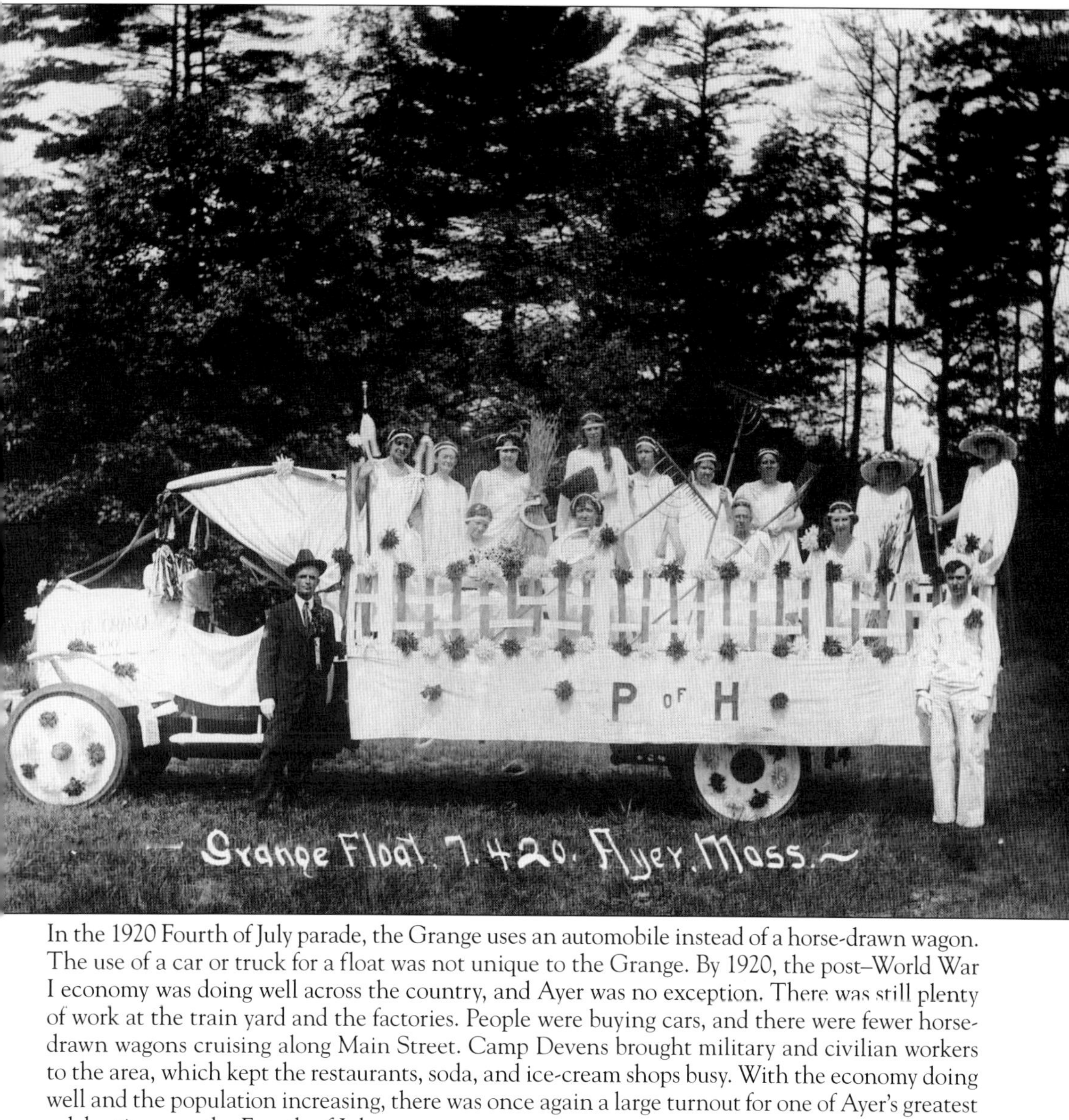

In the 1920 Fourth of July parade, the Grange uses an automobile instead of a horse-drawn wagon. The use of a car or truck for a float was not unique to the Grange. By 1920, the post–World War I economy was doing well across the country, and Ayer was no exception. There was still plenty of work at the train yard and the factories. People were buying cars, and there were fewer horse-drawn wagons cruising along Main Street. Camp Devens brought military and civilian workers to the area, which kept the restaurants, soda, and ice-cream shops busy. With the economy doing well and the population increasing, there was once again a large turnout for one of Ayer's greatest celebrations on the Fourth of July.

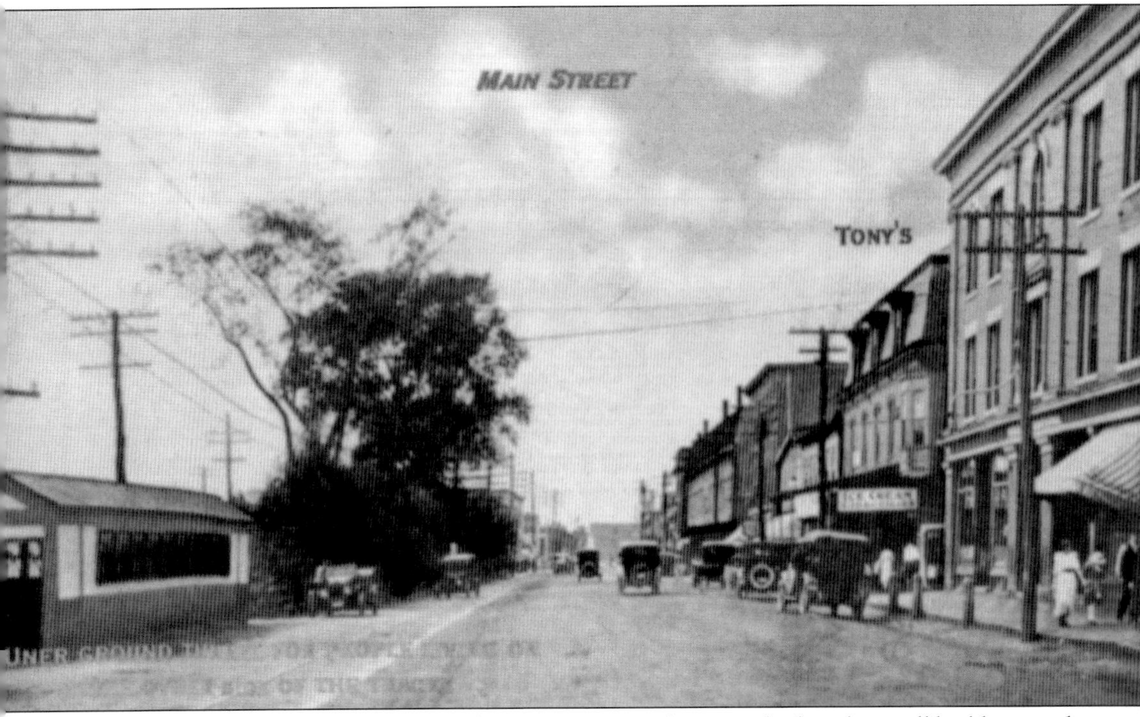

This postcard from the 1920s shows the Main Street underpass, which is the small building on the left side of the card. Initially, there was discussion to either build a subway or a pedestrian overpass. A committee was formed to look into both options. The committee first looked at subways in Fitchburg and Somerville, then a subway and a footbridge in Boston. The underpass was built by the railroad in 1908 at a cost of $6,500. The underpass allowed pedestrians to walk from Main Street to Forest Street by going underneath the railroad tracks. The subway entered the tunnel from the end of the concrete sidewalk at the train depot and connected at the midpoint to the main tunnel. The subway was closed in 1977 and demolished in 1978.

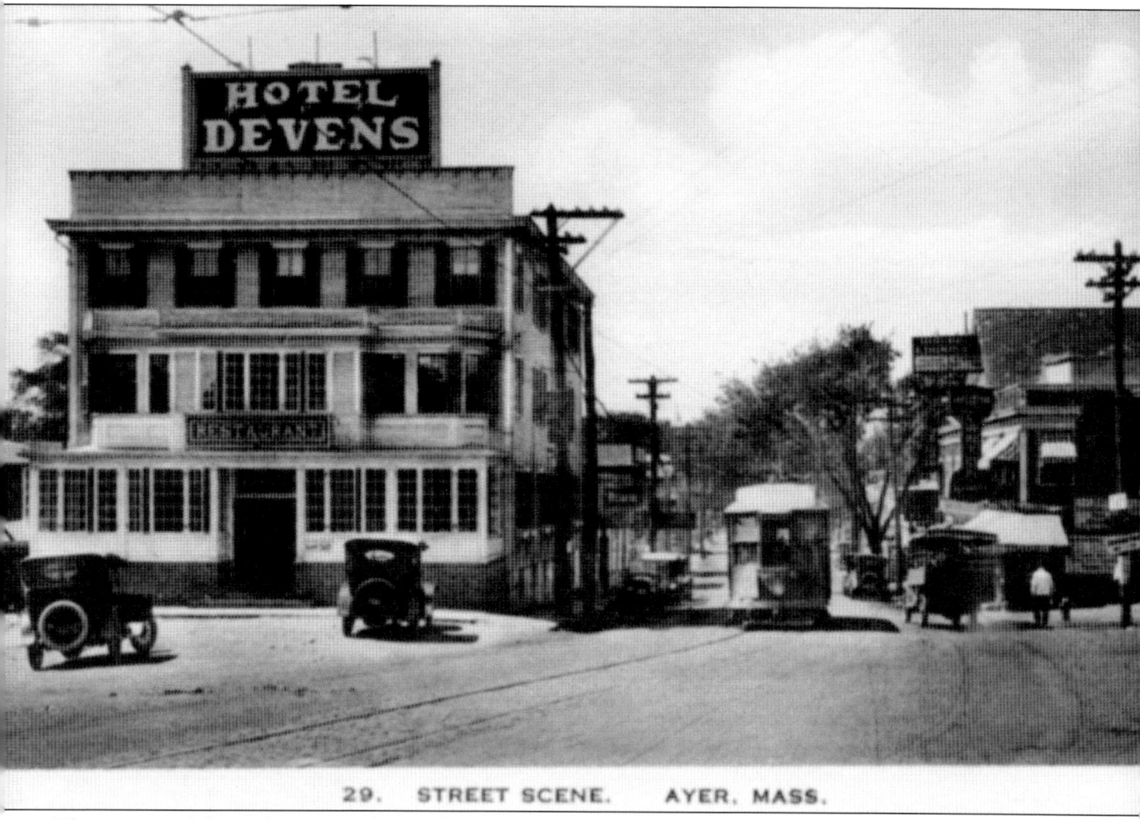

This postcard from the 1920s shows the trolley on its way to or from Leominster by way of West Main Street. Note the hotel has changed its name from the Globe to the Devens. In later years, it would change its name again to the Lincoln Hotel, the home of the Wigwam bar. The firehouse from the days of the hook and ladder and hose companies, although barely visible, is directly across the street from the hotel on the corner of Park Street and West Main Street. It is the site of the present-day Central Fire Station on the corner of West Main and Park Streets. That area also had clothing stores, restaurants, tailors, and souvenir shops. The clothing and tailor shops catered to the men based at Camp Devens. The presence of the camp came at a good time, as the railroad that had been an economic boost to Ayer since the 1850s closed its maintenance shops and freight yards in 1927.

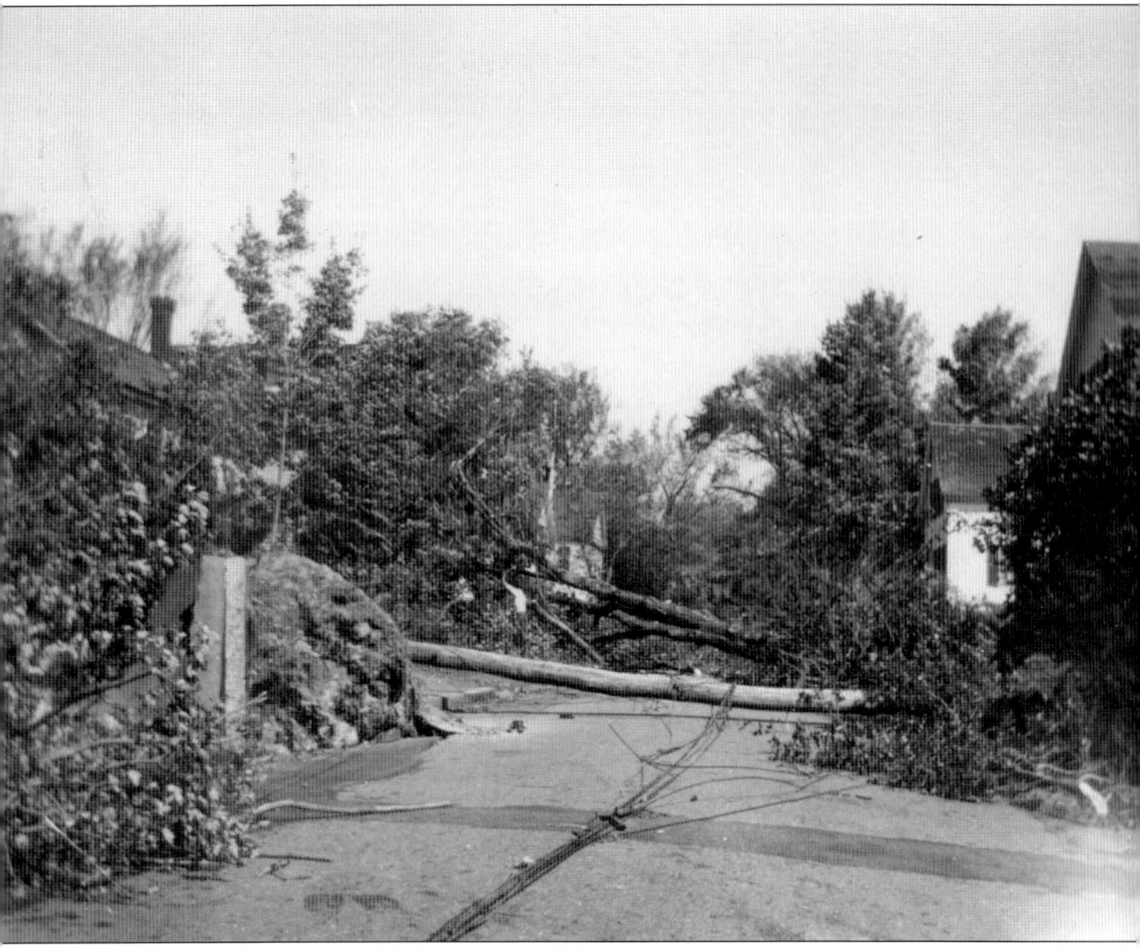

In 1938, a hurricane wreaked havoc in Ayer as it did in so many other towns. Here, Pleasant Street is visible on the day after the hurricane. This street was only one of many that were stripped of its trees. The leafy elms lining East Main Street were uprooted. West Main Street was under water, and the bridge at Mitchellville was threatened with the rising height of the Nashua River. In the Sandy Pond area, hen houses owned by Eric Kohler and John V. Henry were almost completely destroyed. In the hill section, chimneys were knocked from roofs by felled trees. A tree fell on the Cottage Restaurant on Main Street. The town was without power for three days after the hurricane.

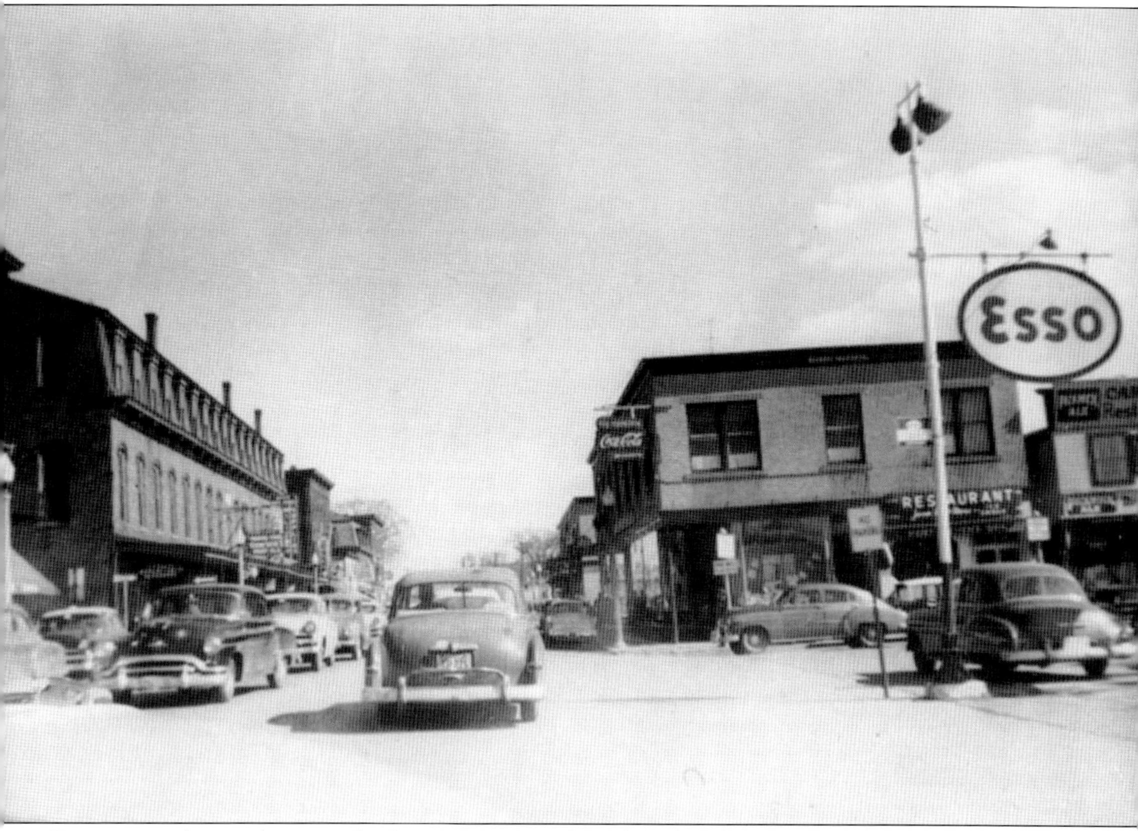

Downtown Ayer is busy in the late 1940s to early 1950s, shortly after World War II. On the corner of Park and Main Streets, a gas station stands where the Medicine Shoppe is today. Here, the traffic is bumper to bumper. It was said that at times one could not cross the street without the assistance of a police officer. Past the Esso station is the Fort Devens Spa on the right of the photograph. Ayer has gone through many changes in its short history but has always remained strong in its desire to rise above any adversity.

Discover Thousands of Local History Books Featuring Millions of Vintage Images

Arcadia Publishing, the leading local history publisher in the United States, is committed to making history accessible and meaningful through publishing books that celebrate and preserve the heritage of America's people and places.

Find more books like this at
www.arcadiapublishing.com

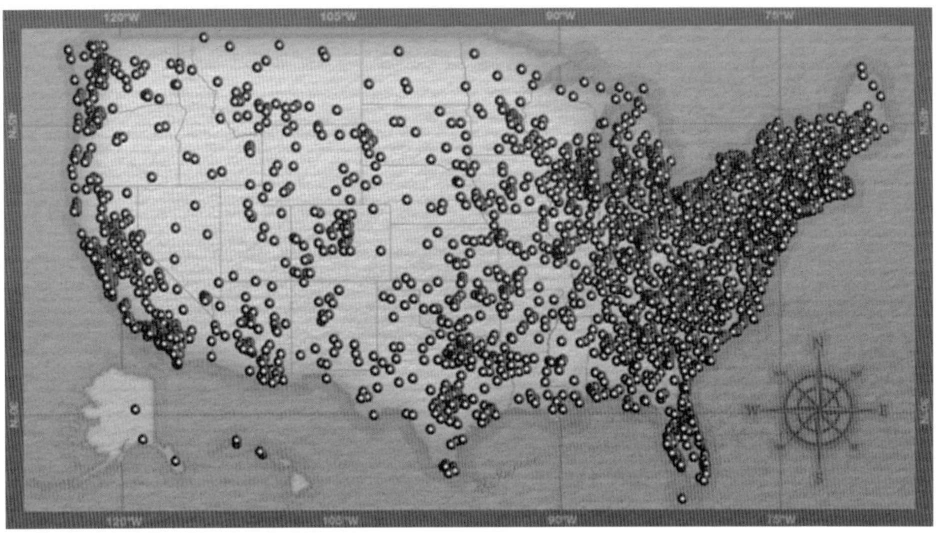

Search for your hometown history, your old stomping grounds, and even your favorite sports team.

Consistent with our mission to preserve history on a local level, this book was printed in South Carolina on American-made paper and manufactured entirely in the United States. Products carrying the accredited Forest Stewardship Council (FSC) label are printed on 100 percent FSC-certified paper.

MADE IN THE USA